AFFECT INTOLERANCE IN PATIENT AND ANALYST

STANLEY COEN

JASON ARONSON INC.
Northvale, New Jersey
London
Ken King, M.D.

This book was set in 11 pt. Adobe Garamond by Pageworks and printed and bound by Book-Mart Press, Inc. of North Bergen, NJ.

Library of Congress Cataloging-in-Publication Data

Coen, Stanley J.
  Affect intolerance in patient and analyst / Stanley J. Coen.
    p. cm.
  Includes bibliographical references and index.
  ISBN 0–7657–0364–5
    1. Psychotherapist and patient.   2. Affect (Psychology).   I. Title.

  RC480.8.C64 2002
  616.89'17—dc21

                                                                    2002019949

Printed in the United States of America on acid-free paper. For information and catalog, write to Jason Aronson Inc., 230 Livingston Street, Northvale, NJ 07647–1726, or visit our website: www.aronson.com

For all my family, present, past and future,
with love, appreciation, and gratitude

T his book incorporates, in thoroughly revised form, material previously published elsewhere. Grateful acknowledgment is made to the *Journal of the American Psychanalytic Association* for permission to adapt and revise the following articles: "Barriers to lover between patient and analyst" (1994) 42: 1107–1135; "How to help patients (and analysts) bear the unbearable" (1997) 45: 1183–1207; "Perverse defenses in neurotic patients" (1998) 46: 1169–1194; "The wish to regress in patient and analyst" (2000) 48: 785–810; "Clinical discussants as psychoanalytic readers" (2000) 48: 471–495; "Why we need to write openly about our clinical cases" (2000) 48: 449–470; the *International Journal of Psycho-Analysis* for permission to adapt and revise "The passions and perils of interpretation (of dreams and texts): an appreciation of Erik Erikson's dream specimen paper" (1996) 77: 537–548; the *American Journal of Psychotherpay* for permission to adapt and revise portions of "Love between therapist and patient: a review" (1996) 50: 14–27.

Contents

Part III
Helping Therapists' Affect Tolerance through
Talking and Writing About our Work   177

Preface

This book aims to help psychoanalysts and psychotherapists manage feelings better—our patients' and our own. To do so, I've drawn on my own affective struggles with those patients I've found most difficult and challenging. Affect tolerance and intolerance in patients and therapists are at the core of such dilemmas. I'll describe how I've been able to help myself and to get help from colleagues with such difficult therapeutic encounters, especially by writing about them. I fully believe that public presentation of our most difficult work offers the chance for colleagues to show us some of what we could not fully grasp for ourselves, as well as what we could not see at all. Such learning doesn't go only in one direction. Presenters, discussants, and members of the audience can each contribute to the other's clinical learning. I encourage you to draw on the affective struggles I describe in this book in myself in order to identify something similar in you. This book is written in such a spirit of collaborative exploration toward the goal that we can learn together how to do the best work of which we are capable with our patients.

My clinical writing in this book is deeply personal. I'll tell you about the problems I got into with patients with whom I found it very difficult to work. That is how I work and how I engage with colleagues about such problems so I and they can learn from such experiences. This voyage of discovery cannot be reduced to the influence of relational and interpersonal psychoanalysis on our field or on me. I eagerly acknowledge the multiple influences on my clinical work, but most of this change is not in my theory but in me and in my ways of working with patients. Nor can such changes be attributed primarily to less rigid adherence to received wisdom—in our field or in me. The story I want to tell is not that relational psychoanalysts have now managed to convince more traditional analysts that they need to include themselves in the therapeutic field. My view is rather that during this past decade the most skilled clinicians, whatever their theoretical persuasion, have been focusing on how best to help our most challenging patients.

This is not a story that has already been told. Rather, by raising questions about our clinical work, we begin to reshape our story. I would not write this book if all I had to convey was that I've become a more flexible clinician during the last ten years. Instead, I assume that I can help you to explore dilemmas in yourself similar to the ones I've had to confront, with the goal of improving your affect tolerance with patients who dread their feelings.

So my focus is a highly pragmatic emphasis on affect tolerance in the clinical situation—in both partners—not a competitive struggle among different theories. In this book I eschew such competition among different theoretical schools so as to integrate the most efficacious clinical approaches. But before I set aside my own theoretical competitiveness during the rest of this book, I want to declare that the relationalists have not already been here! This book is not just written to show the traditional psychoanalytic community how it needs to change its clinical work. The clinical problems I raise apply to all clinicans' work, psychoanalysts' and psychotherapists', with difficult patients. I want all of my colleagues, whatever your orientation, to try on the dilemmas I show in myself to help expand your own therapeutic skills by increasing your tolerance for painful affect in your patients and in yourself. Although I certainly do think that the relationalists have helped, I believe that many of us have been going in the same direction, for which they do not deserve all of the credit. We sometimes talk differently and argue polemically about different theories, but I think many of us practice very similarly, especially when we're challenged by our more difficult patients whose affect intolerance requires that we contain their terrifying feelings.

By describing my feelings and wishes with my patients, I certainly do not aim to shock my readers. Rather, I hope to motivate you to consider similar feelings and wishes in yourself in order to expand your own affective repertory at work. I fully believe that the more of our feelings and wishes for which we can be responsible, the more we can tolerate, contain, and eventually interpret what our patients find unbearable. I believe this is true for our work with all patients, but that it especially applies to more difficult patients. To be able to work with them, therapists need sufficient access to their own psyches. As I'll make abundantly clear, I do not aim to disclose and enact my feelings and wishes with my patients, unless there is a very good reason, when ordinary interpretation has not been effective, to use *something* of my affective experience in order to better assist my patient.

I'll describe in detail how I work with my most difficult patients, trying to engage them as deeply and fully as they and I can tolerate. I do so no matter what the frequency at which I see my patients, whether they are in four-time-per-week analysis on the couch or once or twice weekly psychotherapy, or something in between. This book is aimed at an audience of psychotherapists and psychoanalysts who want to join me in exploring how to work most effectively with our most difficult patients. You will see that I no longer make such sharp differentiation between psychoanalysis and psychotherapy because I am always trying to use all of my clinical skills with all of my patients. Hence, the problems in the treatments I describe, whether psychoanalytic or psychotherapeutic, apply to all of our clinical work with our most difficult patients.

To be most effective with our more difficult patients, we need to learn from each other what does and does not work well. Such learning needs to involve not only therapeutic approaches familiar to us, but more importantly, ones we haven't yet considered. Some colleagues may already have learned what we still don't know. Hence, I've sought to broaden my traditional psychoanalytic perspective, which has always focused on object relations. I've tried to integrate into my clinical work aspects of contemporary British Kleinian, relational, interpersonal, and child developmental perspectives. I bridle when I'm asked to define to which psychoanalytic school I belong. Any answer I give feels misleading. I fear that my pledge of allegiance may be misused against some other group.

Still, I consider myself a traditional analyst who practices passionate analysis, involving both patient and analyst. I believe that change through treatment requires mobilization of much intense feeling, hating and loving. To help our patients with their affect intolerance, we need to contend with our own. Hence we should esteem anything that helps us to tolerate, contain, and manage our own feelings, toward the goal of helping our patients. This includes alternative approaches to clinical work, study of our own and of colleagues' clinical cases, empirical research, peer supervision study groups, consultation with colleagues, and even, if needed, more analysis.

This book contains my analytic journey during the last decade. The clinical chapters, which have been revised from my current perspective, emphasize problems of intense feeling and need between the treating couple—hating, loving, desiring. I especially focus on what clinicians have to do to help patients to tolerate feelings, wishes, and needs that seem, and have always seemed, unbearable to them. Over the past decade, I've come to accept more responsibility than I had previously for the therapeutic work with my more difficult patients. I'll describe how I've come to be much more patient, to tolerate and contain, for an extended time, what I would have expected to interpret far sooner in the past to my more difficult patients. I do so because I fully believe that my therapeutic path is not idiosyncratic, that sharing my own experiences can help colleagues identify similar dilemmas in themselves. So, reader, I hope that you will identify with me, at least to some degree, as your read this book, so that you can use my experiences for your own clinical enhancement.

The section of this book about writing and discussing colleagues' cases is offered with a similar spirit and aim of enhancing our collaborative sharing and learning about our similarities and differences. I strongly believe that we need to study each other's cases, and our own, in order to learn what is and is not efficacious with our more difficult patients. To do so, we need to modify our climate of presentation and publication of clinical work, so that, for the most part, we contribute to, rather than injure, each other. You'll see me apply such a fanciful, hopefully respectful, attitude toward colleagues' clinical psychoanalytic writing.

Many people have helped me with this project. Foremost has been my wife, Dr. Ruth Imber, who has lovingly supported me as a partner and as a colleague. I appreciate and admire her wise counsel. I thank my children—Gwen, Jennifer, Michael, Debbie, and David—for their love, care, and tolerance of my writing. I thank both Michael and David for their computer help and for encouraging me, finally, to get a new computer. I'm delighted to be able to share pleasure in writing with Michael and Debbie. I'm proud and pleased with Gwen and Jennifer's families and accomplishments, within which Andrew is a featured player.

Too many colleagues have helped for me to be able to thank all of them. I thank my patients, especially those who have contributed most to the clinical problems considered here, for what they helped me to acknowledge in myself, before I could help them. I want to acknowledge the help, support, critical thinking, and friendship of Salman Akhtar, Rosemarie Balsam, Paula Bernstein, Richard Fox, Glen Gabbard, Burton Lerner, Alan Melowsky, Morris Peltz, Harry Penn, the late David Raphling, Owen Renik, Arnold Richards, Arnold Rothstein, Eleanor Schuker, Theodore Shapiro, and Jerome Winer.

Introduction

My own need to find better ways of working with more difficult patients has been an important motivation for writing this book. Writing about and presenting the process material of these difficult patients to colleagues invariably helps me understand and manage what has been transpiring between me and the patient during the therapeutic process. In the process of writing about a patient, fresh perspectives on our interaction become possible—it's like getting a consultation from myself. Presenting to others and seeing an interaction through their eyes opens up what I may have seen but have not been able to fully grasp by myself—as well as what I have not been able to see at all.

The contemporary perspective is that therapists should talk and write openly about difficult patients so that we can all learn together how to work most effectively with them. More and more therapists are beginning to discuss not only therapeutic successes, but also their problems and difficulties so that we can all study them collaboratively. Then we can try to decide what works most and least effectively with different patients and different colleagues. Chapters 7, 8, and 9 encourage an open, collaborative presentation of psychotherapeutic and psychoanalytic work in a spirit of playful, constructive discussion. The joy of playful interpretation is the focus of Chapter 11. Chapter 10 plays with the spirit of the young child in the adult patient, as it considers how far to go with adapting child development research findings to adult treatment.

I have written on the clinician's need for active intervention in the stuckness of pathologically dependent patients, who, terrified of change, were all too content just to remain in treatment. I view pathological dependency as a compromise formation for holding onto a vitally needed object, reducing terror of loss and destruction, stifling one's independence and autonomy, and turning rage and destructiveness against oneself, away from the other(s).

The clinician's task is to tolerate and to draw out the patient's rage and hatred in the transference to modify such stuckness. Pathological dependency is fueled by fears of being on one's own and of managing one's own internal contents, especially one's destructiveness. When a patient is terrified of what's inside of her, she will be tempted to surrender and cling to someone else who is to be responsible for her own dangerous contents.

Much of my earlier focus was on the clinician's need to engage the pathologically dependent patient's rage and hatred that had been turned against the self. Therapists were encouraged to tolerate and draw out the full intensity of the patient's dependent attachment in passionate transferences towards them. Many clinicians, fearing their own childlike, dependent yearnings, keep patients from bringing the full force of their hunger close toward themselves. The goal was not re-parenting, but the opportunity for the patient to modify her defenses against attachment and need, so that she could now let herself want from the therapist what she felt she still needed from her parents. Dependent patients can be differentiated into those who could enjoy their dependent attachment to the therapist from those who dreaded and avoided it.

My goal was to help clinicians and their patients tolerate and enjoy need, and the emotions of love and hatred as they played out between the couple. Struggling to make sense of what had gone on between my more difficult patients and me, it become clear that I needed to change my expectations with some of them. I had been trained to sharply differentiate patients who could tolerate intensive exploratory treatment, psychoanalysis or psychotherapy, from those who could not. Once a patient was selected for analysis or intensive psychotherapy, she was presumed capable of working with her internal conflicts, which were expected to become accessible via the clinician's consistent interpretation of defense, resistance, and transference.

When I first started working as an analyst, treatment parameters were much narrower. If the analyst's initial assessment appeared erroneous when certain patients seemed unable to explore their internal conflicts, then we would usually give up on analysis or intensive psychotherapy and shift to a more supportive psychotherapy, or even decide that any treatment was ill advised. My 1989 paper, "Intolerance of Responsibility for Internal Conflict," was aimed at understanding why three treatments did not proceed as far as I had expected. I expanded my examination of the difficulties certain patients had in exploring themselves into my 1992 book. In the last decade, I and others have focused much more on the analyst's role in what seems difficult with patients whom the analyst regards as difficult. I heartily agree with my friend, Arnold Rothstein (1998), that a difficult patient is a patient who is difficult for a given clinician to treat. This present book continues exploring the analyst's difficulties with so-called difficult patients.

It can take considerable work to remain patient and tolerant with difficult patients who seem unable to tolerate responsibility for their own conflicts. When I wrote my earlier book, I was not consciously aware that the contemporary British Kleinians make the axiomatic assumption that patients in the paranoid/schizoid state are indeed unable to bear responsibility for conflict, and that it is the clinician's task to help them *eventually* achieve such tolerance.

Since then, various other psychoanalytic influences have come together to modify my approach, including a general shift further away from a position in which the clinician is presumed to know everything about the patient and her conflicts toward one in which the clinician must contend with all of the difficulties in the consulting room—his, the patient's and the force-field between them.

This book describes treatment processes that do not seem conventionally productive, and that even seem to be destroying the basis for a treatment. Treatments will be reported in which difficult patients oscillate in and out of emotional contact with the therapist over prolonged periods and during which they seem incapable of collaborative exploration. Clinicians need to persist with such difficult treatments even when they sense little change or progress. In these challenging situations, clinicians need to continuously assess why the patient avoids genuine engagement with them and with his own feelings, needs, and conflicts so that eventually they can talk together about these difficulties. The clinician should be prepared for treatment situations that seem highly unconventional for very long periods of time.

Professor J. (from Chapter 1) was certainly not your ordinary patient. His treatment came to represent an encounter between analysts trained to work analytically with disturbed patients and those of us who had been trained to keep such patients off our couches. The help I got from hospital-based analysts and therapists to whom I presented his case at the Austen Riggs Center enabled me to tolerate his extraordinary need for control over his attendance at, and participation in, the treatment. These colleagues contended that Professor J. was like many of their hospitalized patients, who had had multiple prior failed treatments, and whose psychopathology required the clinician's caring and creative acceptance and intervention. They advised me not to try to differentiate my work with Professor J. as psychoanalysis in contrast to psychotherapy, but to simply try to help him, accept that I needed to sustain this treatment and expect much less of him. It was fascinating that the hospital-based analysts disagreed so sharply with the office-based analysts, *all of whom* eagerly agreed with me that Professor J. did not in fact seem to be analyzable.

Yet I had chosen to work analytically with some very difficult patients because it seemed that intense analytic treatment offered their only hope for change. Still, I hadn't realized that I had gone on expecting the same of these much more difficult patients as I did of more ordinary ones. Now, however, I shifted focus with Professor J., as with other patients, away from asking whether this was a productive analytic treatment toward pondering what needed to be done to help my patient. Even though I had asked myself such questions previously,

I had been expecting too much of my more difficult analytic patients. Hence I would become too easily frustrated and dissatisfied with their difficulties as patients and with my role as analyst.

I became aware that I expected all of my analytic patients to be capable of working collaboratively with me at exploring themselves. I had not appreciated that I was expecting all patients, and some very difficult ones, to be capable of ordinary analytic work. I did not then appreciate sufficiently that I needed to help them contain what they could not manage on their own. I no longer differentiate so clearly between psychoanalysis and intensive psychotherapy. Instead, I keep trying to gauge what my patient can and cannot tolerate and how I can enhance her ability to bear what seems unbearable.

I now adapt my treatment approach to what my patients seem to need. Together, we decide on optimum frequency and intensity of treatment based on their needs, conflicts, motivation, goals, talents, strengths, and the limitations imposed by their psychopathology. Four-times-weekly psychoanalysis is not for everyone. Some patients don't want it; some don't need it; some can manage with much less; some can't tolerate it. My desire to practice psychoanalysis should not be the reason it be recommended for those of my patients for whom it is not the optimum treatment.

I do a lot of intensive psychotherapy, in which I enjoy practicing my analytic skills, but I do not feel diminished as an analyst. Some readers may not appreciate how much some psychoanalysts believe that analysis is the optimum and only treatment for most, if not all, patients. For these analysts, it is incumbent on them to work with the patients' resistance to engaging in what the analyst thinks is "best" for them. I thoroughly disagree with this attitude.

On the other hand, for those patients for whom psycho-analysis is the optimum treatment, if they agree with my treatment recommendations, I work to tailor the treatment to their needs, fears, limitations, and strengths. I focus on what I can *do* to help them further. "Doing" certainly does include acceptance and containment, silence, following their lead, and so on.

I have now worked analytically with a number of patients

whose treatments differ from any analysis I had been taught to expect or than I'd heard presented. It has helped to present material to confidential peer study groups, especially away from New York City, to colleagues who could not identify these patients. A number of these colleagues have agreed that, although some of the presented cases are unlike any they've conducted or heard about, they have been very productive. Indeed, these colleagues were surprised how much could be accomplished analytically with these very difficult patients, within analytic processes that were hardly expectable. Colleagues' encouragement has helped me to tolerate with more equanimity my questions and doubts about these treatments. But as expectations of standard analyses conducted with standard technique have changed, we've shifted toward focusing on how to enhance each treatment as unique in its own right, and are much less concerned with deviation from some mythical norm of an ideal analysis.

Indeed, well-conducted psychoanalysis can be a very potent and effective treatment for patients whom psychiatrists might despair of being able to help other than with medication—patients whom colleagues had given up on as untreatable, not just as unanalyzable. That patients require medication to manage mood and anxiety does not necessarily preclude their being helped by analytic treatment.

I've just completed a treatment consultation with a woman who began the final consultation session revealing, hesitantly, that she felt angry and mistrustful with me because I had failed to ask her if she'd taken psychotropic drugs. She didn't tell me this until I asked her about her reactions to our last meeting, implicitly reminding her again that I was eager to hear how she felt being with me. "If you can't remember to ask me about medication, how can I trust you to know what I need," she said. I wasn't going to be treating this woman myself and so wasn't concerned about whether she needed medication but with how well she and I could engage her difficulties, and each other, during the consultations. I responded: "I'm sure I've forgotten to ask you many things, not just about medication. Whether you've been on medication just wasn't on my mind. You seem both to want to tell me more about your mistrust of me and yet hesitant to do so." She then spoke, with anxiety, sadness, and resentment, about her concerns that I and the therapist I'd select for her, like her parents previously, would fail to attend to her needs. It was impressive that she trusted me enough to try telling me about her mistrust and to explore whether we could both tolerate her doing so.

I argued in 1993 that idealized adherence to a standard model technique of psychoanalysis inhibits and constricts creative work with difficult patients. Even then, I believed that we clinicians needed access to all of our feelings towards our patients, and that we get into trouble when we cannot tolerate certain wishes and feelings with patients. This book aims to help clinicians tolerate their hatred and love for their patients so as to help patients bear their feelings of hatred and love toward them. The following chapters make more explicit how to use feelings of hatred and love to advance our patients' treatments.

Chapter 1 addresses avoidance of loving feelings in the therapeutic couple, while Chapter 4 focuses on dangerous desire and need between clinician and patient. Chapter 3 describes the management of intense rage and hate in the treatment setting. Chapters 2 and 7 aim to help therapists augment their patients' capacity to bear affects that feel unbearable. The therapist's role in such affect management is stressed throughout this book. Chapter 5 considers the use of perverse action in patients (who do not have obligatory perversion) when ordinary defenses are insufficient to manage what is threatening. Chapter 6 describes mutual regressive wishes between the therapeutic couple that are used to avoid intolerable affect, especially depressive hopelessness currently being relived in the treatment, and the underlying destructive rage and hatred.

It is surprising that a number of highly capable traditional analysts have expressed their fear that my approach brings clinicians toward the "slippery slope" of action rather than helps us manage our wishes and feelings towards patients for the sake of the treatment. These colleagues needed to be reassured that I don't enact my feelings and wishes with patients. On the contrary, the more I am able to be in touch with my feelings, wishes, and protections with my patients, the better I work and the less I enact what is outside of my awareness.

Other traditional analysts fear that I now advocate a radical departure from standard analytic technique in which I disclose and share my own inner experiences with my patients, and that I'm going over the top in fanning the flames of passion between the analytic couple. They insist that analyses are, and should be, quieter and calmer than mine. They contend that I exaggerate how much anger needs to be opened up in intensive treatments, that productive treatments need not be so stormy. But treatments of pathologically dependent patients require mobilization of considerable anger to break apart their willing dependent attachments. I do fully believe that for most patients to change, they must feel deeply and strongly—not feel just a bit.

A commonplace example can remind us how readily our own affect intolerance leads us to collude with our patients' protections against their feared affects. A younger colleague was relating the penultimate session before her summer vacation, and immediately associated her patient's dream reference, of a religious memorial service, with death. She told about the violent references in her patient's dream—a snarling attack dog, robberies, and muggings—and a locked-out child seeking a comforting home. This therapist certainly understood and interpreted her patient's connections with the impending separation from her. However, even though she could see this, she stopped short of talking with the patient about her angry, attacking feelings. Another colleague had even predicted her patient would have intense fantasies of attacking the therapist's body. She understood that it would be far better for her patient to move from attacking her own self and body toward attacking the therapist. But this seemed too dangerously irrational, not a place this younger therapist had yet been, nor a place to which she was comfortable helping her patient go. She needed help to get there.

It is a major premise of this book that both patients and therapists have difficulty tolerating intense affects, loving and hating, and a central aim of this book is to help both to do so. Chapter 2 explores patients' fearful fantasies about how and why they regard certain feelings as intolerable. The patient is helped to differentiate between feelings of disability and feelings of refusal—"I can't" from

"I won't." They come to connect affect intolerance with fears of relinquishing a pathological object relationship, within which certain key feelings had seemed unbearable to both child/patient and parent.

With such intolerable affects, the clinician needs to experience, contain, metabolize, and at some point find ways to return intolerable feelings in modified form to the patient. This book aims to help therapists take the pressure off the patient to feel what she cannot bear to feel, and off themselves to confront the patient's affect intolerance. While exploring the patient's affect intolerance, the therapist should be well prepared to *feel with and for his patient*, over a prolonged time, what she finds so terrifying. Containment of the unbearable has to come long before attempts at interpretation. Otherwise, we prematurely return the unbearable to the patient.

As therapists struggle to stay with these intolerable feelings, they seek to find creative ways to talk with their patients about how and why these feelings have become so terrifying. The therapists' task is to assist these difficult patients through their own capacity to bear what their patient cannot. Therapists must contend with their own affect intolerance, struggling with their own protections and avoidances against feelings they, too, find threatening. Especially difficult for patient and therapist alike are feelings of hopelessness, intense rage, and hatred.

Seven patients who had psychologically intrusive parents have taught me to become exquisitely attuned to their extreme sensitivity of being intruded upon by my own feelings, expectations, and needs. Such patients will inevitably involve the therapist in a repetitive invasion and undermining, as roles alternate throughout the treatment. Much of the exploration of these patients' mistrust occurs as they confront their sensitivity to feelings of the therapist's intrusion, dismissal, and obliteration of their perceptions, feelings, and needs.

With certain patients who are terrified of allowing themselves to need the help of another person, it is difficult for therapist and patient to preserve a joint focus on any particular problem. No matter what such patients consciously proclaim, their need for protection overrides their need for help. Even as a patient shows her difficulties and seems to ask the therapist for help with them, she flees contact with the therapist about what had just been addressed, so that the two keep losing their focus. Then she will not be trapped, intruded upon, used, robbed, hurt, or do the same to the therapist. When therapists cannot preserve therapeutic focus with a patient, they need to explore, first for themselves and ultimately with the patient, the patient's terror of allowing the two to look together at her problems.

Such difficulty with preserving therapeutic collaboration becomes a problem for the therapist to manage rather than an expectation that the patient now magically do what she cannot. As the therapist struggles to tolerate not being able to help his patient— who cannot tolerate accepting his help—he needs to feel his patient's terror about wanting to show him what is wrong in order to get his help. With such endangered patients, the therapist's empathic appreciation and interpretation of how awful it is that the patient needs the therapist's help, while so terrified of feeling vulnerable in accepting it, won't change the patient much. It becomes incumbent on the therapist to respect the patient's terror and understandable avoidance of vulnerability to the therapist's influence.

The clinician should not continually seek to preserve emotional connectedness with such patients. Consistent connectedness is more than they can tolerate. Sometimes, the patient's need for detachment, distance, control, and self-sufficiency must be respected, not discussed. Sometimes, patient and therapist can explore how each feels impinged upon by the other, because impingement will go both ways between them. And sometimes, they can indeed talk together about why the patient has needed to disconnect emotionally from the therapist.

If I become doubtful about the wisdom of having assessed a patient as genuinely in need of intensive psychotherapy or analysis as the treatment that offers her the greatest potential for change, I spend much time trying to understand my hesitation. I work with my negative feelings towards the patient to understand what's now wrong between us. I'm now much more eager than I used to be to investigate optimistically within myself and with my patient such doubt, disappointment, and defeat between us. A therapist's most essential task is to persist in feeling with and for patients their terrors of their own feelings and of their needs for the therapist. But some patients do not have sufficient motivation or capacity to change where they've become stuck. Not until a patient and I have struggled mightily for a considerable time with *our* stuck, unproductive situation do we decide to discontinue intensive psychotherapy or analysis. Both of us need to investigate, within each of us and between us, what's gone wrong.

I do not attribute such difficulty solely to the patient's limitations, unwillingness, or disability. I'm especially eager to explore the dynamic functions of our negative feelings about the treatment, both their expressive and defensive aspects. I seek to understand the effects of the patient's negativism on me, to contain, and later to interpret what his negativism expresses and defends against. Much better than before, I now tolerate, sometimes even enjoy, working with patients who continue to insist that they want nothing from me.

Part I

What Makes Affect Intolerable for the Patient and Therapist?

1

Barriers to Love Between Patient and Therapist

It should be no surprise that the most intense passions, love and hate, have been difficult for both patients and therapists to manage in their clinical encounters. In intensive psychotherapy and in psychoanalysis, we want both patient and clinician to become caught up in strong feelings, within oneself and between self and other. At the same time, we require that therapists be able to process and understand what they are feeling, so as to understand and analyze the patient. We have good reason to fear that therapists may be unable to manage the strains of their passions, either closing themselves off emotionally or misusing feelings primarily for their gratification rather than to assist patients. I believe that therapists cannot carry intensive treatments to successful conclusion unless they have access to their own strong loving and hating feelings. This is especially true for patients who have needed to defend themselves vigorously, by extraordinary measures, from intense feelings of love and hate. Various barriers can be used between patient and therapist as protection against the full range of loving and hating feelings.

Psychoanalysts have always been ambivalent about the role of loving feelings between patient and analyst: whether they are necessary, genuine, and therapeutic. Is love resistance or the vehicle for change? How much love (and how much hatred) must patient and clinician feel toward each other for a treatment to be effective?

When and how do such passionate feelings between the treatment couple interfere with change? Are loving feelings between the treatment couple merely neurotic wishes in each which must be relinquished or do they facilitate growth? If loving feelings do assist change, how do they do so?

I remember being taught as a psychoanalytic candidate in the late 1960s that I should not want or need my analysand to improve, that I should merely interpret conflict, leaving it up to the patient what she or he would do with such interpretation. Although the supervisor, who told me this, quite reasonably wanted to help me avoid burdening my patient with my own needs, this dispassionate mode of analyzing became fixed conflictedly in my analytic ego ideal (cf. Schafer 1992). It had tended to interfere with my freedom to enjoy feeling a variety of passions with my analysands. Contemporary analysts have encouraged a more positive, optimistic *analytic* use of our feelings in the analytic setting. We have been welcomed to experience the full range of our feelings with our patients and *then* to subject them to self-analysis, in order to sort out their relevance to the present therapeutic work with a particular patient.

I am concerned that the therapeutic ego ideal of most analysts and therapists remains intolerant and critical of loving and hating feelings toward patients. I was especially struck by the apparent discomfort of our most highly skilled psychoanalysts in discussing their loving and hating feelings toward patients. At the panel on "Hate in the analytic setting" (Panel 1994; see Chapter 3), each analyst seemed relieved to be able to move away as quickly as possible from the patient's hatred and his own. Most of the clinical vignettes involved only brief episodes of anger, not sustained chronic hatred. The one case that did involve ongoing hatred and destructiveness was mired in sadomasochistic enactment, patient and analyst both attempting to avoid full acknowledgment of their feelings. I need to stress that such discomfort with hatred in the analytic setting is not an artifact of an outmoded traditional psychoanalytic approach. These were excellent clinicians who still tended to move away from the full force of their patients' hatred toward them. It is an illusion that a shift of theory is sufficient to allow clinicians to manage the passions of the consulting room more comfortably. Hence, I want all clinicians, whatever their theoretical orientation, to be prepared to catch their own vulnerabilities and discomforts with their patients' passions.

Similarly, at the panel, "Love in the analytic setting" (unpublished), we did not hear much about analysts' loving feelings toward their patients. The distinguished analysts seemed uncomfortable with revealing feelings of love for their patients. The exception was a moving description by Gabbard (1994). When his male patient talked of exciting lusty wishes for homosexual fulfillment with him, Gabbard analyzed easily. But when his patient suddenly began to speak much more directly about really wanting the analyst to love him, Gabbard shares with us that he began to interpret the patient's longings toward his father. After a while, Gabbard became aware that by bringing the father into the room, he now felt safer, less threatened by his patient's (and his own) wishes for love between them. He was then able to correct his escape and distancing from his patient. Isay (1985, 1986, 1987a, b) makes clear that many gay men in analysis with a gay analyst are similarly frightened of loving closeness and so must fight it off. Kernberg (1994) describes how a sadomasochistic engagement between himself and his female patient protected both of them from their erotic feelings toward each other. Kernberg acknowledges his own reluctance for a time to explore his erotic feelings toward this woman patient.

THERAPISTS' AMBIVALENCE TOWARD PASSIONATE FEELINGS

When I was about to present an earlier version of this chapter at the American Psychoanalytic Association, a close friend, after reading the abstract, urged me not to present the paper. He insisted that I could not possibly love my patients the way I loved my wife. Of course that is true but irrelevant. Surprisingly, this friend, as a member of a peer supervision study group, not only had heard me present detailed process material of the woman patient I discussed in the paper, but he fully endorsed my analytic work with her. What he objected to was my getting up in public and talking about loving feelings between us, which he regarded as unseemly.

This essay has elicited intensely polarized feelings from colleagues. There are those who have praised my discussion of problems in tolerating and sustaining loving feelings with patients, even those who contend that I am still too held back in talking about love between patient and analyst. And there have been others who have been critical of this paper on several counts: (1) that the feelings I am describing run counter to analytic neutrality and so must be countertransference impediments, which I should have analyzed in one of my analyses; (2) that I am using an emphasis on loving feelings as a defense against feelings of hatred and destructiveness in myself and in my patients; (3) that I am really talking about the vulnerability I acknowledge in myself to feeling unappreciated and dismissed rather than about loving and being loved. I think these objections serve to block us from talking about our common difficulties with loving feelings in the treatment setting. So I advise readers of this chapter not to stop at these objections but to persevere with the argument.

My intention in this chapter is not to advise therapists to love their patients but to focus carefully on mutually constructed barriers which serve to prevent loving feelings in the therapeutic setting. I deliberately do not attempt to define what I mean by loving feelings in the therapeutic setting. I leave this somewhat open and ambiguous so that the reader is free to resonate with a wide variety of responses and with his or her discomfort to one or another loving feeling in the therapeutic setting as described here. Nevertheless, I shall try to describe the variety of loving feelings I felt toward my patients and some of the obstacles with which I contended. It is now clearer to me that we clinicians can feel uncomfortable not only with intense passion and desire toward our patients but even with more benign caring feelings. One function of our clinical theory is to help us with our discomfort in the treatment setting by providing us with therapeutic legitimization for such uncomfortable feelings (Basch 1981, Coen 1981, 1987).

HOMOSEXUAL FEELINGS BETWEEN PATIENTS AND THERAPISTS

In 1994, The Columbia University Center for Psychoanalytic Training and Research held a faculty retreat on problems in the treatment of homosexual patients. A number of us were struck by the difficulty many of our presenters had with talking about loving and sexual desire between themselves and their patients. Our retreat was moving and sad as a number of colleagues talked about ways they now feel they had harmed some of their gay and lesbian patients. In our small group discussions, some colleagues were able to talk about problems of intimacy and closeness with their patients. In a number of presentations at our faculty retreat, it seemed clear that skilled analysts had moved away from intense love and desire between their patients and themselves. Several colleagues found talking about this helpful. Following a respected colleague's sad and moving personal presentation about many analytic experiences with gay men, the discussant, who had even been consulted by this colleague, shifted the focus to issues of theory. This seemed to derail the group's affective experience, thereby blocking us from talking more personally about our feelings in work with gay and lesbian patients. And it seemed that most of the group were perfectly willing to be so derailed from more intimate and personal discussion about intimate engagement with homosexual patients. My attempt to restore our focus in the large group, by commenting on how willing we were to be derailed from sharing deeply moving personal feelings, was unsuccessful.

A woman colleague candidly described her discomfort with a lesbian patient staring, longingly and seductively, at her legs and thighs. She reported that she enjoyed male patients gazing at her seductively but that she felt anxious when a woman, so openly, revealed desires for her. I was delighted that my colleague could talk about this at our faculty retreat, but I was also pained that she was uncomfortable with her homoerotic desire. In our small discussion groups at this faculty retreat, many colleagues spoke of their discomfort with longings that were discordant with their gender and with their sexual object choice. Men were uncomfortable with feminine wishes; women were uncomfortable with masculine wishes; most of the heterosexuals were uncomfortable with homosexual wishes; unfortunately, the small discussion groups I attended contained no openly declared homosexual analysts. I've been delighted, subsequently, to hear a lesbian analyst publicly describe how her training analysis helped her to become more comfortable with her own heterosexual longings toward her analyst and her patients. I have recently enjoyed the opportunity to discuss the analysis of a lesbian patient by a lesbian analyst at a workshop sponsored by gay and lesbian analysts at the American Psychoanalytic Association. It was impressive that the analyst began this work as a supervised analysis while she was an analytic candidate. We had a very constructive open discussion with the gay and lesbian analysts eager to counter their social isolation within their local professional groups. I was especially pleased that the group was eager to consider mutual concerns about loving closeness within this therapeutic dyad, as we would do with any therapeutic dyad.

Hence, I believe we need to talk much more openly about therapists' discomfort with loving feelings toward our patients. You should not misunderstand my emphasis on love between patient and therapist. I do not advocate a love cure. Rather I seek the conditions under which the therapist can help the patient analyze as much of his or her protections against loving feelings (and hating feelings) as possible. I believe that it is better for the therapist to be prepared to experience *some* love and desire for his patient in order to assist his patient than to feel he has transgressed his therapeutic ego ideal by having such feelings.

HISTORICAL BACKGROUND

The early psychoanalysts, pioneers in a dangerous uncharted world, insufficiently analyzed and trained, needed restraints on what they could allow themselves to experience with their patients. A number of them were led astray into actualizing, rather than analyzing, wishes and feelings between patients and themselves. Schafer (1977) reports an idea of Charles Rycroft's that Freud's motivation to emphasize repetition compulsion in erotic transference was, in part, to diminish public disapproval of loving and erotic passions within the analytic setting. Others have been here before. Plato warned that passionate sexual love is dangerous because it tends to lead to disregard for the "character of the beloved" (*Laws*, VIII, p. 837). Love of the soul is far safer because it esteems temperance, courage, magnanimity, and wisdom. In classical Greece, love was divided into Eros (lust), Philias (brotherly affection), and Agape (spiritual love).

TRANSFERENCE LOVE: FREUD'S VIEW

As we reread Freud (1915), we certainly can sense his struggle as to whether transference love should be regarded as real and genuine or as an *unreal* transference repetition. Freud's emphasis is on the analyst's capacity to preserve his analytic attitude in the face of the patient's neediness to be loved. In the consulting room, by regarding transference love as *unreal*, analysts can try to keep themselves from becoming caught up in such passion. Freud's concern was that analysts would join their patients in sexual enactments. Such concern precluded consideration that analysts could move in the opposite direction, toward remoteness and uninvolvement with their patients, at times leading to iatrogenic exaggeration and worsening of the patients' (narcissistic) disabilities. Since the patient opposes the analyst's aims for the treatment, the analyst is to argue with his patient that her loving feelings for him cannot be *genuine*. That is, Freud notes the patient's hostile demandingness in such love claims toward the analyst.

We begin to sense that therapists do have needs of patients and that patients' and therapists' needs can conflict with each other. Having argued that transference love is unreal, so that analyst and patient would accept analyzing rather than acting upon these feelings, Freud then allowed that transference love is, at the same time, real and genuine. Now the tension increases for Freud and his followers. The transference becomes "the strongest weapon of the resistance"

(1912, p. 104). To overcome such resistance, the analyst uses the transference to motivate the patient by *suggestion*. For the sake of the analyst's love, the patient is to relinquish her loving attachment to the very analyst she now loves! That is not quite how Freud put it, although it is how Friedman (1991, 1997) now understands Freud's advice that the analyst *use* the patient's transference love to overcome resistance (loving attachment) by [the analyst's] suggestion and [the patient's] compliance.

Freud (1912) claimed that the analyst could indeed make use of suggestive influence over the patient through the "unobjection-able" part of the transference. He did not acknowledge that the analyst's use of suggestion would have repercussions that would themselves require analysis. Others (McLaughlin 1981, Stein 1981, Wallerstein 1993) have since pointed out the risks of regarding part of the transference as "unobjectionable"; what is seemingly "unobjectionable" and beyond analysis easily becomes a hiding place for conflicted feelings. Wallerstein (1993) notes that the patients Freud refers to in his (1915) "Transference-Love" paper tend to be sicker than the ordinary neurotic patient. Clinging to their sticky longings for maternal nurturance from the analyst, they relinquish them only with great difficulty. By opening up multiple and opposite meanings in positive and negative transferences, Wallerstein makes Freud's dichotomy more complex. And he too warns us of what is objection-able in the seemingly unobjectionable transference.

Schafer (1993) plays with the tensions in Freud's (1915) contradictory views of transference love as both genuine and unreal. He argues that Freud would not preserve the analytic relationship as separate and apart from ordinary life outside the consulting room. Freud demolished the boundaries between transference love and "real love." Freud, according to Schafer, was then unprepared to confront the implications of what he had opened up between patient and analyst. As a result, Freud restricted his position on transference love to the unreal repetition of infantile wishes. He did not acknowledge that transference love can *also* offer possibilities for creative interpretive transformation, for change and progress in new modes of relationship

(Schafer 1977, pp. 18–20). Indeed Schafer (1993) suggests that Freud was uncomfortable with patients' love, which he sought to avoid by emphasizing a rationalistic, argumentative, and pressuring attitude with his patients. Alternatively, Schafer proposes, analysts can seek to intensify patients' erotic transferences for the analyst's own needs: to enhance self-esteem; to avoid hostile aggression, intense maternal longings, or acknowledgment of the patient's emotional deadness. In his considerations of transference love, Freud was preoccupied with women's desires for their male analysts, neglecting other varieties of transference love.

Searles's (1959) paper, "Oedipal love in the countertransference," was remarkable for the revelation that, during successful analysis, the author developed loving and sexual desires for his male and female patients. Searles candidly described his surprise at his passion, for which he had not been prepared by his training analysis, psychoanalytic institute training, or the psychoanalytic literature. We have now been able to critique the emotional constriction that analysts were encouraged to feel toward their patients during the 1950s (Panel 1994b). For example, one distinguished analyst told how preoccupied he felt, as a candidate during the 1950s, with a patient who kept sitting up on the couch; he had to get her to behave herself like a proper analytic patient so that he could feel like a proper [candidate] analyst. We hope that the personal analysis of contemporary analysts and therapists has emphasized the need to become relatively comfortable with the variety of loving and hating feelings we all have with our patients. We are now freer, to some degree, to tolerate our feelings and needs with our patients than were analysts in the 1950s.

Friedman (1997) argues that Freud's papers on technique shift the focus of analysis from the patient's opposition to remembering to his or her conflicts over desire toward the analyst. He extends his argument by opening up the tension between what patient and analyst each want from the other. Friedman contends that the present generation of analysts, in competition and rebellion with our predecessors, are now ready to examine more openly what we want from our patients. He emphasizes the tension in the analyst between what she wants from the patient and her attempts to get outside of such wants or demands of the patient for the sake of analyzing the patient. The analyst has the power of a psychological seduction that she offers the patient. Other aspects of the analytic setup serve to "cushion . . . that discomfort." The patient is "led to expect love while the analyst, in Freud's words, plans to provide a substitute for love. Admittedly the love-substitute is something very special with secrets we have yet to fathom, but it is not the love the patient is imagining" (1997). The ambiguity of the analyst's personal interest heightens the emotional tensions between the analytic couple. "The demand structure of psychoanalysis" has varied from the analyst's wanting patients to remember, to tame other wishes, to face the truth/resistances or to grow up in treatment. Friedman would have us face what we want from our patients rather than continue trying to conceal such wishes/demands by the illusion of objectifying analytic technique, as by imagining that the analyst's interpretation can be free of her desire.

THERAPISTS' DEFENSE AGAINST PASSIONATE FEELINGS

Gabbard (1994) argues that analysts' focus on distinctions between love in the transference and outside of it tends to serve as an obsessional defense against our discomfort with intense loving feelings between patient and analyst. Gabbard's frank discussion of his discomfort with loving feelings between his male patient and himself shows that it may be much safer for patient and analyst (especially of the same sex) to focus on erotic feelings than on wishes to love and to be loved. I agree wholeheartedly with Gabbard's demonstration that the analyst must be able to tolerate intense loving feelings between his patients and himself in order to be able to work with them analytically. If the therapist cannot tolerate such loving (and hating) feelings in himself or herself, the therapeutic couple may tend to become mired in unproductive sadomasochistic repetition that closes off the path toward change through new and dangerous experience of loving and hating feelings between them.

In Searles's (1959) groundbreaking paper, he still reported that he ended the treatment of a man who made him uncomfortable by loving him too intensely. We noted above Kernberg's (1994) acknowledgment that his discomfort with erotic feelings between himself and his female patient perpetuated a defensive sadomasochistic relationship between them. Kernberg (1994) claims that narcissistic resistances (and enactments) against dependency and envy and sadomasochistic resistances (and enactments) against oedipal wishes interfere with the development of transference love and desire. Smith (Panel, unpublished) contends that there is no question that analysts do love their patients. The question, however, is what analysts do with such loving feelings (Brenner 1982, Schafer 1997). I certainly agree with Smith that the issue is whether the analyst can draw upon loving feelings to understand the patient (and oneself) better and so advance the analytic work. If the analyst is not capable of such self-inquiry, then transference/countertransference love will hinder analytic exploration. Jacobs (Panel, unpublished) similarly claims that the analyst's dilemma is not just to be the object of the patient's love but that, to varying degrees, the intimate analytic setting invariably stirs up the analyst's own wishes to be loved by the patient.

Contemporary psychoanalytic authors encourage passionate engagement between the analytic couple and acknowledge that the analyst will tend to lose his place frequently, acting rather than reflecting. Indeed Renik (1993) claims that the invariable route by which the analyst becomes aware of countertransference is through recognition of neurotic *action* with the patient. But Renik is optimistic that if analysts can tolerate such knowledge, then they can learn from new developments in the countertransference in order to assist the patient. More than twenty years ago, when this was still startling news, a distinguished analyst told a public audience that he draws upon his fantasies of having a love affair with his female patients to understand them better by imagining what would go wrong in each affair. Nor did he hide that such fantasy affairs were fun for him, part of his legitimate analytic gratification.

Contemporary psychoanalysts have become embroiled in extensive debate, generally unproductive, over whether conflict or object relations should be our central focus. Some analysts, myself included (1992), prefer to integrate conflict and object relations. Similarly, analysts debate the therapeutic role of the analytic relationship in contrast to greater mastery and integration of conflicted intrapsychic wishes. Wishes to be loved easily enter into such debate. Few would argue that it is not therapeutic to indulge a love cure that avoids analyzing conflict by reassurance and (loving) gratification from the analyst. Most analysts would be concerned that an analyst's loving feelings for a patient may interfere with the analytic posture of neutral interpretation equidistant from each of the psychic functions. We question when love between the analytic couple is defensive against more threatening affects and wishes.

Analysts debate whether deprived patients need an initial phase of treatment in which, to a degree, they can live out a kind of loving acceptance with the analyst. Some would argue that such a "loving" initial phase of treatment indulges the deprived patient's claims for reparation and entitlement, making them harder to analyze and relinquish. Others contend instead that in analyzing the deprived patient's conflicts about wanting to be loved, it is inevitable that there will be a phase of treatment in which the patient opens up such intense wishes to be loved with the analyst. It may even be that some analysts argue against such fostering of the deprived patient's wishes to be loved in the transference because the patient's regressive wishes threaten their own defenses against similar childlike longings for caring.

My loving feelings for my patients especially involved my resonating with them about conflicts I had resolved in my analyses, which I enjoyed resampling. I appreciated the help I had received and I was pleased to be able to assist my patients' attempts to work their way out of similar conflicts. The clinical vignettes that follow are intended to show something of each patient's and my own wishes for, and defenses against, wanting and giving love in the analytic transference. My clinical material for this study includes presentations by colleagues at panels (Panel, 1991, 1992, 1993) of the American Psychoanalytic Association in which I participated. I emphasize how common, temporary or longlived, barriers of angry, critical feelings are between the therapeutic couple as *joint* protection against feelings of love (and hate), even in ultimately successful treatments. In the vignettes that follow, therapists seem to protect themselves especially against fully feeling intense need, love, and hate between the therapeutic couple or against narcissistic vulnerability when the patient either refuses to be loving or shifts abruptly from a loving to an unloving attitude.

CLINICAL VIGNETTES

Ms. X., a young single woman raised in a Muslim country, sought consultation about her grief, which she feared would be endless, two months after the accidental death of an older brother. Ms. X. expressed her hunger for emotional and physical contact in her pleading stare that seemed to beg for response; in frequent silences, incomplete, incomprehensible, or inaudible sentences; in her touching and holding the couch pillows and couch fabric; and, eventually in her curling up on the couch in my direction, sneaking a peek at me, or lowering her head off the pillows onto the couch like a kitten wanting stroking. On the other hand, Ms. X. felt frightened of her intense wishes for closeness with me and kept running away, emotionally and physically. She found being on her own very difficult; she sought human contact in telephone calls, radio, television, and visiting her mother and sister in the city where they lived. As she became more involved with her analysis and with me, she would tend to be depressed at her first session of the week; her depression would lift during the course of the session and usually not continue during the rest of the week.

    I wondered whether she could tolerate analyzing what she wanted from me in the analytic transference rather than either just trying to get it or to deny such need with me and seek to get it fulfilled by others. Ms. X. emphasized her deprivation: other than the brother who had died, during her childhood no one in her family had spent much time with her; both parents seem to have been depressed; the nanny who raised her provided perfunctory care, without the parents objecting; she was the fourth child, a girl, in a family ill-prepared to care for her; her family and country devalued women, tending to keep them subservient. Ms. X. had memories of being locked in her dark room as a young child, the blinds shut, banging her head against the wall so someone would come to her. At a slightly later age (3-4 years old) when she felt ignored, she would station herself in the central hallway of her home; as others walked past her, she would bang her head against the wall, hoping that someone would pick her up. Instead, her mother seemed annoyed with her for being so poorly behaved that she needed to show others how she felt. Indeed, proper respect, manners, and deference to authority were insisted upon. Not until college in the United States did she appreciate that she was bright; mother seemed to regard her as stupid and to expect little from her. When Ms. X. considered business school, her mother suggested secretarial school so that Ms. X. could become a typist.

Ms. X. became engaged at the start of this analysis around her difficulty managing on her own and her hunger for human contact. I linked these themes with her sense of deprivation, narcissistic vulnerability, insecurity, and her feeling deficient, unlovable, and unloved. Much of what opened up and fueled the beginning phase of this analysis was Ms. X.'s sense of my concern about her feelings and needs. Her wish to have me like her determined much of her early treatment behavior, including her compliance and, at times, her acceptance of my interpretations. Indeed Ms. X. perceived correctly that I liked her and enjoyed working with her; I lowered my fee to make analysis possible for her. For some time she and I liked each other, except when she would feel hurt, rejected, and angry at me for not being sufficiently caring or available. What I liked about Ms. X. included the intensity of the analytic process related to her ability to tolerate feeling her powerful angry hunger for caring, her terror of this hunger, and the liveliness of her running toward closeness with me and away from it; she allowed me to feel creative in my analytic work with her; I enjoyed working with her potent hungry desires; I liked being able to help this bright, talented, attractive woman reclaim her assets; and I enjoyed feeling needed, wanted, desired (and hated) and caring, loving, and desiring (and hating) as I resonated with her wishes to be loved by a mother and by a father. That is, I liked feeling with her as deprived child and as rejecting, caring, loving, and desiring parent. Her foreign/exotic qualities and background evoked my own oedipal and pre-oedipal maternal wishes, which I now enjoy sampling.

The task at the start of this treatment was to bring the patient's wish to be loved into the arena of analyzable conflict, where it had not been. That is, Ms. X. originally felt entitled to insist that others demonstrate their concern and caring for her. When others failed this demand, even in minor ways, she would feel very hurt, disappointed, rejected, and angry. Ms. X. needed to relinquish her sense of entitlement to reparations of unlimited care and loving for her to understand, rather than *justify*, the childhood sources for her present feelings and needs.

Indeed, Ms. X. was able to shift from dumplings (Freud 1915) to fantasies and to gain greater perspective on the multiple meanings and derivatives of her wishes to be loved. As she succeeded in relinquishing the entitled expectation that I would actually give her what she had missed, she became less terrified of actualizing her transference wishes. Her entitled expectations, she learned to her surprise, could not magically compel me to gratify her. Now Ms. X. could feel more responsible for what she wanted with me rather than to dread merger or incest as external dangers to which she could succumb. She felt safer to want me to love her sexually once she could accept that her wishes would not automatically be granted. That is, Ms. X. could enjoy fantasies and feelings of my loving her once she could relinquish her entitled demand for action and reparation in the treatment setting. That a sultan, genie, or now I as the analyst would grant her wishes because of past misfortune was a fairy-tale version of her wish to be loved.

A significant shift occurred when she began to feel that she could gain my acceptance not only through what was wrong in her but through what was good about her. It scared her to realize that she wanted me to admire, love, and desire her. But she preferred the anxiety of her now more erotic transference to her earlier masochistic stance as deprived victim. She now wanted to exhibit what was good about her, including her attractive body, and to go after what she wanted much more actively and assertively. She began to enjoy her anger and aggression, as she moved from passive helplessness to a more demanding insistence on the satisfaction of her needs. She obtained a significant promotion at work and began to have men pursue her.

The meanings of Ms. X.'s organizing wishes to be loved changed through the course of this treatment. At first, she craved signs of interest, response, and human contact, which she equated with caring. This young woman scrutinized and gauged the quantity and intensity of my speech and the expressiveness of my face and gaze. She hungered continually for lively response to reassure her against fears of abandonment, rejection, and feeling unwanted. Her original wish to be loved had been generalized, stripped of more intimate, passionate, sensual, and loving desires. I was, first, as analyst, just to be an interested older man who showed my concern about her feelings and needs. With analysis of resistance to awareness of the transference, her wishes for concern and caring from me grew to wishes for closeness, physical contact, and love. As Ms. X. could tolerate her attachment to me in the transference as a family member, she wanted much more from me: what she felt she had not gotten enough of from her family. The brother and father transference to me as analyst brought, under considerable resistance, sensual and sexual desires into the analysis. As Ms. X. could confront her feelings of insecurity, she could now open up, in a more angry, demanding way, how much she desired the sexual love of her father and brother. She could begin to tolerate her angry, competitive feelings with other women, including her mother and sister, and want to rob and destroy them, so that she would be the only one to be loved sexually by the father/analyst.

Ms. X. wanted me to pursue her through active intervention, which she sought to encourage by the many provocative ways she would refuse to be responsible for herself. Certainly I interpreted Ms. X.'s attempts to get me to tell her what she could indeed tell herself. Much of her dependency involved hiding her abilities and presenting herself as incapable so as to involve the other in some caretaking role with her. She and I needed to monitor how and why I participated with her in the treatment, so as to allow her to discover all she could do for herself. From this perspective, her hungry and angry demand for caring and vindictive refusal to become responsible for herself was a major contributant to her early formidable resistance to awareness of the transference and her ongoing exaggerated passivity and helplessness.

Ms. X.'s anger and aggression emerged in the transference from behind the screen and camouflage of *only* loving feelings. Just as she needed to feel loving, loved, and lovable with me, so too did she need to be able to hate me and to tolerate my hatred of her. Initially a battle for power, authority, and control appeared with me as both mother and father. Then the battle focused along gender lines with dreams and fantasies of castrating and seizing for herself the penis and prerogatives of men, especially with me in the transference. Ms. X. sought to dominate and control me so that she herself could run the show as boss, with me in an inferior, degraded position. Loving feelings left the consulting room, replaced by hatred, envy, and competitiveness in and between us. Of course, she would continually shift away from her anger and aggression to her more comfortable position as passive, meek, seductive, or loving, as she would curl up on the couch, exposing her thighs, undoing her destructive wishes toward me.

Then, Ms. X.'s infantile, extractive, and exploitive qualities became clearer in and out of the analytic transference. During this period, I often felt angry, dismissed, and taken advantage of. Her reduced fee contrasted with the money she and her mother considered using for an expensive wedding and for the jewelry and gifts that would make Ms. X. feel like a queen. She now felt freer to draw upon family funds and her own. She feared that both she and I would want whatever was available; this insatiable greed and envy frightened her in herself and in the other person. We saw how she had identified with her mother's infantile greed, envy, and entitlement, which she had compounded by her own angry sense of deprivation. Here, to be loved meant extreme indulgence, that she could have whatever she wanted without limitation or delay. Ms. X. would often dismiss my interpretations that she was avoiding addressing important conflicts in the treatment. She frequently would arrive late, enjoying being unpredictable, wishing that I would wait at the door for her, escort her in, and then close the door for her. Many times Ms. X. would not tell me clearly about her business trips so that I would not know when she would return. We learned that business colleagues and friends (and I) resented her selfish, irresponsible ways. At a party several months after she married, a friend asked her with some annoyance why she had not offered to help serve the meal. In a huff, Ms. X. retorted, "I'm a bride!"

Given how loving the consulting room had felt, I was somewhat surprised when I found myself hating Ms. X., experiencing her as selfish, extractive, and exploitive. Indeed for awhile, at times, it was hard for me to see beyond these feelings and images of Ms. X., as if we had reached the core of her psyche. Fortunately, I was presenting this case to a peer supervision group at the time; my colleagues helped me to preserve more consistently the perspective that Ms. X.'s ugly character traits could be analyzed so that something else could emerge from her. I had felt disappointed and angry that she was not more appreciative and accepting of my analytic help, that she did not just somehow change into someone different from who she was. She too felt disappointed and angry that I was not as accepting and caring toward her as I had previously been. But my angry feelings had led me to close off temporarily, at least in part, my fuller perception of Ms. X. and my caring feelings for her. When we worked actively with her infantile, extractive, exploitive qualities, which were now becoming less acceptable to her, and agreed on a systematic schedule for raising her fee, I felt less angry and dissatisfied with her. I could again become (lovingly) optimistic that Ms. X. could relinquish her selfish and destructive attitudes, which precluded her being loving and lovable.

Later, we could again see that Ms. X. was more comfortable with negative response than with acceptance, love, power, and success. Her selfish, exploitive, irresponsible character traits had simultaneously served as a sadomasochistic barrier against such positive wishes. That is, feeling safer in the treatment situation, she felt freer to reveal her ugly character traits, which she then exploited (successfully) to keep us from enjoying each other. As we analyzed her guilty competitiveness about defeating her mother to become a genuine queen, who no longer needed jewels to feel authentic and accepted, loving and sexual feelings returned between us.

I want to contrast Professor J., who would not relinquish his entitled demands that others, including me, owed him reparations for his childhood trauma. Similar interpretive strategies with Professor J. did not lead to a productive analytic process as with Ms. X. I did not succeed in alarming Professor J. that his control of the treatment and refusal to analyze his entitled position threatened the success of the treatment. Instead, Professor J. would claim that he too doubted the treatment would really change him and so dismiss my attempts to engage him on where he was stuck in the treatment. After many years of analysis, Professor J. still continued to come late, to miss sessions frequently, and to struggle against allowing me to occupy a prominent position in his mind. But Professor J. had been this way with his wives, girlfriends, male friends, and colleagues. Until he was about to lose a woman, she did not have much importance to him. He wanted to feel the woman's or my presence but at a considerable distance; he felt more comfortable with his computer than with a person. Especially when he had just been frustrated, Professor J. would become angry, demanding, insulting, insistent that others provide him with care. Otherwise, it was much more difficult for him to hold still and feel how much he wanted another person to actually care for him. Control was much more important for him than was caring.

Professor J.'s mother died when he was 4½ years old; she had been seriously ill since his infancy. His father, older brother, and a part-time housekeeper had helped to look after him. After mother's death, he was placed in foster care and moved among numerous homes during the next five years until his father remarried. Presumably, his anger, needy demandingness, and aloof withdrawal had made it impossible for foster parents to find him lovable.

Indeed, as an adult he resisted allowing himself to feel vulnerable, needy, and lovable. He would easily become enraged at me for charging him for a missed session, insisting this was an illegal exploitation that he might report to the state attorney general. Or he would become furious that I was wasting his time by announcing "administrative details" such as when I would be away for summer vacation. He could feel that I understood him better than had his previous therapists, that I was bright and verbal, perhaps with the condescending implication, which he did not quite express, that I might not be a bad student in one of his classes. He would laugh warmly when I described how impossible he could be in his demands and dismissal of me. Sometimes, he would miss me, and he certainly understood intellectually what I had interpreted to him.

He could grasp my telling him about his vindictive destructiveness with me and with others, that he would not now allow anyone to really be helpful to him, that he would find various rationalized ways to reject the help I offered him. At times, he could work with his destructiveness as a kind of refusal to let the world off the hook for his childhood trauma. But I had the sense that what touched him most at such times was my concern about him, that he would not really change. I felt that he remained in treatment largely because he liked my interest in him. Unlike with Ms. X., however, interpreting to Professor J. that what seemed most important about his work with me was that I seemed concerned about him did not lead very far. He could easily agree with me and yet simultaneously dismiss and deny the full emotional significance of his wanting me to like or love him.

Professor J. once became excited when he met a cousin of mine at a meeting. He would have enjoyed learning more about me so that we had a "real" connection, but he would not allow himself to imagine about me. Or, one Sunday when he felt lonely, he used his computer to search a psychology data base to find what I had written.

He was pleased that, in the abstracts he reviewed, I had seemed thoughtful. But here too he resisted imagining further about me and so drawing closer to me. Unlike with Ms. X., the craving for dumplings, or more accurately, the rage that dumplings were not automatically supplied, continued in Professor J. We could not really interrupt this despite Professor J.'s intellectual understanding of his entitlement and of his narcissistic defenses against genuine human need. He could complain that he now seemed much angrier than he had in the past, that his friends told him they did not like this in him. He just did not become genuinely responsible for working with and containing his rage. Unlike Ms. J., he would not relinquish his angry fairy tale that the analyst/genie should now fix his life for him.

Professor J.'s narcissistic defenses against human need, vindictive rage-filled rejection, and entitlement were much more intense and resistant to analysis than Ms. X.'s. In contrast to Ms. X., Professor J. could not open up his needy vulnerability in the treatment transference in an ongoing way and hold still with his intense wishes to be loved. Instead, he continued to indict everyone, including me, for failing to love him. He remained protected behind his rigid, angry shell, seemingly terrified to feel, more of the time, the needy child in himself. Ms. X. had felt safer, despite her considerable terror, with allowing herself to open up her dependent attachment to me. Less traumatized than Professor J., Ms. X. was more able to take a chance in the treatment with opening up and exploring her multiple wishes to be loved.

I have made clear that it was much more difficult for me to sustain, in an ongoing way, feeling close and caring with Professor J. than it was with Ms. X. Certainly I could resonate with his sadness, loss, deprivation, bitterness, and wishes for caring, when he allowed himself to feel the horrors of his mother's illness and death and his being shuttled from one foster home to another. I liked working with his loneliness, sadness, rage, and demandingness. I wanted to help this highly intelligent, articulate, thoughtful man feel better about himself and be able to manage a loving relationship with me and with a woman. I enjoyed his allowing himself to connect with me as brother, mother, and father. But his enormous need to control both our relationship and his needs of me would, over and over again, reduce my role with him almost to nothingness before he would again allow himself to make use of me. And my persistent interpretation of his need to control and destroy his relationship with me did not lead to significant change in his treatment behavior. So my hating Professor J. for his rejection and destruction of me interfered with my being able to preserve my liking and enjoying him. Although I could grasp and interpret that we were tending to enact roles in which mutual rejection protected against liking each other, I kept losing my footing.

When I presented an earlier version of this chapter at the Austen Riggs Center, a number of colleagues accustomed to working with hospitalized patients insisted that I was too pessimistic about Professor J. They agreed that I needed to emphasize his attempts to destroy the treatment process and good feelings between us but that I had moved back from him, so that, unlike with Ms. X., I was no longer fostering mutual loving between us. One colleague asked why I could not love Professor J. and let him love me the way I had with Ms. X. On the other hand, colleagues in the audience who practiced office-based analysis *unanimously* disagreed that Professor J. could be analyzed; they shared my concern and pessimism. The office-based analysts and I saw little or no indication that Professor J. was changing his way of relating to me or to others; he did not seem able to keep open a constructive analytic process. Our hospital-based colleagues compared him with hospitalized patients who had had multiple prior unsuccessful treatments. In effect, they recommended that instead of expecting Professor J. to adapt to an analysis, that, through my feeling caring toward him, I needed to find ways to try to keep him engaged in the treatment. They insisted that I and my office-based colleagues were expecting too much of him and had given up too quickly. This would have to be a long, demanding treatment, which I, as the therapist, would largely have to sustain with optimism, confidence, and caring.

I was indeed having difficulty preserving my conviction that there could be loving closeness between us even as I interpreted Professor J.'s terror of allowing such intimacy. After the Austen Riggs presentation, I felt less angry and disappointed by Professor J.'s recurrent retreats and attempts to spoil what had gone on between us, less concerned about the outcome of his treatment than I had been previously. At least part of my sense of stalemate with him derived from my feelings of anger and disappointment. My previous attempts to alarm Professor J. that he was destroying the treatment, as I was trying to get him to be different with me, contained more anxiety, helplessness, and resentment. He would respond with interest to such efforts to engage him but it was harder for us to preserve a consistent focus on his wanting to torture me through his provocativeness. But even more importantly, I kept losing my perspective on the defensive goal of his being an "impossible" child/patient, on how effectively this barred close, loving feelings between us.

As I interpreted such events more hopefully, focusing on Professor J.'s terror of continuing to enjoy feeling close to me, at least some of the time, he was less antagonistic, easier, warmer, more troubled about his angry destruction of all his relationships. I talked with him about his hesitation to appreciate and to feel pleased with what he got from me. I told him that he was afraid to relax and enjoy what was good between us, that he felt safer when he could criticize angrily what he did not get from me so that he quickly shifted from close moments to spoiling and destroying such closeness. Nevertheless, he would still insist that the treatment was worthless, that he had not changed, and that he would leave at the end of the month.

But he could respond to my interpretation of his need to fight with me by acknowledging how much more comfortable he felt punching me than wanting me to care about him. We heard about times when he felt touched and grateful for the concern of others, when he had been capable of tender caring: with his stepmother, a terminally ill friend, and his two cats. Each time one of his cats died, he called to speak with me on the telephone, in effect wanting me to comfort him. I could show him how he then needed to close off and devalue his tenderness with his cats and with me.

Once we could acknowledge that he was capable of some loving feelings, it became easier to preserve a therapeutic focus on exploring his defensive need to destroy loving feelings, especially now between us in the transference. With such loving feelings came considerable sadness, not only about what he had missed but especially how much of his life he had spent eradicating, rather than cherishing, memories of tender concern. He would feel moved and nurtured when he allowed himself to treasure moments of caring between himself and another rather than to fight about what was missing. Nevertheless, we were both keenly aware how quickly he would revert to his well-rationalized need to distance and spoil what he had just esteemed.

Earlier, I had interpreted Professor J.'s unconscious efforts to reverse roles with me, to have me feel for him what it was like to deal with inconsistent people on whom he could not rely, to have me rather than he be the uncertain, vulnerable one in our relationship. This was manifest in my being unable to know what to expect with him: whether or when he would arrive for a session, even whether he would call me if he was not coming; how long he would stay interested and available in what we were discussing before he would disappear emotionally or physically; when he would suddenly turn on me, angrily destroying and denying what had just been valuable between us. I had told him that I thought he was afraid of feeling overwhelmed with sadness and an addictive hunger for caring. The Austen Riggs presentation helped me to preserve my loving feelings of concern for Professor J. without allowing them to be destroyed by the rage and hatred he and I would periodically feel between us. The hospital-based group's encouragment that I modify my analytic expectations with Professor J. enabled me to counter my analytic ego ideal in working with this traumatized man. I was not frightened by homosexual tensions between us nor by mutual wishes for loving care. But I was put off by his destruction and devaluation of our work and our relationship. How many missed sessions in a row would I or should I tolerate? Indeed, I would need to tolerate my helplessness with

Professor J. and seek ways of showing him why he needed to reduce me to this position with him. I would tend to lose my perspective on his defensive need to destroy our work and instead, angrily and helplessly, feel like agreeing with him that his treatment was futile. I kept wanting to conclude that he was incapable of loving, allowing himself to be loved, and of being treated. I was getting back at him and protecting myself as I closed off the treatment and gave up on him, rejecting him and feeling superior to him (as unanalyzable, unlovable, unloving) as he did to me. How much better it would have been had I been able to preserve a more consistent interpretive focus on his angrily and defensively trying to push me away, to have me be the angry, disappointed child, so that we would be unable to keep open between us feelings of love and concern.

Without presenting additional clinical vignettes, I want to note briefly some reflections on colleagues' analytic work (Panels, 1991, 1992, 1993, in which I paricipated), which support what I have reported about myself. Even when skilled colleagues report their work, there often tends to be evidence of their discomfort with feeling caring and loving with patients. The colleague may tend to remain distant, critical, and rejecting or collude with the patient in persistent sadomasochistic struggles. As reported publicly, the function of such behavior by the therapist seems to be to protect against mutual caring between the therapeutic couple, when such caring appears to be dangerous and forbidden to the therapist's therapeutic ego ideal. That is, antagonism and fighting remain safer than loving for the therapeutic couple. Further, sadomasochistic provocation offers each partner the illusion of control over the other and over one's needs of the other in contrast to the vulnerability of loving and wanting to be loved. Each partner settles for the excitement in being able to provoke the other rather than risk the vicissitudes of caring and loving. For the therapist to disengage himself from the enacted sadomasochism, he needed to confront his hatred of his patient's destructiveness with him and their mutual avoidance of loving feelings between them.

In many examples, the patient's neediness in the therapeutic setting appeared to be exaggerated by the unavailability of the therapist's love. As I tended to do with Professor J., the therapist's pessimistic, negative judgments of the patient's analyzability served to keep apart the therapeutic couple. That is, the therapeutic couple would collude to a degree in *closing off* the possibility that the patient could indeed tolerate his or her passions in the transference. And the therapist remained unable to acknowledge as legitimate the patient's complaints of not getting enough from the therapist and that something was indeed wrong in the treatment, not just in the patient.

DISCUSSION

What seems most to impede the clinical work in these examples, mine and colleagues', is collusion between the treatment couple that forecloses the possibility of change. That is, when the therapist agrees with the patient that he or she is as fixed, damaged, narcissistic, unlovable, hopeless, fragile, or ugly as the patient insists, treatment has been closed off. To move forward, the therapist would have to focus consistently on the multiple functions and meanings of the patient's predominant images of self and other as bad. The therapist's hurt, disappointment, and anger can easily contribute to destructive collusion in closing off exploration, instead settling for the negative status quo. My vulnerability to feeling unappreciated and dismissed by my two patients had contributed to my [less than conscious] resentful rejection of them, preventing me from continuing to want and expect closeness between us.

In each example, when I could become aware of having closed off a fuller, more loving set of feelings between me and my patient, I could regain my perspective as well as these more accepting, loving feelings. Like my colleagues, I too got caught up in a persistent, if temporary, attitude of criticism and rejection toward my patients. There is some element of sadomasochism in what happened between my patients and me in our willingness to remain within such negative feelings between self and other, foreclosing other more favorable possibilities toward the other and oneself. More significant, however, in my own examples than the sadomasochism was the persistence of my critical attitude toward each patient that so much narrowed my view of who this person could be and of how we could be together. I am impressed with how different the analytic setting felt once I had succeeded in interrupting my tunnel vision.

My synopsis of the literature and my clinical material indicates that persistent negative, critical feelings between the treatment couple, including sadomasochistic engagement, seek to block access to more intense passion, loving and hating. I am emphasizing an unconscious destructive collusion between therapist and patient that *closes off* possibilities for change and love, within and between them. Chronic hatred can serve as a relatively stable human bond (Bollas 1984–1985, Coen 1992, Pao 1965) or it can prevent and destroy human relationships. Either way, chronic hatred is safer than the vulnerability and gain of risking loving and wanting to be loved. I believe that when I was able to preserve my loving feelings for each of the patients I have described, I was then able to see and to help the patient see beyond where he or she had become stuck. Put in other words, I could then extract myself from and show my patient other possibilities than the images of self and other that were then so predominant in the consulting room.

To preserve loving feelings in the consulting room, it was necessary to focus consistently on how each patient and therapist tried to destroy such possibilities, especially by wishing to preserve a negative relationship, often sadomasochistic, which emphasized the impossibility of loving and being loved. Sadomasochism is not the only barrier to loving, although it is present in many of the examples I have used in preparing this chapter. Whatever fixes the treatment couple, not just the patient, on negative, hopeless, bitter, rejecting, defeated feelings can serve as a barrier to optimism, change, and love in the consulting room.

I do not intend to put loving feelings in a secondary position to hate, as merely an antidote to hate in the treatment setting. Nor do I mean to say that love should be used to avoid hatred. But love does need to temper hatred sufficiently that hatred between patient and therapist can be enjoyed and seen as a path forward. Hating a patient can indeed be loving, if the therapist can see beyond his or her and the patient's hatred and even love the patient in their mutual hatred (cf. Bollas, 1984–1985). I assume this is what Loewald (1960, 1970, 1975) meant by the analyst helping the patient to move to new levels of integration, beyond what the patient had yet been able to envision. It can be loving and accepting, of oneself and of the patient, for the therapist to tolerate similar appalling feelings in oneself as those in the patient. To separate oneself from one's patient (or oneself) as impaired, untreatable, and hopeless is far more hateful and destructive. Thus I would differentiate two kinds of hatred. Malignant hatred seeks to destroy possibilities for change, love, and acceptance within and between self and other. It is rooted in vengeance, bitter rage, and refusal/rejection of what others offer. The other aspect of hatred, although destructive of what is hated, does not seek to obliterate everything before it; while destroying, it is able to preserve a hope or demand for change or replacement. I have drawn upon Gabbard's (1991) concept of malignant transference hate, in which the patient, having lost the as-if quality of transference, insists that the therapist really deserves his hatred.

Schafer (1992) warns that idealization of scientific rigor in clinical technique precludes the therapist's being resourceful by encouraging him to conform to absolute standards; it invites misuse by his conscience to torture him for innovations in his work. Such idealization of, and concern about deviation from, imagined ideal technique may interfere with therapists' ability to tolerate loving and hating their patients. Most of us now no longer are so afraid that having strong feelings with our patients means that we need to return immediately for more analysis. Nevertheless, despite Searles' (1959) paper almost thirty-five years ago, we still do not easily admit to loving our patients. To a degree, our theoretical advance, that counter-transference feelings are a necessary and potentially helpful part of treatment has not been fully integrated into our daily work so that we can tolerate our passions with our patients. There still seems to be an aspect of our therapeutic ego ideal that precludes loving and hating our patients.

Some might contend that with the "narrower scope" patient, the therapist's concern with feeling loving toward patients would tend to make treatment overly and inappropriately interpersonal, outside of standard technique. I would disagree. Instead I would favor a therapeutic emphasis on how to help the patient gain as much personal autonomy as possible, from his own persistent conflicts and from reliance on the therapist. I would argue that whatever tends to close off the therapist's access to all of his feelings, wishes, perceptions, and expectations, even with his healthier patients, will interfere with their growth and change.

My conclusion is not that love between patient and therapist is curative but that it is necessary to facilitate therapeutic change. I would say the same about hatred. Therapist and patient need to be free to feel all the passions between them, loving and hating. When patient and therapist tend to be dissatisfied, critical, finding fault with each other or with oneself, *somehow* they need to be reminded to wonder what lies behind this for the other and for oneself. What I am describing is self-evident except when the therapeutic couple becomes blind to such possibilities for growth and change within and between them. Certainly there are treatments that therapist and patient, after considerable exploration, will assess as hopeless. But one aspect of therapeutic stalemate is precisely this need of the treatment couple to close off what could be good and loving within and between them, including mutual acceptance of loving and of hating. From this perspective, hatred can be loving when it allows for the possibility of transformation into something better. Hatred is only absolutely destructive when it refuses to see beyond itself.

How much love and hate do patient and therapist need to feel toward each other for therapeutic change to occur? I disagree with those clinicians who object that love and hate in the transference/countertransference are necessary to facilitate therapeutic change. These clinicians may be correct that certain affectively constricted patients may change in treatment even if their treatment has not been passionate. But I think the clinician would have to expect such passions in the intensive treatment of more rigid patients in order to develop a passionate treatment. I would argue that the therapist, if he or she is comfortable with such passions, would have to consistently analyze the patient's protections against feeling and expressing intense loving and hating feelings toward the therapist for them to flower in the therapeutic setting.

  I have been asked what the therapist is to *do* with his loving feelings for his patient. My answer would be the same for the therapist as for the patient. That neither is to *do* anything with loving feelings. Instead each is to feel them and to explore their meanings and uses. We now seem to agree that the therapist needs to feel a certain degree of caring, concern, and optimism for his patient to be able to help him change and grow. In my clinical examples, this seems to be especially necesary in order to analyze negative, hateful, rejecting, exploitive aspects of the patient. Otherwise, the patient will tend to experience (*correctly*) the therapist as judging and condemning him rather than attempting to assist him with change. As I learned with Professor J., I needed to help him (and myself) to establish, not just to preserve, loving feelings between us. I had to learn that analyzing his destructiveness with me was not enough; I had to help him learn how to tolerate a caring relationship through my ability to remain caring even when he attempted to spoil and destroy my concern for him.

  We seem to argue more about whether it is necessary that the therapist feel romantic and sexual desire for his patient. If I do not respond with *some* loving and lustful feelings to a patient who feels this way with me, I take for granted that something is in my way. Further, I expect to learn about my patient's not-yet-fully acknowledged wishes and desires through my own feeling responses, including my loving and sexual feelings for my patient. If we take seriously contemporary psychoanalytic emphasis on the inevitability of interaction and enactment between the therapeutic couple, we need to acknowledge that the therapist will play an emotional role in most intense affective developments in the therapeutic situation, including loving and sexual feelings. Better that the therapist be prepared to experience such feelings in order to assist his patient than that he continue to feel he has transgressed his therapeutic ego ideal by feeling *some* love and desire for his patient.

I do believe that deprived patients, like those I have described, need assistance with analyzing their protections against feeling the full force of their emotional hunger with the therapist. My strategy is to open up as fully as possible such need in the treatment setting. This is not intended as a cure by love but as the therapeutic condition for the patient now becoming able to be responsible for his wishes, desires, and feelings. Opening up passionate transference hunger with the therapist need not preclude exploration of rage, destructiveness, desire, and wishes for competence and autonomy. On the contrary, the more passion is drawn into the treatment setting, the more opportunity there may be to experience a variety of passions. I believe that for the therapist to work productively with such intense transference hunger, he must be able to resonate with both the deprived child and loving (and rejecting, hating) parent aspects of his patient and himself. The therapist's emotional tolerance for his loving feelings toward his regressed, deprived patient will facilitate his ability to analyze his patient's conflicts over such transference need of the therapist. I do believe that some therapists oppose the therapeutic strategy of cultivating the deprived patient's wishes to be loved in the transference because such intense regressive wishes threaten their own defenses against similar infantile longings. One aspect of the rigidity of the therapist's therapeutic ego ideal is this need to protect himself from what he cannot tolerate feeling in himself. And one goal of this chapter, and more generally of clinical theory, is to help the therapist tolerate what is difficult to bear in the therapeutic setting.

2

How to Help Patients
and Therapists Bear
the Unbearable

Since my earlier paper (1989) on intolerance of responsibility for internal conflict, I have continued to puzzle about why some patients seem unable to tolerate certain affects and certain conflicts so as to be able to address these in treatment. I have struggled with how to differentiate an inability to process feelings and face conflicts from a hesitation or unwillingness that can be more easily analyzed into component irrational fears and wishes. Either way, with inability or with unwillingness, I go on wondering about what makes it so difficult for certain patients to do what most other patients seem much more capable of managing, that is to analyze conflict, face feelings, change, and grow. It certainly can be painful and frightening for all of us to have to confront what seems most awful within, but most of us are ultimately able to manage this therapeutic task.

In two patients with such apparent inability to face their feelings and conflicts in analysis, I highlight conflict about their intense dependent attachment to me in the treatment. Each man could acknowledge a benign aspect of his needy dependency, but each was terrified of facing his more malevolent desires to possess and destroy me. Each patient felt very attached to me but

simultaneously kept running away from his hungry and angry desires toward me. One aim of the seeming treatment disability and
impasse was a *covert* angry wish to transform the therapeutic
relationship into a version of an unsatisfactory mother/child
relationship. With the patients I described in my earlier paper (1989),
their intolerance of affect and conflict was expressed through endless defensive transference repetition. They would avoid responsibility
for what was wrong within. Unlike the present patients, these earlier
patients had much more difficulty with acknowledging the benign
aspect of their dependency on me as therapist. With the present
patients, both patient and I remained unsure whether the apparent
treatment disability was really an inability to tolerate and process
affect and conflict or could more readily be analyzed into component
wishes and fears, especially in the transference with me. However, unlike my earlier patients, these two men's therapeutic disability
existed alongside the capacity for responsible self-examination,
attachment, concern, and love for himself and others, including me
as analyst. I examine shifts in these two patients between the ability for responsible self-inquiry and what seemed like therapeutic
disability.

When over a prolonged time the patient seems unable to
process key affects and conflicts and cannot acknowledge the therapist's
interpretations of his angry wishes to stay locked into a mutually
unsatisfactory relationship with him, the therapist may well feel
hopeless and defeated, as the patient unconsciously intends. How do
we decide whether this is an analyzable patient who can ultimately
bear responsibility for what has so far seemed intolerable? How does
the therapist help such a patient to bear the unbearable? What
determines those times when the patient seems capable of responsible
self-inquiry in contrast to his apparent therapeutic disability?

Each patient and I found it difficult to know whether he
could function better in his treatment and in his life than he was at
present. What was most useful was consistent attention to each patient's
unconscious attempts to eliminate the most valuable aspects of the
treatment relationship by regarding them merely as repeating in

transference what had come before rather than also as offering new possibilities for change and growth (Schafer 1977). Each patient desired and invited me as therapist to penetrate and own his body and mind. Terror of engulfment led him to fight vigorously against such wishes to surrender to me. Unable to acknowledge such transference longings, he *enacted* these transference wishes. Presenting himself as a disabled patient he invited me as therapist not only to assist him but to take him over. This living-out perpetuated the quasi-delusion that I as therapist could, if only I would, omnipotently protect the patient forever against his exaggeratedly destructive views of himself.

I shall consider the difficulty I, as therapist, and each patient had in grasping and preserving our therapeutic focus on understanding each patient's apparent treatment disability. Such examination should help us to differentiate patients' treatment disability from analyzable unwillingness to face conflict and to differentiate the therapist's collusion in perpetuating such impasse from more constructive efforts to help the patient move forward. My either/or attitude toward analyzability, at times, tended to interfere with my ability to shift flexibly between being an interpretive analyst and needing to provide holding, containing, and affirming functions for my patients without being able to interpret such need. I suggest that either/or views of analyzability may lead to overconcern with seeming treatment disability rather than to persistent understanding and facilitation of treatment process. Therapist and patient can become bogged down in the rigidly narcissistic trap of analyzable/special versus unanalyzable/worthless.

I needed to shift my view of treatment process to include prolonged oscillations away from expectable therapeutic collaboration toward profound narcissistic retreat, disavowal, and other defensive avoidance of conflict. I now favor more fluid, dynamic, and shifting perspectives of therapeutic engagement as well as of the patient's defense and integration. Otherwise, we may become trapped in static assessments of analyzability from within which we tend to exaggerate either the patient's progress or his impasse. I now believe that substantial analytic work can be accomplished with patients who oscillate for prolonged periods between emotional connection with the therapist and detachment and between acknowledgment and disavowal of conflict. Following Krystal (1975, 1978a, b), I advocate tactful challenging of patients' affect intolerance as entrenched in childhood attitudes, fantasies, and experiences that are no longer tenable. To bear the unbearable, patients need to gain the confidence that painful affects no longer will be as overwhelming as they had once seemed.

CLINICAL VIGNETTES

As Professor A.'s analysis progressed, he came to feel very proficient in his work: strong, capable, and bright. Conflicts over separateness and autonomy continued so that he felt terrified to be on his own, although he often covered this over with denial, attempts at omnipotent control, and counterphobic maneuvers. Professor A. now seemed to hesitate with actively taking the lead in his analysis, with making connections between sessions and themes. This contrasted with his earlier pleasure in contributing constructively to the work of the treatment. Unlike my second patient (Mr. B.), Professor A. had been a fine analytic patient; he and I had enjoyed our work together in this treatment for some time. But now the treatment situation suddenly changed so that Professor A. seemed inaccessible to analytic exploration. He stepped up his sexual activities, which now seemed to separate him from the treatment and from me. Earlier, these sexual activities had not been a barrier but a useful contributant to the treatment process. I again became concerned whether Professor A. would ultimately be able to tolerate separateness without severe regression, which we both had good reason to fear at the start of this treatment. In retrospect, both of us grasped that once termination was in sight, Professor A. became afraid to really rob and destroy me, to consolidate and appreciate his gains, to finish his treatment, and to go his own way.

When Professor A. especially feared being on his own, he would seek out women to serve as sexual substitutes.[1] He had begun this behavior some time ago, soon after his mother's death, especially when he felt alone. We had been able to work with his attempts to replace me and his intense feelings about me, in intense maternal and paternal transferences, with an endless succession of anonymous substitutes when he felt he could not wait to be with me again. We saw his repetitive attempts to turn his hurt, disappointment, and anger with me for leaving him on his own into sexual excitement. For a while his longings for contact and sexual gratification moved into the transference as I became the heterosexual and homosexual partner. Sometimes when Professor A. felt hopeless, bereft, and alone, he felt helpless to control his spending many hours searching for the one woman who would make him feel wanted and whom he would not hate.

When Professor A. learned about police raids on some of his haunts, he became terrified that his inability to control his driven search for a woman would endanger his academic career and his relationship with L. I shared with him Myers' (1994) recommendation that the underlying mood disorder in patients with sexual addiction be treated with antidepressant medication. Myers regards the pressured search for sexual activity as the patient's attempt at self-healing of his depressive affects. He advises that such patients must feel less depressed to hold still for therapeutic work. Resistance to facing their terror of dependent attachment in the transference to the therapist kept Myers' patients from decreasing their sexual activities. A psychopharmacologist concurred with Myers and placed Professor A. on antidepressant medication. Professor A. now felt more supported and protected against his sexual temptations both by his medication and by what he felt as my concern and that of the psychopharmacologist. I had felt that, *in part*, we were tending to give up on analyzing his behavior,

---

[1]To protect my patient's confidentiality, I have omitted details of his sexual behaviors. However, I want to focus here primarily on the defensive aspects of these sexual behaviors.

because of my disappointment and resentment at those times when
we could not work with his transference hunger.[2] I would have
difficulty switching between working in a collaborative, interpretive
way with Professor A. and needing to tolerate and contain his
regressions. I had to become comfortable with the fact that I would
need to keep shifting between these two positions. Sometimes I
could interpret expression of and defense against his enormous
transference hunger. When he was more regressed and more heavily
defended, I needed to tolerate that he had to enact his longings without
being able to work with them interpretively. The psychopharmacologist's intention with antidepressant medication was to reduce the
compulsive aspect of the patient's sexual behavior; he did not seek to
modify either the patient's depressive mood, which was neither intense
or consistent, or his separation anxiety. In retrospect, I am not
convinced that the antidepressant medication accomplished much
other than temporarily enhancing the patient's feeling that I and the
psychopharmacologist were concerned about him. Other than
immediately after beginning the medication, Professor A. did not show
much change in his sexual behavior, his moods, his separation anxiety,
or in his ability to manage these.

I want to contrast the last session before my summer vacation
with the preceding three weeks. In this final session before the
separation, Professor A. suddenly and dramatically again, unlike this
earlier period, seemed able to examine himself responsibly. Is he trying
to win my acceptance and love before the separation or has he
genuinely again become capable of responsible self-inquiry? And if
he can now tolerate being responsible for his own feelings and conflicts,
why had he seemed unable to do so during this preceding period?
How long will this more mature attitude last?

Professor A. had resumed his sexual seeking in the context of
feeling unbearably alone when apart from L., from exciting work on

---

[2] I use the term transference hunger to refer to parental wishes toward the
analyst that feel insistent, impatient, urgent, and demanding (see Coen 1992).

his new book, and from me, although he insisted on deemphasizing the importance of separation from me as being only one of several factors. He continued to crave attention and admiration from others. I tried to engage him about his sudden return to seeking sexual substitutes when he was alone in relation to the July 4th holiday, to my forthcoming vacation, and to the fact that he had been playing down his attachment, anxiety, and resentment in losing me. He then missed the next session, having gone to bed very late after going to one of his haunts. He reported that during the sessions with me he feels unable to stop himself from thinking about these women; by doing so he can totally tune out any other feelings. In contrast with much of this treatment, in these sessions he and I do not really get to what he is feeling and work with it. He indicates his angry refusal to do the work of the treatment and to do his own writing, wanting instead that I should have to chase after him the way he felt he had to pursue his mother to preserve her involvement with him.

He declares: "It's striking that I went to an X[3] straight from here yesterday." As he seems to move away, I ask whether he can take seriously his noting that he went directly to an X from here. "Like I wasn't going to let you reach me," he responds. I add, "Like today." He says, "You changed my appointment for me but it doesn't feel like enough. You still send me away at the end of each session. L. sends me away too. Nothing's ever enough, I never feel satisfied. I feel very self-critical about it." I say that it seems as if he just moved from strong feelings with me to turning on himself. He knows that he's been behaving in an angry way with me, he says, but he feels afraid to hold still and experience such angry feelings with me. In the next session he refers to wanting the women to dance on his string. I interpret, "You want me to dance on your string and you get enraged with me when I don't." He responds, "I feel that I want everybody to dance to my string. I feel insatiable. It seems like I can never make you dance to my string. The only power I have over you is the power

---

[3]X will designate the patient's sexual scene.

I have over myself." He moves away and I remind him that yesterday he said that I would not get through to him, that I wasn't going to have any influence on him, that I was going to feel helpless and useless with him while I watch him get himself in trouble like he felt with his mother. He talks about how helpless he feels that I can disappear on him for a month. That is the context for his picturing women at an X during the session.

Now here is some of the last session before the summer vacation separation. He describes feeling much better. He says, "I've never really taken responsibility myself for making like a bitter, angry child. I've said instead I'm acting like my mother. She failed in terms of the potential happiness she could've had. She never gave up being a disappointed, angry, depressed person and I guess one of her big failures was to blame everybody else and not to take responsibility and that's what I'm doing now. I can feel it particularly in relation to the last three weeks. I'm sure it has a lot to do with your going away but I experience it as I refuse to really work hard."

As he acknowledges how he has behaved like an angry, demanding child, he reports that he has been acting as if he has no control over anything, as if the antidepressant medication is responsible for regulating his behavior, or by implication, that I as his analyst should be responsible for his fate. I ask if he can bring this closer to him and me so that he can feel his wanting to throw at me how angry and disappointed he's been feeling about my going away. He responds: "It's like you were the parent who substituted for the missing parents and then I wouldn't have to feel bitter and resentful. So when you're leaving, it's like you're taking away my drug, my calming influence, my substitute. I think the thing I've been denying and fighting against most in my analysis for the past year is I really have to come to terms with how I'm feeling now and not just use the past as an excuse. I've come in here so often in the past month feeling I have no control over my feelings. You're saying that's what an overgrown baby does. You're saying, 'Grow up, take responsibility, stop having temper tantrums.' Today I feel so much better that I can do that, I'm not having a temper tantrum, I'm taking responsibility. I'm going to try while you're away to think of you as my analyst who's helping me rather than abandoning me. I'll take responsibility for my bitterness. Now you're more like a coach who's in my corner but very hard on me, not letting me slip backwards, saying, 'Get your ass on the field and fight, stop making excuses for the past.' The next stage is once you understand it not to let it control you but for you to control it. So it's a valuable message you're giving me that I'm able to hear today whereas the previous three weeks I've been talking about falling apart. This message is easier to receive when I feel stronger, then I feel I can handle responsibility."

Until the last session before the separation, Professor A. insisted that he was passive, helpless, and lacked control over his regressive pull toward sexual excitement with his women. In the last session, we see the beginning of his willingness and ability to accept responsibility for his attempts to get at me through such behavior. He now notes the difference between his feeling angry and abandoned by me as an uncaring parent and his feeling responsible for his own bitterness and wishes to attack me. Although he dreamed about murder, kidnapping, and making love before I left him, when he feared wanting to possess me so intensely, he literally ran from such affects and wishes to the distraction and comfort of sexual excitement with his women. An endless stream of easily replaceable sexual substitutes protected Professor A. from bringing his feelings and wishes in close with any one person, now especially with me in the treatment. In each sequence before a separation, he would move from repeated sexual enactment in which he claimed not to be responsible for his behavior and feelings, including his loss of me with hurt, disappointment, longing and rage, to wanting to be my best and favorite patient so that I would love and admire him. That is, to a degree he would move in closer to acknowledge *overtly* his attachment to me in contrast to the *covert* sexualized attempts to engage my concern while he attempted to displace and deny what he felt and wanted with me. Later, he could reveal and acknowledge that the more terrified he felt of homosexual desire for me in the paternal transference, the more he turned to a seductive woman, in dreams and in behavior, to calm and distract him. Professor A. suggested that he functioned better when he was away from me, as in August, when, to a degree, he accepted the need to manage himself. In my presence, he regressed to insisting that I could be responsible for him. When it became clear that I would still leave him, no matter how he acted up, he would then handle himself more responsibly. He believed that he could not tolerate feeling sad and lonely in my absence so that he needed to go into (sexual) action, as he had much of his life. Repeatedly examining his profound conviction of his affect intolerance and need for action, and the underlying identifications with both parents, helped him to learn, despite his terror, he could tolerate sad and lonely feelings.

Was Professor A. moving slowly through a mourning of the loving nurturance he felt he missed as a child toward acceptance of limitations and limits? Or would he keep insisting that his needs must always and continuously be satisfied? How do we differentiate between the patient's difficulty with managing separateness and separation and his rage-filled vindictive attacks on the therapist as the inadequate, insufficiently loving parent? How do we differentiate "I can't" from "I won't"?

In contrast to Professor A., Mr. B. seemed incapable of being an engaged patient throughout most of his long analysis. He rarely followed through in his sessions or conveyed a sense that he really wanted to work out some conflict in his treatment. He seemed content to feel my presence so long as he could feel in control, not too much in need of my help or too aware that he really did have emotional problems. For the longest time, he would be offended when I would refer to his problems. He wanted to be my colleague, supervisor, or guru, but not have to be a patient in his own right. Even when I could move Mr. B. to tears in individual sessions by telling him that he was content just to remain in treatment forever with me without really wanting anything and without really changing, his concern did not seem to last more than a day or two.

Certainly, we explored Mr. B.'s treatment impasse from many different perspectives. Much of his need for control derived from his relationship with an intrusive, possessive mother who often overwhelmed him with accounts of her feelings, wiped him after his bowel movements until he was eight years old, and insisted on his not having a full door to his room when he was an adolescent. Mr. B. felt that his penis, and the rest of his body and soul, belonged to his mother (cf. Novick and Novick 1987). As an adolescent, he had masturbated without taking his penis in his hands, by rubbing his penis against his bed. We did much work on Mr. B.'s arrogance, grandiosity, and insistence that he was perfect, problem free, as defense against his feeling crippled and incapable. He had a quasi-delusional belief that I wanted to criticize, cripple, and keep him subservient forever, as he felt his mother had done with him, his father, and his two sisters. Or Mr. B. would play the role of the grandiose, omnipotent one who would control and possess the other person.

All his relationships were contaminated by concerns about dominance/submission, as he alternated between these two poles, with the dangers of rejection, enmeshment, and enslavement on the one hand, and intrusion, devouring, and possession on the other hand. If he did not stay "on the roof," as he put it, aloof, superior, and unconcerned, he feared how vulnerable he would be to his needy craving for caring, which he pictured as disgustingly infantile, like he and his mother had been with each other. This metaphor of his being "on the roof" derived from early adolescent experiences in which he pretended to "be cool" by hanging out on the school roof with a few other boys who were too shy to approach girls during dances. When we could talk constructively about his pretending to be "on the roof" with me so as to distance himself from what he wanted from me, we could make emotional contact with each other. But I would have to contain such human need for him and interpret repeatedly his protection against needing me.

Much of his enormous envy of my importance in making interpretations related to his sense that only one person could be important. So Mr. B. refused to ingest and metabolize my interpretations. If I was indeed helpful to him, then he hated and envied my being valuable and important while he then felt relegated to the role of my lackey. He could connect such feelings with his sense that only his mother's needs, opinions, and feelings had mattered in his home; he felt he had had to cater to her needs for caring and aggrandizement. From time to time, he could acknowledge that he felt that I really was different from his mother, that I did seem to want to see him change and grow for himself rather than for me. But he still clung to the belief that he had to fight against me and my malevolent influence, which would cripple and possess him. He would not take the horror of his charge that I was a destructive mother seriously enough to continue to hate me; hence he could neither leave me nor destroy his image of me as malicious.

I made quite an issue out of his attempts to deny reality, especially about his business dealings, his insistence that reality should and would conform to his wishes. This was a pattern he had learned from and shared with his mother. So it did not mean much to Mr. B. when I spoke to him about how he was not using the treatment and not changing. For the longest time he would not take seriously what I told him was wrong in his treatment. He would insist, that, as the patient, he knew better than I, as the analyst, did about his treatment; he would proclaim that he was indeed "getting value" out of his treatment.

He would be very touched when I showed him in many different ways how hard it was for him to imagine that I really wanted to help him change and grow, including by acknowledging his strengths and abilities. Even when he could grasp how much he had given up on himself and feel enraged about it, he would not persist with his angry feelings nor would he seem to care about what had just seemed so horrible to him. We worked extensively with his attempts not to care, with his destruction of meaning in the treatment, with his not wanting to understand clearly. No matter how we approached his lack of depth and meaning, he would soon be back at the same place emotionally. It certainly seemed that he was repeating the pattern he had learned with his mother of not questioning her and her difficulties, of not looking below the surface of things to see what was wrong (cf. Joseph 1975, 1983, Roth 1994), what he and his wife called his "going unconscious."

When Mr. B. allowed himself to grasp that I really did want to see him thrive, grow, and change, he would immediately contrast the differences in the relationship with his mother, fill up with sadness and anger and with the *genuine* wish to be a capable man. He was surprised to discover underneath his arrogance and grandiosity, how much he had held himself back and had surrendered to his mother's terrifying views of the world and to her insistence that he remain under her protection. The magical specialness he and his mother had shared had discouraged his own needs to develop himself autonomously, to acknowledge his deficiencies and limitations so that he could change and grow into a capable person in his own right. He believed that wishing or proclaiming what he wanted should be sufficient rather than patiently and persistently having to work for what he wanted. He would cry when I would interpret that the only positions in the narcissistic world he and his mother shared were either being god-like or worthless. The full range of human need, ability, and limitations was thereby excluded.

NOTES ON THE LITERATURE

The usual explanations for such seeming inability to tolerate affect or conflict are that there is something about the affect or conflict that seems overly threatening, more than the patient can bear; that ego defense and superego judgment are too harsh to permit more than momentary sampling of the given affect and conflict; and that facing and feeling the affect and conflict would threaten a vitally needed object relationship. We wonder why the patient should have come to believe or continue to believe that feeling a given affect or conflict would be too dangerous to bear, especially now in the presence of the therapist. In my earlier paper (1989), I emphasized patients' fears of their destructiveness, superego harshness, and the appeal of imagined dependent protection. Later, I (1992) elaborated versions of this appeal of dependent protection to which patients cling. I wrote about patients' attempts to get rid of what is wrong within by attempting to make someone else responsible for it, especially by denial, blaming, externalization, and sadomasochistic attempts to put one's own badness into another person. Many of these patients have identified with a parent's defensive style of avoidance of facing conflict by such interpersonal defensive maneuvers. They have come to believe that facing what is wrong within is unbearable, as it once had seemed to be for a parent. I emphasized fears of destructiveness in the patient and in the other who is imagined as vitally needed. Destructiveness in self and in the other are then hidden under the cloak of a relationship in which each one clings to the other as protection from the dangers of life and death struggles.

Certain themes stand out in the literature on intolerance of conflict. Early trauma can lead to predisposition to anxiety (Greenacre 1953), with persistent terror of being overwhelmed by affects; defensive efforts lead to severe affective constriction, even to the point of emotional deadness. Such defense is often buttressed by addictive behaviors (drugs, alcohol, people) that aim to obliterate feelings (Krystal, 1975, 1978). The ego's defensive aims range from avoidance, riddance, or isolation, to efforts at organization and integration of what had been previously regarded as intolerable (Coen 1989, 1992, Dorpat 1987, Gill 1963, Klein 1976, Rapaport 1953, Valenstein 1971). In contrast to affective constriction, healthy development leads to the capacity to tolerate anxiety and depression, a requirement for analysis (Zetzel 1949, 1965). Externalization of responsibility for conflict is thought to derive especially from aggressive conflicts and severe guilt (Sandler and A. Freud 1985). Externalization in the transference provides illusions of safety and magical protection, especially because of anxiety and guilt about separateness (Giovacchini 1967, Modell 1961, 1965, 1971, 1976). Certain patients need others to provide what they feel they lack and what they also tend to destroy (Khan 1962, 1964, 1965a, 1965b, 1969, Winnicott 1956). Hence, therapists need to help patients contain affects they cannot manage on their own (Bion 1962, 1970, Modell, 1990) or, at times, to provide "psychically dead" patients (Modell 1990, p. 73) with a sense of affective aliveness. Kohut's (1971) view of disavowal and externalization of unstable narcissistic structure emphasizes patients' defenses against the shame of primitive, grandiose longings for affirmation from their analysts.

Certain models (Gedo 1979, 1984; Killingmo 1989) dichotomize need and wish, need as pre-conflictual, wish as embedded in conflict. Need then cannot imply intentionality or subjective awareness and hence must be outside of patients' introspection. I believe this strategy seeks to help therapists tolerate those situations in which we cannot interpret unconscious conflict but must clarify instead for our patients *and for ourselves* what our patients now *need* from us. Most authors readily acknowledge how difficult it can be within the clinical situation to differentiate need from wish and how easily needs become drawn into conflict.

Krystal (1975, 1978a, b) notes that affect tolerance is significantly influenced by patients' attitudes toward affects. He considers a variety of factors that interfere with patients' assumption of maternal comforting functions, especially the need to idealize the mother, who becomes the exclusive owner of such caring functions. This avoids rage and indictment of her as deficient. I have used Krystal's advice to question and tactfully challenge patients' beliefs about their affect intolerance so as to address the infantile, irrational, and traumatic contributants. From the perspective of adult capacity, these unrealistic beliefs exaggerate the danger of feelings.

The contemporary Kleinians of London (e.g., Joseph 1983) believe that the patient in the paranoid-schizoid position is *unable* to bear responsibility for his own conflicts so that another person is needed to contain these conflicts. Patients in the paranoid–schizoid position are assumed to have intolerance of separateness, autonomy, internal conflict, and external reality and as needing to avoid, deny, and destroy conflict and reality. The therapist then needs both to contain the patient's unbearable conflicts and to show the patient how he destroys conflict and reality. I have found helpful such detailed attention to the functions the patient requires of the therapist and to how he tends to destroy the latter's usefulness. Although I think that we are addressing a similar problem, I would want to question, more than our Kleinian colleagues, rather than *primarily* to assert and accept, why a patient cannot be responsible for a given feeling or wish. I would want to investigate with the patient his conviction that he cannot tolerate a given affect, how this intolerance has developed, what it repeats from his relations with his parents, as well as how it now functions dynamically with the therapist. I would not feel constrained to wait to broach this subject until the patient first showed signs of introducing consideration of his affect intolerance. I would try to shift flexibly between addressing the patient's conflict and containing it for him. I would prefer to engage the patient in examining his conflicts rather than assume that I could know that he was incapable of doing so. The risk here is of the therapist *impatiently insisting* on putting back into the patient what the therapist cannot accept in himself and what the patient feels he cannot yet bear to claim as his own.

DISCUSSION

Toward Treatment Process as Oscillation

Tolerance of responsibility for conflict requires that the patient be able to know and feel clearly and persistently what is wrong so as to be able to address the conflict and attempt to resolve it more satisfactorily. Such active affirmation or acknowledgment of what is wrong (and what is right) contrasts with varied defensive efforts to move away quickly from a temporary and often passive acceptance of the therapist's interpretation of that conflict. In this sense, acknowledgment contrasts with defensive maneuvers of denial, disavowal, and isolation of affect. My patients certainly knew what was wrong and what they needed to address in their treatment but they would *close off* such awareness and persist with their usual ways of protecting themselves and relating to others. Each man attempted to tune out what seemed unbearable as much as he could: not to care, to be distracted, preoccupied, or otherwise stimulated, Professor A. with sexual substitutes, Mr. B. by being "on the roof." Freud (1927) described disavowal as protecting against an unacceptable idea or perception rather than an affect. Thus disavowal does not sufficiently capture my patients' need to deal with their intolerance of affect and need but can be complemented by a defensive technique akin to *partial* detachment, dissociation, a splitting off of one aspect of oneself, or a *partial* psychic retreat, in Steiner's (1993) terms.

Humphrey Morris, as an editorial reader, recommended that oscillations in the treatment process between acknowledgment and disavowal be understood as expressing either/or dilemmas as described by A. Kris. He suggested that the goal in such treatments should be to modify the extremity of narcissistic withdrawals rather than to acknowledge conflict. Kris (1977, 1983, 1985, 1990) suggested that narcissistic patients make "small alternating steps" (1983, p.446) during free association between seemingly either/or positions in their incompatible wishes. These patients fear total loss of the wished-for position that is temporarily neglected. In treatment, the patient oscillates between opposing positions, learning through a kind of mourning that he does not have to fully renounce his lost object or his temporarily unacknowledged wish. Kris regards either/or dilemmas as related to failure of developmental progression, modulation, and integration. He notes terror of loss in tolerating either divergent position and he uses mourning as a paradigm of the dilemma. Terror of loss and disappointment were central determinants of my patients' retreats from therapeutic collaboration.

I would not privilege narcissistic withdrawal as more significant than the ability to face conflict. Nor would I separate either of these from regressive/progressive shifts; angry refusal to be responsible for oneself; sadomasochistic fighting; affect intolerance; terror of separateness from the therapist and from one's original objects; and all the rest of patients' fears and needs. I believe that my patients had much more difficulty with being patients than those referred to by Kris. With the kind of patient I am describing, clinicians do indeed need to be prepared for substantial oscillations in the patient's capacity and willingness to be a therapeutic collaborator. I was surprised that my two patients could achieve significant therapeutic gains despite such profound disruption in what I had regarded as expectable therapeutic collaboration. I have shifted my perspective on treatment process to include such substantial oscillations away from the expectable emotional engagement between the treatment couple to include long periods when the clinician cannot be sure that his patient is involved in a constructive treatment. Similarly, I now regard my *static* designations of my patients as acknowledging or disavowing as both too either/or and as not sufficiently fluid to capture their shifting stances. The path toward facing, resolving, and integrating conflict certainly can involve repeated detours through avoidance and riddance just as the path toward love and intimacy can proceed through profound narcissistic retreats.

It is better that the clinician not need too much for such patients to acknowledge their conflicts or modify their narcissistic withdrawals. Such therapeutic goals or needs of the therapist can .contribute to an adversarial either/or struggle between the treatment couple. For the patient to modify his extreme positions, the clinician needs to tolerate substantial variation in his patients' therapeutic collaboration, to modify his own exaggerated expectations of how such patients change during treatment and to bear his uncertainty more gracefully. Whether we talk about either/or dilemmas, narcissistic retreats, oscillations in relatedness, intolerance of conflict and affect, and so on, at least some of the time, we are giving ourselves explanations for what we do not understand and cannot predict–the course of intensive treatment with such inconsistent patients.

WHO IS INTOLERANT OF WHAT?

When I hear patients claim that that they cannot bear to face a certain feeling or conflict, I become interested in what they mean, how they know this, what they imagine will happen if they do have the feeling, what has happened in the past when they have had this feeling, and so on. That is, I want to focus on patients' sense of their inability to tolerate affects in order to help them understand and modify such felt inability. When I hear other clinicians report similar intolerance for affect or conflict in a patient, I wonder how they know this. I certainly wonder which treatment partner cannot bear the given affect or conflict, how well the clinician has facilitated the patient's efforts to explore the problem or colluded with the patient at avoidance, and how to help one or both partners. I remember vividly when I presented a version of my 1989 paper, a sensitive, skilled analyst/discussant (the late Paul Russell, M. D. of Boston; see also Chapter 7) insisted that what determined a patient's affect tolerance in treatment was how safe the clinician could make the treatment situation. I believe that there are limitations to patients' tolerance of conflict and affect and to therapists' abilities to assist such patients, no matter how safe the therapeutic climate may be. I think our best approach to such therapeutic intolerance is to investigate the therapeutic situation between both partners. Thus I have attempted to explore some of my own contribution to my patients' difficulties so as to assess whose intolerance this really was and how best to help with it. I, as the therapist, would, at times, find it difficult to decide between actual limitations in each patient's ability to function in the treatment and conflicted inhibition or unwillingness which could be interpreted satisfactorily. I, at times, would feel ineffective, more so with Mr. B. than with Professor A., and angry and critical of the patient as well as of myself. I certainly did interpret such wishes to keep us locked into an unsatisfying parent/child bond in which the couple stays together despite how angry and critical we each feel, thereby repeating aspects of the mother/child relationship.

However, when such interpretations did not seem to have much effect over an extended time, I could revert to believing these were actual limitations in each patient. With Mr. B. *at times and to some degree*, I could collude at living out sadomasochistically an unsatisfying parent/child relationship. Certainly Mr. B. blamed me for his not changing and growing while he continued to keep me unhelpful and ineffective. He could acknowledge briefly his destructiveness toward me and our joint work and then feel gratitude for my concern and help. But no matter how moving one session would be, he would dissociate himself from it quickly, so that, over time, there was little sense of integration and change. On his own, Mr. B. would not or could not want anything from me and from his treatment; he would not persist with focusing on any given conflict. No matter how much we talked about his sense of triumph over me, his omnipotent control over his needs and me, his need to make me impotent, his many fears of being human and vulnerable, by the next session, he would be back in his usual place "on the roof."

I thought that I had good reason to feel discouraged that he would change, little cause for optimism about the outcome of this treatment. I believe most colleagues would neither have begun an analysis with him nor continued it. I was frequently tempted to either terminate the analysis or to convert it to a supportive psychotherapy. However, when we discussed such options, it seemed clear to both of us that a more limited, supportive psychotherapy would foreclose the possibility that Mr. B. would really change. My efforts to enhance his motivation to struggle with his problems, to a degree, gratified the sadomasochistic tensions between us, as if I wanted something from him that he would not or could not provide me. He would encourage me to feel dissatisfied and critical of him so that I should pressure him to try harder. On the other hand, we both felt deeply moved when Mr. B. would genuinely acknowledge how little he allowed himself to treasure and preserve the good and valuable stuff he got from me, from his wife, and even from himself. When Mr. B. showed genuine affect and concern about himself, I enjoyed working with him and he with me.

I am not sure that I contributed to Professor A.'s therapeutic intolerance or that we could have proceeded more rapidly to his becoming responsible in an ongoing way for his wish to hold onto me and for his destructiveness between us. Most of the time, even when I felt frustrated that we could not analyze his affect intolerance satisfactorily, I enjoyed working with him, especially when his hunger, anger, and destructiveness were clearly available in the transference with me. There was no question in my mind or Professor A.'s that he was growing and changing in this treatment or that much of the time we could work interpretively with his rage and hunger for which he could usually accept responsibility. Professor A. could be difficult when he would deaden his needs and his image of me, closing himself off emotionally from our joint work, but I could expect to be able to reach him again soon except during those prolonged periods of sexual action when we were relatively unable to work together interpretively.

Given how productive the earlier part of Professor A.'s treatment had been, it was not hard for me to be patient for a long time about his difficulties in the treatment situation. Initially, I was intrigued by the meanings and functions of his sexualized behavior. We could link his pressure to act, rather than to feel, to identifications with both parents. But then he began to indicate that he really could not bear to sit still and feel when he was left alone. Sometimes we could work on his fears of finishing his treatment, leaving me, and managing on his own. However, frequently he simply felt or believed that he could not control his frenzied actions, sexual and otherwise. Even with my keen awareness that Professor A. was terrified about moving forward and terminating his treatment, somehow the two of us temporarily kept losing this focus.

In retrospect, it would seem that once Professor A. could imagine being out of treatment and on his own, the therapeutic difficulties began. The more real the threat of actual separation and aloneness became for him, the more he had to struggle against moving forward in the treatment. Even though Professor A. and I had worked very well together, given what I knew of his history and our seeming impasse, there was also good reason for me to suspect that we might not be able to go further. I need to stress how difficult it can be to differentiate between fixed and modifiable therapeutic disability when we can see little change over an extended time. Needless to say, I quickly regained my therapeutic optimism and enthusiasm when each patient could acknowledge his yearnings for me and his vindictive wishes to stay locked in combat with me as an inadequate parent. I needed to keep shifting flexibly back and forth between a position where I accepted that the patient could not do otherwise and one in which I would try to engage my patient in wondering whether he could indeed modify his therapeutic position.

Both patients wanted me to be caring, persistent, tough, intrusive, and dominating, while they also attempted to fight off my penetration and ownership of their body and mind. Because each man found it difficult to acknowledge such transference longings, he enacted these transference wishes through seeming disability as a patient, thereby inviting me to assist him. Each patient found it difficult to imagine that he could feel close and caring with me and still proceed toward developing himself separately and capably. The dangers of desire, possession, and destruction seemed too great for each patient to tolerate coming and staying close with me (and his partner) long enough to feel responsibly his powerful desires toward me (and his partner). Hence each man seemed unable to bear responsibility in an ongoing way for his conflicts toward me so that he wanted me to be responsible for him and for them. Each man seemed committed to obliterating the differences between the therapeutic relationship, which was aimed at health, growth, and change, from the mother/child relationship, which seemed to have been aimed, at least in large part, at preserving a relationship in which neither person could function alone satisfactorily. Important therapeutic work focused on each patient's attempts to move away from acknowledgment of the substantial differences between the current treatment relationship and the previous pathological mother/child relationship.

The patient needs to move from holding on vindictively to an ancient, unsatisfying relationship without acknowledging what is good, valuable, and loving in oneself and in the other toward the capacity to feel both loving and destructive with those he loves who deserve his love. I think that much of what seems like intolerance or inability to bear affect and conflict derives from an angry clinging to an unsatisfying parent/child relationship. Responsible hating requires responsible loving. Unless the patient acknowledges that the other deserves his love, he cannot acknowledge the inappropriateness of his hatred and destructiveness. Once the patient can acknowledge that the other deserves his love, he can admit that he is capable of some loving feelings toward another person, and then he can struggle more responsibly with his hatred and destructiveness. Otherwise, the other person simply deserves his hatred and destructiveness. I believe the therapist needs to make a therapeutic issue out of the patient's unloving, unappreciative attitude as largely reflecting a vindictive refusal to acknowledge what is good. I certainly would also agree with Joseph (1975, 1982, 1983) that in being unloving, the patient seeks omnipotent protection and control in the present over genuine human need.

Each patient's wish that the therapist could and should manage his conflicts for him perpetuated the quasi-delusion that the therapist could provide omnipotent protection. The counterpart to the therapist's question of whether the patient "won't" or "can't" do better was the patient's unconscious insistence that, if only the therapist cared more, he would omnipotently protect the patient. Because of his terror that he would lose control of his greed and rage, turning into a violently destructive monster, each patient clung to the quasi-delusion of the therapist's omnipotent protection. Much of his dread of his own omnipotent destructiveness related to images of father and mother as too vulnerable to survive his aggression. Because of his fear that he would actually crush me, each patient would hide his competitiveness with me, present himself as disabled, or insist he was not responsible for his behavior.

In retrospect, I did not appreciate and tolerate sufficiently each patient's regressive needs and defenses against wanting me to be an accepting and containing parent rather than an interpretive analyst. At those times, each patient and I could share the same polarized view of him as either capable/analyzable or disabled/unanalyzable. I could get caught up with each patient's narcissistic views of himself as either special or worthless and hopeless, more so with Mr. B. than with Professor A., so that it could be difficult for each of us to preserve a broader view of each man's capacities and limitations. Now it seems clear that such either/or dilemmas tended to derail my therapeutic work with both patients. Each patient sometimes was able to bear the tension of addressing his own conflicts, while at other times he shifted between being unable to do so and refusing to do so. Our work would be interrupted when I would find it difficult to shift flexibly back and forth between each patient's ability to manage his conflicts and his dissociation from them. I expect far less of the "wider scope" patients I treat in intensive psychotherapy; without much frustration, I am prepared to accept and contain their conflicts over prolonged periods. But I have tended, obviously not fully consciously, to have a more either/or expectation with my analytic patients that they should be reasonably capable, over a prolonged time, of addressing their conflicts. Otherwise, we should discontinue the analysis and/or shift to psychotherapy. I believe this rather common polarization of patients as either suitable for analysis or for psychotherapy has interfered with my comfort in tolerating extended periods in which certain of my analytic patients have not been capable of the usual analytic work.

    As I have presented this material in different venues, I have learned that for some colleagues what I have discovered was old hat, while most needed to join me in modifying our expectations of analytic process with more disturbed patients. I was trained to differentiate sharply during initial diagnostic assessment and then continuously during the course of analysis between analyzable and unanalyzable patients. The latter were to be treated largely by supportive psychotherapy so as not to undermine their fragile defensive structure. In contrast, certain colleagues were trained to analyze more disturbed patients with the expectation that much of the time they would need to help to contain, rather than interpret, conflict. This is certainly the position of the contemporary British Kleinians toward patients assessed to be in the paranoid–schizoid position. The rest of us have had to learn to expect substantial oscillation during analysis of more disturbed patients, often for very prolonged periods, in their capacity to tolerate and address conflict. The same, of course, applies to intensive psychotherapy with such patients. Now, with these more difficult patients, I distinguish less whether we are engaged in psychoanalysis or intensive psychotherapy and I'm prepared to carry the treatment for long periods of time. Nor will I expect to be able to interpret soon what the patient is putting into and expecting of me.

I feel surprised that I did not wonder much more *consistently* why my patients had again become seemingly unanalyzable in the sense of being unable to work with me interpretively or why we could not acknowledge together that the patient now needed me to render another function for him, such as affirming, containing, or holding him. On the other hand, it is not surprising to me that I have expected to be able to *interpret* the functions I was providing for my patient rather than just to do so. Akhtar (unpublished), following Killingmo (1989), suggested that my viewing conflict versus deficit in an either/or way may have interfered with my being able to tolerate Professor A.'s regressive periods when he required affirmation of his needs rather than interpretation of his conflicts. I agree with Akhtar that my either/or orientation interfered but I would focus this around analyzability versus unanalyzability and pathological optimism and omnipotence versus pessimism and hopelessness (Akhtar 1996). I have tried to conflate deficit/conflict, need/wish, interpretation/affirmation by attempting to draw in dependent patients' intense parental longings (need and wish) within passionate analytic transferences (Coen 1992). My patients needed to mourn and modify such narcissistic tensions into more realistic and moderate expectations as I needed to acknowledge and relinquish my not-fully-conscious expectation that my patients and I should be able to interpret (talk about) what they were needing of me when they obviously were unable to do so.

Balsam (1997) suggested that the periods of apparent crisis in Professor A.'s treatment may be understood as involving mutual regressions in both patient and analyst (see Chapter 6). Balsam speculated that the psychopharmacologist and his medication may have functioned like a father to help separate patient and analyst/mother. Indeed, I think she is correct that the patient and I became locked in a mutually unbearable, inseparable maternal transference. The optimistic, confident, growth-promoting paternal transference contrasted with the hopeless, pessimistic, maternal transference, in which both patient and I had felt *trapped*. Professor A. sought to transform me into the father who helps him to proceed with his own life separate and apart from union with the disabled mother. *Now* I can see that in the face of separation (summer vacation and future termination), Professor A. regressed to wanting to be together continuously with a maternal substitute, who was and was not the therapist. This maternal union he put in front of me so that it should be my task as individuated father to help him separate. It is also *now* clear that much of Professor A.'s wish/terror of homosexual paternal transference involved wish/fear to turn the strong father into another maternal figure with whom he could merge rather than use to move himself forward.

I suggest that psychoanalytic either/or polarizations tend to interfere with our therapeutic capacities by arbitrarily limiting the range of human function. Better that we view human potential on a more continuous gradient within which patient and analyst can both shift positions. My attempts to differentiate so-called analyzable from unanalyzable behavior in my patients tended to foreclose my persistent analytic understanding of why they would at times seem unanalyzable. From this perspective, it would seem very difficult to assess analyzability during an ongoing treatment. Hence, I would now contend that once an analysis or intensive psychotherapy is in progress, rather than focusing on and worrying about a patient's apparent analytic disability, we should instead concern ourselves with how best to facilitate an ongoing treatment process.

I do not take most of my patients into analysis, both because of what they do and do not need as well as what they can and cannot tolerate. But once an analysis is begun, better that analyst and patient not become trapped in either/or polarizations of what should be. It was especially helpful to address my patients' hopelessness about modifying their affect intolerance and the narcissistic rigidity of their expectations of specialness versus worthlessness. I suggest that analysts' either/or polarizations about patients and analysis share these same primitive narcissistic differentiations of valuable and worthless. Once patient and analyst become mired in such narcissistic polarities, we may try to reclaim the high ground by insisting that it is the patient who is stuck instead of struggling to extricate both of us from this narcissistic trap.

3

Managing Rage and Hate in the Treatment Setting

A major aim of this book is to help all of us clinicians, myself included, to tolerate and manage loving and hating passions in the treatment setting. In my 1992 book, I commented about my discussion of the 1991 panel, "Hate in the analytic setting", at the American Psychoanalytic Association meetings (Winer 1994). Each of our highly skilled analysts seemed relieved as soon as his patient had moved away from hatred to some other feeling. Even at a panel on hatred, three of our most capable American analysts showed little of their patients' hatred and even less of their own. The late Merton Gill was prophetic about the tenor of this panel as he jumped up from the audience to protest that he felt insulted that the chairman hadn't included him in introducing the panelists as "the most hated analysts in America." Unlike the analysts in this panel, Gill was loudly proclaiming the pleasures of being hated: an honorable distinction, a badge of courage, fun. He was facetiously helping to set the stage for talking about hatred in the analytic setting. To do so, clinicians need to tolerate, enjoy being hated.

Merton Gill championed analysts' need to process our intense feelings, so that we do not have to remain emotionally remote from our patients, so that we can analyze them most effectively. None of the presenters at this panel actually focused on feelings of hatred— the title and ostensible focus of this panel. Two analysts presented cases involving brief bits of anger in treatments not otherwise distinguished by rage. One case involved a sadomasochistic stalemate. This analyst revealed to us that his patient's angry attacks on him had made him uncomfortable. Hence he attempted to placate and distract her by interpreting that her angry provocative attacks on him were defensive against loving transference feelings toward him. Again, Merton Gill arose to object that my colleague was a wimp. This colleague was able to help himself and his patient get out of their sadomasochistic stalemate *only* when he was able to tell his patient that they *both* needed to address what they had each been getting out of fighting with the other. Previously, the patient would object *correctly* that his interventions about *her* needs to fight with him left him out of what was going on between them.

Clinicians' discomfort with rage or hatred impedes patients' direct expression of rage and hatred, encouraging a shift toward sadomasochism, as occurred with my colleague at that panel. Most patients are all too willing, because of fears of violence and concerns about the therapist's vulnerability, to be diverted from angry affects. Pathologically dependent patients (Coen 1992) redirect anger and aggression against themselves, surrendering their capabilities to the other person who is deemed the capable, valuable one. Sadomasochism, one form of pathological dependency, serves as a complex defensive operation for containing and managing rage, destruction, and loss, by provoking another to act as the controller/dominator/critic under whom one willingly serves. To help such patients reclaim the ability to manage on their own, therapists must tolerate, and help them own, the rage and hatred previously turned against the self, which is now newly focused on the person of the therapist.

I've been asked many times how much anger patients need to express in order to change, whether there aren't many successful treatments that are relatively quiet affectively, less expressive of angry passion. I'm skeptical that patients can change significantly without feeling deeply and strongly very angry feelings, in all their many variants, during analysis or intensive psychotherapy. As supervisors, it is certainly easy for us to see younger colleagues deflect patients' expression of anger. It is more disconcerting to acknowledge that most of us clinicians, *at times*, seem to do the same thing. Yes, of course, *sometimes* we can bear patients' rage and hatred without inhibiting it. But it would be psychoanalytically naive to assume that we clinicians could simply remain immune to our patients' intense destructiveness without having our own affective responses. How can we tolerate our patients' anger more comfortably? Do most of us need to return to the couch or should we turn to peer supervision groups, consultation, or discussion with a colleague? I think that with the chronic rage of our most difficult patients, now stimulated also in us as therapist, many, if not most of us, need someone else's help. I think it is very helpful for us to talk and write openly—a major aim of this book— about our difficulties tolerating patients' rage and hatred toward us so that we can manage better such destructiveness, in ourselves and in our patients.

So, when I've had trouble with patients' rage toward me, I've sought help. I might try to write out something about the difficulties my patient and I were having in the hope that I could provide my own supervision, if I could gain some distance from my troubled feelings. Indeed, my recent clinical writing, as you can see, has served, to a degree, to help me manage such clinical troubles. Not only did writing help me with the difficulties with which my patients and I were contending but I also profited from public presentation and publication. Numerous colleagues offered helpful perspectives from which to understand these affective dilemmas. At other times, I've turned to trusted colleagues, including my peer supervision study group. I want to strongly encourage my readers to seek help from colleagues you trust and respect when you sense that you're feeling threatened by your patients' passions. Otherwise, outside your awareness, you're going to have to turn down the intensity of your patients' affects.

CLINICAL VIGNETTES

Perhaps the most impressive management of rage and destructiveness I've heard presented was Peter Fonagy's (1998) analysis of a murderess. Most of us would never have attempted to treat, let alone analyze, such a traumatized, violent woman, who was terrified that one analytic partner would kill the other. I use this example to emphasize the obvious—even Dr. Fonagy, who seems to handle murder with equanimity, reveals one vignette of his being thrown, as we all are at times—here, by envy, the patient's and his own. Before he is about to leave her, his patient blames him for what she has not gotten from him, envying what she might have received from a more senior colleague, in comparison with whom he is a "disaster." Dr. Fonagy, referring to his envy of this colleague (presumably Betty Joseph), imitates her style, he suggests, as he interprets that his patient is trying to destroy his ability to think and help her. Enraged, the patient, attacks him as too young, inexperienced, and vulnerable. She storms out of the session, declaring the analyst and the analysis dead.

I too idealize and envy Betty Joseph, so I can easily put myself (or any other analyst) in his place—a place I quickly relinquish— with this virulent, unappreciative patient. I wouldn't, couldn't, have treated this woman. Dr. Fonagy thinks, in retrospect, that his patient did not want to destroy him but to provoke him to respond with irritation. But since she complains bitterly that he can't "*cope*" with her angry, envious attack, perhaps she simply needed him to bear, contain, and interpret her rage and envy at missing the good (Betty Joseph) parent. I suspect that in the next session, as he interprets her *need* to see him as evil, he rejects her anger and disappointment with him as the self-concerned analyst/parent who is unable to bear her feelings and needs. However, both patient and analyst are able to *recover and process*, not avoid, their experiences, so that he survives her attack on him as evil and unconcerned with her, and she can move toward ownership of her bitter hatred for the father/analyst.

Mr. N.'s (for negativistic) (also see Chapter 7) chronic rage was frequently in the room with us, as he'd arrive furious about what he was not getting from life, what others were asking of him. He often conveyed the expectation that if I could not find a way to help him feel better quickly in the session, he would lose control of his rage and attack me with it. Indeed, his rage was so often in my face, that I had little choice but to manage my own resentment toward him so that we could work with his rage and its defensive functions. For example, one day, he jumped up, rushed toward me, screaming in my face, to show me, he claimed, how his father continually got in his face. He did this so rapidly that I didn't have time to stop him. Afterwards, he insisted that he had merely intended to show me how violent his father had been with him. Of course, I could talk with him about his sadism with me, his identification with his father as cruel aggressor, his wanting to dominate and intimidate me and avoid needing and caring about me. But first, I had to contain and manage my own resentment at him. I felt violated—he had run into my space, screamed in my face, taken me unawares of what he was about to do to me. I felt like screaming back at him—he could not scream in my face. I wanted to attack him, set limits with him, tell him I was boss! When I could feel the temptation to fight sadomasochistically with him about dominance/submission (and thereby stay connected), then I could work with Mr. N. about the rage at his cruel father that he was now feeling toward me as father/analyst.

This certainly was not the first time I had felt violated by Mr. N. One day, before I knew him well enough to anticipate what he might do, he felt enraged at a noisy pigeon on top of the air conditioner. Jumping up suddenly to drive the pigeon away, he ran quickly to the window, violently pulled apart the Venetian blinds covering the window and banged the window. Not surprisingly, he bent the Venetian blinds. I felt enraged with him for having intruded on me with his rage, seeming to have damaged my Venetian blinds. Or, when he felt angry, he would scream in the office, claiming that he was merely venting his frustration, letting off steam, so he would feel better. I felt I needed to be vigilant to protect myself by interrupting his destructive behavior, and so that we could instead talk about his rage and destructiveness. Sometimes, he would seem to whip up his anger so that he would erupt, contending that he needed to unleash his anger so as to feel better. He would whip himself up into a frenzy, screaming, banging the chair, as he seemed to tear to pieces whatever he thought about. It became clear to me that there was nothing useful for his treatment in our tolerating his living through such scenes— scenes we came to call "swirling," like a frenzied devil. We could talk about the omnipotent destructive power he sought to feel as he destroyed everything he touched, especially how this omnipotent illusion protected him from intense feelings of helpless need and vulnerability, which, from an adult perspective, were highly exaggerated. Then he would calm down, become much softer, and allow himself to want my help—help he otherwise despised and rejected.

Early in the treatment, I had reduced my fee with him because of financial difficulties at his business, with the proviso that he would let me know when he again earned a certain sum, whereupon we would restore the original fee. I discovered, after having had to question him, that, by omission, he had lied to me, not letting me know when his salary had increased. He responded that he was just protecting himself, that no one would look out for him, that everyone exploited the other. He was taking advantage of me before I could take advantage of him, which I would do if I could. I felt angry, taken advantage of, feeling once more that I needed to protect myself better with Mr. N., to anticipate and remain vigilant about his destructiveness with me. Shouldn't I have anticipated this outcome? On the other hand, it seemed far more constructive for me to treat Mr. N. respectfully rather than continually try to catch him at wrongdoing. I felt disappointed that he had misused me, that he hadn't been appreciative and respectful with me.

I used my own feelings of resentment, disappointment, intrusion, and disrespect to talk with Mr. N. about his similar feelings with both parents, especially his father. He was genuinely touched that I didn't stay fixed on berating him, as his father would have done, that although I felt angry with him, we were talking constructively about what had happened between us. Surprised that I expected *some* feeling of appreciation and respect from him, he felt sad that he had felt so little appreciated and respected by either parent. Mr. N. felt that his distrust of others' intentions toward him was warranted because of his experiences with both parents. Exploration of his dishonesty, exploitation of me, cynicism, and entitlement were productive. It was difficult for Mr. N. to fully accept responsibility for his projection of his greedy, extractive wishes onto me and others.

He would be moved to tears when we would talk about his attitudes toward me in contrast to the reality of how I had been with him, that I did not deserve his mistreatment of me. He would melt as we talked about how lonely and uncared for he had been feeling, and allow himself to want me to care for him. But he rarely preserved the hope or wish that I provide him with something he felt he lacked. He would dismiss what he wanted from me. He attempted to focus concretely on the difficulties of his life, about which I was to give him advice or commentary. Or he would complain about his situation at work so negativistically that I could not possibly be of help to him. So often he would just complain about what was wrong, claiming he needed relief from his pressured day. He would make no connection to any issue we had been discussing, the current session seeming to be totally disconnected from any place we had been together recently. I had to use my angry feelings at Mr. N.'s unappreciative, dismissive, rejecting ways with me—his negativism in all its forms—so that I could talk with him about his not letting himself want anything from me. Then he would feel sad that he had been keeping his distance with me, and struggle with his enormous fears of staying close and in need of me.

I would so often feel angrily discouraged when Mr. N. would once again merely complain about what was wrong, even about how bad his memory was, so that he did not remember anything we had discussed recently. I would feel tempted to agree with him when he would again complain that he was not changing in this treatment, that he could no longer afford it, and that he should now try cognitive therapy. He would insist that it was time that he faced the fact that he could not effect change in this treatment. He'd taken notes after certain sessions, which he'd read and reread, devised mantras to try to remember key points of our work, all to no avail. Nothing stayed in his mind. I'd feel disappointed at how unappreciative he'd be during such tirades. I could hear nothing that he had preserved of our work together. But most of the time that was his presenting style: I could find little connection to our previous work. Perhaps he was correct that he just could not use this treatment to achieve lasting change in himself.

But once I could extricate myself from my angry discouragement, then I could wonder with him about what he was doing with me. I would talk with him about his showing us through his behavior toward me what it was like for him to grow up with so little ongoing encouragement, admiration, and support from either parent. He would link his failure to persist with some positive acknowledgment of what he and I had done especially to his relationship with his father. Often in a rage, his father would attack him critically, showing him up. Mr. N. could get father's attention by serving as father's mirroring audience, listening to father boast about *his* accomplishments. Mr. N.'s example of his father teaching him a new skill was that father taught him to shine father's shoes. He felt pleased at father's participation with him until I asked him why father hadn't taught him to shine his own shoes.

Sometimes, he would misuse my invitation to explore himself to instead attack both of us for his shortcomings. Often, however, I could sense his surprise and appreciation that, rather than condemn him for his apparent failure, I seemed to view him as much more potentially capable than he viewed himself. Then we could get to much more positive expectations and capacities *and* his wish that I be the admiring, affirming parent, of which he had had so little. Then, of course, I no longer hated him, nor did he hate me. As the room swelled with much richer possibilities, we could each feel appreciative and loving toward the other.

The previous day we had again gone through his destruction of meaning and value of the treatment. Once more he insisted he should end the treatment, and I felt tempted to agree with him. But, as we were able to talk about his destroying anything good between us, he could join me collaboratively in reflecting on what he had done to our relationship. The next day, in trying to engage him about what he'd missed as a child and now needed, I told him about my brief "talk" the previous evening on the telephone with my two-year-old grandson in another city. I said it was very sad that my grandson regularly could expect to get what Mr. N. had gotten so little of—parents, or me as grandparent, enjoying and admiring him, in this example, my grandson's beginning ability to exchange a few words on the telephone with me. Mr. N. was touched both by my example and by my sharing my experience with him. He was especially touched that I did not remain angry and rejecting of him for how dismissive he had been with me the previous day.

Because I did not join him in mutual attack, he experienced me as a new developmental object, different from his rejecting parents. Instead, he experienced me as reaching out to him, warmly encouraging new possibilities for him. I talked with him about the beating he and his self-esteem had taken as a child when his father would go at him the way he so often went at me, like yesterday. It was no wonder he remained so mistrustful and kept himself so aloof, ever ready to retreat into his shell. We used his ongoing lack of appreciation for me and our work to talk about the horror of his similar experience as a child: the lack of a consistently positive parental attitude affirming him as someone good and valuable, worthy of respect.

He would wonder why sometimes when we were apart, he was able to imagine me with him, whereas most of the time he felt disconnected from me, as from everyone else. Some years ago, when he had felt lonely at New Year's on a western ski trip, unexpectedly, when he imagined me with him, he felt better. He was now well aware how anxious he became when he felt close to me. But he was surprised when I (again) suggested that he try to tolerate his anxiety in feeling closely connected with me, rather than to immediately disengage. He felt encouraged by the prospect that he could strengthen his emotional capacity to bear his anxiety. While we worked on the intensely destructive forces within him, Mr. N. seemed to need me to imagine greater possibilities for his competence. Or, another day, I told him a bit about an experience from the previous day with another patient, rather like him—a flighty, anxious young woman who continually ran away from me and from everyone else. Meeting again for the first time in person rather than on the telephone because she had been far from New York, she described her surprise and pride that she really had let herself feel attached to me in a caring way. Here too, Mr. N. felt encouraged that he could also take pride in his newfound capacity for caring feelings with me. How different this was, he mused, from his father's critically dismissive attitude toward dependent need. Although he enjoyed being able to do what father could not, he still felt tempted to regressively retreat from caring relatedness with me to his identification with his father.

One day he described that he'd written notes about the previous day's session, something he hadn't done for a while. I was surprised that he hadn't just mechanically written another mantra that he would soon discard. This time he'd written a short poem to highlight two key points. He had wanted to bring the poem to read to me but hadn't had time to return home to get it. He played with the first image he'd elaborated in the poem of himself as an artichoke, the tough, hard, spinny outer core protecting the soft stuff within. Here his images were highly evocative, well wrought verbally. This was not the Mr. N. I had known. Mr. N. so rarely allowed himself to be playfully creative in his sessions with me. When he talked about not having wanted to get out of bed that morning, although he knew that the sun was shining, I too joined in playing with his images. We'd long known that Mr. N. had turned to mother nature instead of his own parents; for example, as a very young child he'd lie on the concrete pavement soaking up sunshine. I said he needed to be warmed by human sunshine and that he hadn't fully let himself know he wanted my encouragement and admiration for his creative elaboration of our work, which also made him anxious so that he hadn't brought the poem with him. Mr. N. then could open up more of his exhibitionism, wanting me to admire him as capable, even as he joined both parents in condemning such "selfish" display in himself. The irony here is that his father had so often exhibited himself for the patient's admiration while condemning similar, developmentally necessary, behavior in Mr. N. This easier, warmer, playful, enjoyable tone between us alternated with the more customary remote, constricted, critical, negative one. I certainly did tell Mr. N. that his allowing both of us to play creatively and enjoyably with each other was an important new step for him.

Mr. R. (for rejecting) (also see Chapter 7), a workaholic businessman, skipped his sessions, especially on Thursdays, or came very late to them. Feeling overworked, he wanted to reduce the frequency of his treatment. He wanted to drop the Thursday session, which he, in effect, did by not coming or calling to let me know he was not coming to it. Indeed, it seemed unclear that he was continuing the treatment, which he appeared to have given up on. He had been distant all along, fearful of needing and loving me or his partner. I felt angry, dismissed, uncertain of my role with him and of his availability with me. We certainly had talked about his reversing roles, so that I was to feel his anxiously insecure position with his father and with his mother, too. He could feel sad about what he had been through as a child and what he was now putting me through. But he continued to allow only a few minutes of a session, when indeed he did come. I was tempted to give him a limit-setting ultimatum, to attack him, throw him out of treatment. I struggled with my angry feelings so that I could instead talk with him about the war he sought to have us fight out with each other. He felt surprised that I didn't go at him; he encouraged me to attack him, or implicitly criticized me for my tolerance of his destructive behavior toward me and the treatment. Here, he seemed to be stoking the sadomasochistic currents between us, a sadomasochism in which he had been stuck.

It certainly seemed that it would not be in his best interests for me to try to force him, as I felt tempted, to comply with my needs of him in the treatment; he had been far too masochistically compliant with everyone. His anger toward me, as the helper who was not worth being with, was now so much louder and clearer. We both felt that he and I needed to tolerate his rage at me as the bad, deficient parent, father and mother. He talked about how much of a struggle it had become for him to come to the sessions, which he didn't want, preferring to oversleep or make deals. We both knew that we needed to avoid sadomasochistic protections against his experiencing his anger now with me in the transference as his distant, uninvolved, depressed mother and as his violent, selfish father, whose availability he could never take for granted.

I had to contend with my angry, dismissed feelings, when he again wouldn't show up or call or would arrive with only five or ten minutes left in a session. I knew that Mr. R.'s previous treatment had foundered very quickly, he thought, because his analyst had become angry and impatient with him. One Thursday as I sat waiting for him, I read a draft of G. Katz's (1998) paper emphasizing that patients need to enact in behavior what they cannot express in words. When Mr. R. arrived with five minutes left in the session, I could empathically talk with him, as I certainly had other times, about his wanting to have me feel for him what it was like for him to wait, never knowing when his father would return home. I needed help getting myself out of feeling angrily discouraged, wanting to retaliate at Mr. R. by rejecting him, so that I could try to talk with him optimistically and constructively about what was transpiring between us. I could not know how much Mr. R. would be able to tolerate working with, talking about, how enraged he now felt with me, while allowing himself to make use of me.

He felt sad, and excited, as he allowed himself to imagine wanting to torture me by having me sit helplessly, waiting for him, not knowing if I would ever see him again. And he felt sad seeing himself repeating with me and his partner what his father had done with him. He could now feel with conviction how much he wanted us to hate each other, to feel bitterly discouraged that there could ever be *anything* good between us, that *we both feel* the depressive hopelessness he had felt with his father and mother.

COMMENTARY

We certainly have been taught during our training that our patients must hate us for so many reasons: we disturb their psychic equilibrium by consistently focusing on what they have spent a lifetime avoiding as we interpret protections against feelings that seem especially painful, unbearable, intolerable. We frustrate our patients in so many ways. We open up our patients' attachment to us as fully as possible, yet set firm limits to our availability. We encourage passionate transferences, full of love and hate, that we interpret instead of gratify. Yes, of course, all this helps with growth toward mature, reasonable expectations but not without much disappointment, hurt, betrayal, and rage. We all know this, yet, when we need to feel valued and appreciated, we don't want to be hated. It's all too easy for us to lose our perspective, to return back to our patients the "badness" they attribute to us, to deflect critical attacks as unmerited. It is so much more difficult to draw patients out in great detail over an extended time, so that we can listen from their perspective, about how and why they hate us, long before we attempt to "interpret" such hatred. It's impossible to do so when we've been dislodged from our position as containing and interpreting therapist, as when we're threatened with loss of the patient, when our superego agrees with the patient's criticism, or when we're regressively willing to surrender to the patient's attack (see Chapter 6). When we are vulnerable to a patient's angry attacks and shift to a self-protective or self-gratifying stance, we have lost our therapeutic position. Acknowledging that we all, *at times*, have trouble with chronic rage, in our patients and in ourselves, we seek to know ourselves better by grasping how we have lost or willingly abandoned our position as therapist who contains and interprets.

Of course, it's much easier to bear a patient's hatred when we're more secure that our doing so is in our patient's best interests than when we feel his attacks are derailing the treatment. But even knowing that we need to tolerate negative transference may not be sufficient for us to bear the patient's chronic hatred when it undermines our self-esteem, when we become vulnerable to the patient's attacks. We all have some vulnerabilities in our self-esteem, some fault lines that resonate with patients' hate-filled criticisms. Chapter 7 considers therapists' problems with intensely negativistic patients who induce their therapists to feel badly about themselves. In supervising younger colleagues, it's not difficult to see their discomfort with being hated as a deficient parent. Beginning analysts and therapists certainly can agree that it is progress when their patients feel anger toward them as the parents in the transference. Yet they will still repeatedly deflect and distract patients' expressions of angry criticism toward them, wanting instead to have patients express satisfaction with them. Although we may be able to see our supervisees' vulnerabilities more easily than our own, in order to best manage our therapeutic work, we all need to acknowledge our vulnerabilities to being hated and derided. Nor are love and desire necessarily easier to manage if the novice or skilled therapist feels threatened that they will get out of hand.

We need to differentiate patients' integration of their chronic rage from their merely living out their rage and using it defensively for the illusion of omnipotent control of themselves and of the therapist. Mere expression of anger does not "discharge" anger, as we used to think and as many patients wish, so as to be able to get their anger out of them, once and forever, as if it were an anal expulsion. Mr. N.'s "venting" his anger, in the belief that he would feel better once he had gotten as angry as he could get, was unproductive for his treatment. We could understand that his "swirling" around like a frenzied devil provided him with a sense of omnipotent destructive power. But then we could work with his negativistic protection against his terror of relying on and making use of others, now especially me as his therapist. He needed not to merely give vent to his anger, as was his custom, but to tolerate, contain, and manage it. Then he needed to make his chronic rage his own problem rather than a problem for the rest of us in his world, and to integrate at whom and about what he was angry. He needed to move from his negativistic rejection of his needs of others toward tolerating concern for himself and for others.

And he needed to bear feelings of appreciation and gratitude for others' care and generosity with him. By then, Mr. N. was on the path toward loving relatedness. Of course, the anxiety this roused in him would periodically lead him to retreat back to the safety of his negativism.

Henry Friedman (see Rizzuto 2000) contended at the 1999 Panel, "Rage in the analytic setting", at the International Psycho-analytical Association Congress in Santiago, Chile, that my adherence to drive theory led me to allow Mr. N. to live out his rage with me rather than to provide him with a new, very different model of how people show concern for each other. Friedman also thought that my focus on Mr. N.'s fear of intimacy aggravated the tensions between us. I think my colleague was overly polarizing our positions, in an effort that was more politically motivated than it was clinically accurate. I think that we really do agree, more than we disagree, about how to work with Mr. N. I certainly do not believe that I needed to passively endure Mr. N.'s destructiveness, which would have been counterproductive. On the contrary, I had to show him that he needed me to help him manage and integrate his intense rage and sadism. I certainly do believe, as did Mr. N., that he was terrified of loving closeness, and that much of our effort was to help him tolerate his wishes that I be a helpful, admiring, caring parent/analyst with its concomitant anxiety. Even to the degree that he needed me to be a new developmental object (see Settlage 1994; Tähkä 1993) to teach him a new mode of relatedness to others, he still struggled against the vulnerability he felt when he allowed himself to need such help from me.

Indeed, Mr. N. needed me to help him contain his intense rage and destructiveness so that he did not continually destroy what was good. I served him as a new developmental object by containing my angry reactions to his destructiveness toward me, rather than joining him in mutual attack, as had both parents. While helping him work with his destructiveness toward me, I also showed him his potentials for greater competence and effectance. I interpreted that he had projected much of his abilities into me and then deferred to me as the capable one, just as he had surrendered to his father. By acknowledging his more positive potentials, which he erased and denied, I provided some of the legitimate childhood need for parental admiration, encouragement, respect, and enjoyment, of which he had had so little. I fully believe that merely interpreting Mr. N.'s destruction of the good stuff he got from me would not have been sufficient to help him. I am convinced that I also needed to keep showing him a much more optimistic, caring relatedness than he had known, while repeatedly showing him how, in his anxiety about closeness, he kept eradicating, destroying, what had just been so good between us.

That Mr. R.'s seeming destruction of the treatment could provide the opening up in this treatment that he had so long avoided was a strange paradox. It was understandable that Mr. R. could not bear to feel his childhood depressive hopelessness on his own, that he needed me to feel this for and with him, to contain it, process it, and only then return it to him as a jointly experienced, metabolized feeling that he could accept. This hopelessness could become much too real for me so that I would think that Mr. R. had so disengaged himself from this treatment that it was, in effect, over. What was most helpful with him was my talking repeatedly about how unbearable his hopelessness was for him now, and how even more unbearable it had been when, as a child, he had been mired in it. I imagined with him, from what I felt waiting endlessly for him, uncertain of his engagement with me in the treatment, that his hopelessness had been traumatically overwhelming during his childhood. He would be moved, feel sad, touched by my persistence and patience with him, feel concern and gratitude toward me and his partner. He reacted with surprise and optimism to my suggestion that his need to destroy the treatment could be a positive sign, an opening up of his rage and hopelessness, so that we might now be able to address these heretofore intolerable feelings. But, of course, he would then miss most of his sessions again, occasionally call with excuses about why he hadn't been able to come, but rarely call when he didn't show up on Thursdays.

I would remain optimistically confident for a while that we needed to contain his rage and hopelessness until I would again start to wonder whether we were still hopelessly stuck at sadomasochistic struggle, which Mr. R., and perhaps I too, could not get beyond. I would wonder whether I was trying to delude myself and Mr. R. that we were still meaningfully involved in a treatment from which Mr. R. had long ago withdrawn himself. Was I misguidedly priding myself on my capacity to feel deeply, to bear Mr. R.'s hopelessness and rage, so as to deny the demise of this treatment? Even if I was correct that the paradox of Mr. R.'s destruction of the treatment could be its flowering, could he and I bear his rage and hopelessness sufficiently to work with these unbearable affects in this treatment? I would reassure myself that our goal could not *now* be to work directly with Mr. R.'s rage and hopelessness in our sessions but for me and him to survive and contain their expression in his action, action which seemed to signify destruction of the treatment.

I needed to resist Mr. R.'s powerful invitation that I mistreat him, so that we could instead talk about the safety of his confident expectation that each of us should mistreat the other. It would have been easy to rationalize mistreating Mr. R. I could feel tempted to criticize him for coming late, paying late, not investing himself in the treatment, so intensely wanting to preserve his sadomasochistic relatedness. But even when I was untouched by Mr. R.'s provocativeness, it was difficult indeed to really engage him in meaningful exploration rather than his going through the motions of talking about his fears of needing others, his intense resentment, or his chronic dissatisfaction and willingness to retain it. He seemed terrified to remain emotionally touched for very long, to really want something good for himself, to care about himself or others. Mr. R. had survived his childhood by priding himself on his ability to endure hardship without being tempted by what he knew he could not have. He did not try out, did not even open up, what for him should have been a very special piece of equipment, for over a year, until it was already obsolete. Even now, Mr. R. knew keenly that whatever he pursued would not work out well; whatever he touched had to turn bad. He was very hesitant to allow himself to want anything that could satisfy him. Our job was to keep open his anxiety in taking his chances in really wanting something good from another person. As with Mr. N., here too bitter rejection of the possibility of satisfaction, another kind of negativism, protected Mr. R. from ordinary human need. Rage, hurt, and disappointment had hardened, foreclosed Mr. R.'s hope that he could get anything good from others.

When I have presented some of Mr. R.'s material publicly, highly skilled clinicians sought to reassure me that I should not feel badly about the failure of his treatment, which I should accept by ending it. My capable colleagues insisted that Mr. R.'s sadomasochism was too deeply entrenched for us to modify it. Was I holding on to my patient too long, sadomasochistically trapped with him, or stubbornly denying the reality of our failure? I still don't know the answers to these questions. Every so often we have a session that touches both of us with possibilities for change. But of course such optimistic sessions are followed by Mr. R.'s prolonged absence or uninvolvement. Yet, I persist as I try to preserve my hope that we can extend and enhance our mutual engagement. And I keep reminding myself that Mr. R. is touched when I suggest that because of his anxiety about our making contact with each other, he has needed to retreat. So I again interpret his fearful flight from me and from the possibilities for contentment in his life. At least my optimistic persistence with Mr. R. in the face of his entrenched hopelessness counters his parents' attitudes toward him, showing him a new developmental potential for constructive change. Perhaps at some point he will become able and willing to modify his masochism and emotional retreat from others.

In the past, in agreement with my skilled colleagues, I probably would have told Mr. R. that we should discontinue his treatment because he was insufficiently motivated to change. If his motivation for change increased, then it might make sense for him to return to treatment. By doing so, I would have been making the treatment problem his failing rather than accepting it as a joint problem for both of us. For patients like Mr. R., who have been rejected, criticized, attacked, and blamed, such a therapeutic stance can aggravate the problem, heightening the residues of past trauma in the present treatment. The patient can easily experience the therapist, like the parent of childhood, as making the patient solely responsible for what has gone wrong between them (cf. Bromberg 1983). In contrast, the therapist's committment to joining the patient in struggling with the treatment impasse rather than putting it back on the patient offers a new developmental perspective. Such patients will insist that the therapist, unlike the parent before him, own his contributions to the treatment dilemma. They may seem to torture the therapist forever about his failings with them.

These patients may need to take *a very long time* in which they live out such treatment struggles before they can or want to allow themselves more open and vulnerable collaboration with the therapist. They seem to need to test over and over again the therapist's willingness to persist with them no matter how impossibly they behave. Or, they need or want to live out for a very prolonged period with the therapist the previous sadomasochistic struggles with a parent. The therapist reassures such patients by his ability to endure rather than retaliate, reject, succumb, leave, or die. At some point, such patients may become willing or able to join the therapist in collaborative exploration of what they have lived through together. Then the patient can become capable of bearing responsibly for himself what the therapist has for so long needed to bear and contain for him. I cannot emphasize enough how long such treatment impasses may need to continue before these very difficult patients become able to move outside of them.

Part II

What is the Therapist's Role in Helping the Patient Develop Affect Tolerance?

4

Dangerous Need and Desire

L ike rage and hatred (chapter 3), desire and need can be difficult for both treatment partners to manage. In chapter 1, I discussed therapists' discomfort with loving feelings between themselves and their patients. In chapter 6, I will discuss certain of the therapist's regressive temptations. Here I consider dangers of desire and need for both patient and therapist.

We struggle with our ambivalence about our own personal roles and contributions to our patients' treatments. We remain conflicted about what we need from our patients, about what they need from us, and about how we shape their treatments. We are hesitant to speak openly about which therapeutic gratifications are legitimate and which are not (Fox 1997; see Chapters 1 and 6). How much satisfaction should we derive from our work? Have we become neurotic when we enjoy our patients, when we have erotic feelings toward them, when we hate them? How much passion is the clinician at work to have? Or more importantly, can we contain our passionate feelings for our patients, to be able to explore them in order to understand and aid our patients? The risk, otherwise, is that we will enact our desires or withdraw from them. So long as we are confident that we will not act on our feelings and desires, they are fun.

SOME TEMPTATIONS OF DESIRE AND NEED

Friendship

Some years ago at a social function, I was enjoying conversation with an *analyst, A.*, whom I found very warm and generous, especially in his praise of our hosts. He made a point of telling me what a special person B. was. B. and his wife responded with similar warmth about analyst A. My pleasure was spoiled when I learned that analyst A. had treated B. and that they had become friends. This is a common enough occurrence, and well worth our consideration. Most, not all of us, believe that, after the termination of treatment, transference and countertransference persist and need to be respected. In this example, the analyst may have considered that he wasn't doing analysis, that his psychotherapy had built into it supportive, friendly elements.

Of course, I had no way of knowing whether my concerns were justified that this treatment couple had used friendship to avoid opening up unfriendly feelings between them. But there are too many examples of treatment couples ending analysis or intensive psychotherapy only to become close friends or collaborators. The risk is of foreclosure of persistent transference and countertransference feelings between them that tempt them to want to remain together after the formal end of treatment. On the other hand, after sufficient time has elapsed, and after careful examination of the clinicians' feelings, former patients and clinicians can integrate some of what has transpired between them by acceptance of the fact that they no longer are or will be a treatment couple.

Greed and Envy

When a *new patient* in a second consultation session clearly sees the envy in my eyes as I gaze at his gorgeous white satin New York Knicks jacket, he knows instantaneously that I'm an avid Knick fan. He offers me his season tickets to Knick games when he is away from New York at his primary residence elsewhere. Be aware that these are not just any tickets, as he tells me seductively, these seats are fantastic! For those readers who don't live in New York, you should know that good tickets to Knick games are very difficult to get. Spike Lee-grade tickets are impossible to get. I struggle with my greed and envy so as to be able to say to this potential, occasional patient, in my best therapeutic voice, "That's the nicest offer anyone's made me this week, but let's find out why you need to seduce me like that." This example is relatively easy, although I certainly felt tempted to find a way to rationalize accepting the tickets, especially by focusing on the irrelevant fact that the giver could only be an occasional patient. And I felt considerable disappointment that I could not share these tickets with my youngest child, who would have loved them. Sometimes, it seems that it would have been much easier to have become a cardiologist. On the other hand, I felt proud of myself for containing my greed and envy, and I certainly have enjoyed the slightly more sublimated pleasure of telling about this incident.

Sexual Desire

An *attractive woman analysand*, outstandingly successful and capable, reported a dream late in her session: "I was in here, lying on the couch. I was tired and fell asleep. When I woke up in the dream, you were lying next to me, criss-cross across me. I started nuzzling against you. You asked what I was doing. I lied, saying I was just moving my head, but I was nuzzling, trying to get closer to you. You asked if I was being honest. Then I started kissing you to see what you would do. The dream was fraught with lots of tension and sexuality. You started kissing back so I knew I was safe in this territory. You were on top of me in a protective way, enveloping me. I wanted to feel subsumed, possessed, like not knowing where one person ends and the other person begins. It was very erotic. It reminded me of very passionate feelings I've had at the beginning of relationships. When I woke up, I felt really excited; it didn't dawn on me this was only a dream. When

I realized it was only a dream, I was kind of disappointed. The day of the dream was my birthday and my father had a pacemaker implanted for his arrythmia." My thoughtful patient did, of course, point out, to help us both tolerate our temptations, that I had taught her to wonder about dream elements that seem too obvious, so perhaps my undisguised presence in the dream (not her words) also represented her father, whom she was anxious about losing because of his surgical procedure. My patient had felt afraid that I would not be able to withstand what she wanted from me, that if she wanted to seduce me, I could not resist her. I think to myself that I need to feel the incestuous temptations fully so as to experience what she's after. It is fun to do so without fearing that I will act on my temptations.

DANGEROUS NEED

When needing others threatens patients with dangerous vulnerability, they will, of course, attempt to destroy, deny, at least minimize the need, now with the therapist, rejecting and spoiling whatever "good stuff" they get. Needing others exposes all of us to possibilities of disappointment, frustration, loss, hurt, humiliation, and rage. For some, such threat is more than they can bear because of the tremendous intensity of their need; because of their terrible expectations of what others can and will do, once they've exposed such vulnerable need; because of their chronic rage at past hurt, disappointment, loss, or trauma; because of their own unconscious wishes for merger to ward off threatened loss and destruction of the other and of oneself. The greater the threat, the greater is the patient's need for the illusion of omnipotent control and self-sufficiency, seemingly free of the dangers of human need. Since emotional contact with the analyst threatens to liberate such long-stifled dangerous need in our most rigidly closed-off patients, they must keep us, and their need of us, apart. They do so, as we have all become painfully aware, by attitudes and behaviors that can be very difficult indeed for us clinicians to bear.

With these difficult patients who tend to ignore, misuse, or destroy what we provide them, many clinicians have drawn on the writings of our contemporary Kleinian colleagues of London. We have found it helpful to follow carefully, as they advise, what our difficult patients do, and don't do, with what we provide them. Some American colleagues, such as Kernberg, Schafer, and LaFarge, who write about patients' attempts to hide, devalue, or destroy what is valuable in what they receive from the analyst, have been significantly influenced by these contemporary Kleinians. Other colleagues have written about patients' defensive use of the analyst and the analysis (e.g., as fetish [Renik 1992], for soothing [Peltz 1992], for dependent containment [Coen 1992]), misusing analyst and analytic process in the wish to stay protected forever from the patient's terrifying internal dangers. Not all pathologically dependent patients are comfortable with their need of the therapist. Some have to avoid full experience of need, involving especially tender, loving concern, by rigid constriction, distance, escape, distraction, excitement, angry rejection and attack, sadomasochistic relatedness, and so on.

Another perspective for careful attention to what patients do with what analysts provide them is that of close monitoring of analytic process via focus on the defensive functioning of the patient's ego (Busch 1993, 1994, 1995, Davison, Pray, and Bristol 1986, 1990, Gray 1973, 1982, 1994). Gray and his colleagues have emphasized helping patients observe and modify their automatic defensive activity toward the goal of achieving maximum autonomy from internal constriction and from external surrender to the analyst. They carefully consider how to speak to patients so as to minimize their defensive functioning; they seek to enlist patients as collaborators in observing their own automatic needs for defense. However, these American colleagues have not described their own responses when the patient ignores, rejects, misuses, or destroys what they have interpreted. Gray intends his approach to be applied to "narrower scope" patients who, he believes, are relatively able to collaborate with the analyst in investigating their own defensive functioning. Busch has extended this program to a much broader range of patients; he now promises to describe in detail his approach with more rejecting patients, such as the perverse (personal communication, 2000).

I vividly remember my surprise as an analytic candidate when a supervisor suggested that my perverse patient was *spitting out* my interpretations, refusing to keep them inside his mouth and mind, so as to ward off his terror of my influence. I found my supervisor's bodily imagery highly evocative. My patient began to imitate me as the analyst by making analytic interpretations in a rather pompous style. Soon my patient was pretending to be me, at times briefly losing his awareness that he could not transform himself into me. He would also leaf through my mail in the hallway, announce his absences before I could announce mine, and once asked a woman patient he met in the waiting room for a date. Then my patient elaborated fantasies of our being twins rather than two separate people. My supervisor's focus on what the patient was doing with my words, my body, and my person was very helpful. It was fascinating to observe the shift from this man's initial attempts to keep me outside of him toward pressured wishes for interpenetration, incorporation, and merger.

In my experience as a supervisor, beginning analysts and therapists tend not to consider what their patients are doing with what they, as analyst or therapist, interpret. I try to help my supervisees think about why their patients are not listening to them or not collaborating more fully in the work of the treatment as we attempt to examine what transpires between the treatment couple. We look closely at just that switchpoint at which the patient attempts to move away emotionally and physically, by not listening, distracting himself from, ignoring, forgetting, devaluing, destroying what had just seemed good and relevant. We attempt to consider the patient's needs for protection against his feelings and desires and the uses he is making of the therapist. And we especially explore what it means to the patient to collaborate actively with the therapist in contrast to more passive compliance *or* refusal to make the work of the treatment his or her own.

For example, I was concurrently treating three patients whose mothers died when they were children. Each patient needed to exert an inordinate (so it seemed to me) control over the conditions of the treatment and its process. Mr. A. initially was very argumentative and oppositional with me. He would tell me repeatedly that he would consider what I had interpreted *later* when he was alone or that he would ask a number of his friends what they thought about my idea. He was terrified that I could succeed in influencing him into erroneous ideas if he did not scrutinize what I told him. He made clear that he felt mistrustful and frightened of relying on me or on anyone else. He would attempt to control what he told me or what I told him and insist on deciding what my policy on missed sessions should be. He would then try to dismiss my interpretations of his control and demandingness by pompously lecturing me on current writing on corporate management techniques, of which, he eagerly pointed out, I was obviously ignorant. If he arrived early, he would try to pressure me into seeing him sooner, even when I told him I was waiting for the previous patient. Or he would turn my waiting room into his own office, as he spoke loudly on his cellular phone, conducting business even when I came out to get him. I told him he was playing at being in his own office, so that he did not have to feel vulnerable waiting for me and wanting to be with me in my office. When he could relax his control and guardedness, he would feel lonely, sad, needy, and vulnerable, all of which he would vigorously attempt to reject. If my interpretive focus made him anxious, he would try to bully me that he was considering ending the treatment or at least that he would consider over the next vacation whether this treatment was useful for him.

Even when I was helpful to him, he would minimize or destroy my helpfulness, insisting on his having the upper hand with me. He could be incredibly demanding, intrusive, unappreciative, insensitive, and very angry. He was fired from a substantial job and was repeatedly told by others that they found him arrogant, offensive, domineering, and angry. He would dismiss and justify these criticisms of himself. No matter how he behaved with any of us, he felt entitled to appreciation and caring. He found it very difficult to take his character flaws seriously without feeling depressed and hopeless. Similarly, he could not hold still with his intense passive longings for closeness, caring, and physical contact.

This married man was eventually able to reveal to me his intense homosexual wishes for physical closeness and strength from another man. He could relax his guardedness and control with me long enough to allow himself to feel cared for by me, although he fought such regression fiercely. He would insist that what helped him feel better might have been the treatment, but that he was not really aware of how I had helped him; rather, something good had just happened in his life that had enhanced his self-esteem. I felt angry with Mr. A.'s relative intolerance of working with his entitled demandingness, exploitativeness, and argumentativeness. Instead, he would angrily justify why I should again change his hour or not charge him for missed sessions or not talk to him about how angry and demanding he was. My job was to be supportive, encouraging, give him advice, and do as I was told. I had to remind myself that Mr. A. had initially told me he had chosen me, instead of the three other therapists he had consulted, because I had seemed the most willing to talk with him about what was wrong with him. But he made clear that he would not easily tolerate my confronting him with his psychopathology.

I would try to show Mr. A. why he needed to maintain so much control over his treatment relationship with me and help him to feel and tolerate some of what lay beyond such control. It would have been easier had he been more able to bear his sad, lonely, needy feelings and to preserve the connections to his mother's illness and death and to his father's remoteness. Over and over again, I would interpret his arguing with me as protection against his experiencing what he wanted and felt. Sometimes, I could show him that, in expecting that I wanted to control and dominate him, he was projecting his needs into me. Sometimes, we were able to connect images of mother and father insisting on his compliance to them. He was hesitant to remain aware of his terror in relying on me or on anyone else—I would neglect or abandon him, think of my needs not of his. I would remind him that allowing genuine emotional contact with me both helped him to feel better, yet terrified him. Thus he got rid of his knowledge and desire, returning next session again insisting on control over our interaction. This was not a collaborative patient who could explore with me his ego's need for protection against the fantasied dangers of his desires and feelings. My task was to help him bear these dangers a little more consistently and with somewhat less dread.

DANGEROUS DESIRE

At the 1997 panel on the technical management of highly erotic transference at the International Psychoanalytical Association Congress in Barcelona, only one of three presenting analysts said *anything* about his or her erotic desires toward the patient. I don't know if there is significance to the fact that the analyst who spoke about his discomfort with the desires his patient stirred in him, which she repudiated, was from the United States. It would be interesting to study geographic variations in analysts' disclosure of their affects at meetings. The other two (women) analysts said nothing about their own erotic counterresponses to their patient's intense desires toward them. The American analyst reported feeling "duped" that he had been set up to feel desire for his patient, to play the role of her lover, while she totally repudiated her role in the enactment and would not share this desire with him. I imagined that his "discomfort" came about because his patient had put him in the uncomfortable position where he was helpless about her perverse power to stir up desire in him that she would not also feel and acknowledge.

    The other two women analysands seemed to crave intense responsiveness, caring, and bodily contact but somehow seem to repel, rather than attract, their women analysts. One analyst emphasized her patient's destructive attacks on her maternal analyzing functions— the analyst felt immobilized, paralyzed, projected into. I imagined that when her analysand could not draw this analyst in closer through sexual arousal, she then succeeded in catching the analyst through provocative, sadomasochistic, antisemitic attack. I wondered what interfered with the analytic couple's ability to "play" with the seduction between them. Because the analyst felt controlled by her patient, she may have wanted to return back to the patient the infantile longings she felt had been projected into her. I imagined that the intensity of the patient's wish to live out being cared for by the analyst hindered the analytic couple's ability to regard these desires more playfully. Similarly, the third analyst struggled to tolerate being the recipient of her traumatized, deprived, lonely patient's intense erotic desires toward her. The patient's wishes that the analyst love and rescue her, through a wished-for enactment of writing a letter on the patient's behalf, turned into a struggle between the analytic couple. When this analyst insisted that the patient was trying to seduce and dominate her, I imagined the third analyst, like the second analyst, felt uncomfortable with the intensity of her patient's desire to be loved and rescued.

Gabbard and Lester's fine book, *Boundaries and Boundary Violations in Psychoanalysis* (1995), considers why analysts do, sometimes, act on their desires toward patients. This book is not a superego-ish admonition to analysts to stay away from their analysands. Gabbard and Lester encourage a tension between analysts feeling their passions fully while managing and using them for the benefit of their analysands. Of course, I agree with them, as they invite us to feel and struggle with our inevitable temptations with our analysands, rather than to resist experiencing the seductive pulls between our patients and ourselves. Even as they describe the frightening dangers of analysts transgressing boundaries with analysands, they would have us feel our temptations, so that we can reflect on them rather than enact them. Glen Gabbard, in panels on hate, love, and intense erotic feeling in the analytic situation, has been one of the very few analysts who has not been put off by such intense feeling between his analysands and himself. Instead, he has openly described his own struggles with passionate feelings between his patients and himself.

Gabbard and Lester differentiate transgressing analysts who can be rehabilitated from those who should be helped to leave psychoanalytic practice. We need to get past our own defensive dismissal of transgressing analysts and our wish to separate ourselves from them and from our own frightening temptations with our analysands. We need to differentiate issues of punishment, remorse, and restitution from clinical decisions about which analysts will and will not be able to return to responsible practice. Gabbard and Lester's portrait of severely narcississtic, sadistic, exploitative analysts speaks for itself about why such people should not practice intensive psychotherapy or psychoanalysis. They propose a program for rehabilitating *some* analysts who founder. They describe a mediation process to facilitate healing for both patient and analyst, in which the analyst, who has transgressed, expresses remorse, apology, and offers restitution to the former patient.

Each time I've read this book, I've been especially touched by Dr. K.'s very open report of her painful analytic experience. Every analyst and every analyst-in-training should, I think, read her statement so that it can move all of us to want to do better. Her esteemed senior analyst, feeling lonely and uncared for, tried to convince both of them that intimacy between them merely expressed healthy tender concern rather than inappropriate exploitation. For us to remain intimately involved affectively with our patients, we must feel confident that we will not run the risk of acting on our wishes and needs toward them. Gabbard and Lester want us to be painfully aware how difficult our work is so that we protect our patients and ourselves as best we can. But we should not protect them and us by withdrawal, isolation, and emotional distance. If we need more education, supervision, reanalysis, or less emotionally taxing work, so be it. We should be capable of such self-assessment; that should be the minimum outcome of training analyses.

We should be sufficiently aware of times when we become excessively vulnerable and needy so that we can protect ourselves and our patients from our own excesses (see Chapter 6). At such times we need to be especially wary of our temptations to do and say what we ordinarily would not, to consider very carefully whether our interventions aim to help us to feel less vulnerable and needy rather than to help our patients. Perhaps we need a list, that all of us memorize, of those stressors that put us at additional risk of violating patients' boundaries: threatening illness in the therapist or a close family member; major professional disappointments; separation, divorce, death of a spouse or partner, parent, child, or other significant loss; and the inevitable loss that Gabbard and Lester want us to acknowledge, termination of treatment. We may be tempted to avoid the threat of loss of a patient through termination by varied attempts to preserve a different connection with her. This gets us to the problematic area of asking former patients to contribute money to our institutes, to befriending former patients, to follow-up interviews with former patients, to our questions of how long transference and countertransference feelings persist, and so on. Gabbard and Lester make clear that these are difficult problems, that the practice of intensive treatment is very challenging and gratifying, and that we need to acknowledge our human frailties with our patients in order to best help them and ourselves.

JOINT NEED: ACKNOWLEDGMENT OR AVOIDANCE?

We need to acknowledge, much more than we usually do, how differences in our personalities, therapeutic style, emphases, intentions, goals, and so on, determine how we approach patients. I want to focus especially on how acknowledgment of joint need between patient and therapist helps to open up the affective force-field between the treatment couple. The converse is also true—treatment is hindered, at least to some degree, when the treatment couple does not acknowledge what they want from each other. In order to comment on such differences between therapists, I will draw here on my discussion of a distinguished analyst's process material. Although I respect and admire Dr. R., I use this vignette to argue the advantages of acknowledging joint need between patient and therapist, need that includes preoedipal aspects for each of them. It will be clear that Dr. R., in his emphasis on analysis of phallic-oedipal conflict, views the "homosexual" tensions between his patient and himself primarily as negative oedipal regressive retreat. Dr. R. will acknowledge that, in retrospect, he thinks he did not attend sufficiently to these homosexual tensions. But he doesn't make it legitimate to consider each treatment partner's needs of the other. As a result, it becomes more difficult for each one to feel what he and the other wants. So I, of course, believe that when each partner is freer to experience his wishes, needs, and defenses with the other, we gain greater access to the preoedipal conflicts in our more difficult patients. Dr. R. is an excellent analyst. I present this material to suggest that leaving out joint need between patient and therapist and its preoedipal origins *may* tend to close off the therapeutic playing field. Dr. R. would see it differently. He would provide what he felt his patient needed—"support"—so as to be able to analyze phallic-oedipal conflict.

Some years ago, at the Freud/Klein panel held at the American Psychoanalytic Association, it had been a pleasure to listen to colleagues play respectfully with other skilled colleagues' work. I was fascinated to hear Harold Blum contrast himself as an analyst with Edward Weinshel, who had presented lovely detailed process material. Blum said Weinshel was a much more patient person, one who could wait much more comfortably for the transference to develop than could he. Blum said that he would go after resistance to the unfolding and acknowledgment of transference much more actively than would Weinshel. I was delighted to hear an analyst talk about such personal differences in analytic style. Like Blum, I tend, *sometimes*, not to leave things alone to develop on their own. I tend to jump in more than would Dr. R. Dr. R. expects to conduct analysis most of the time with ease and comfort; he takes for granted that the analytic process will go well. I imagine that even in my own mind, I tend not to leave things alone as much as he would, that I do more scanning and searching of what is going on between my patients and me than he does. And we have different attitudes toward self-revelation with ourselves and with our colleagues. He expects to have to do self-analysis when confronted by a prominent resistance in the treatment contributed to by both treatment partners. I expect to scan my feelings, wishes, needs, and defenses much more regularly for clues as to what is occurring outside of my conscious awareness. I believe much of this has to do with differences in temperament as well as differences in expectations of how affectively involved we need to become in most treatments *and* of what we want to address in them. Some of this is also an issue of differences in our analytic age, although you should be aware that I'm older than I look. But I assume I've been analyzed, supervised, and trained differently than was Dr. R., that indeed Dr. R. and his psychoanalytic contemporaries are the ones who've helped to bring about these differences in our analytic attitudes.

This was an excellent analysis. Dr. R. certainly did help his patient grow and change considerably. I played fancifully with my imaginings of what Dr. R. reported in his protocol, an approach to clinical discussion I'll describe in Chapter 8. Given my bent, I was intrigued that Dr. R. did not consider mutual need between his patient and himself. When his patient returned to treatment, after an interruption, Dr. R. seemed subtly critical that his patient wanted "support" instead of analysis. Dr. R. viewed his patient's wishes and needs for warmth and caring as necessary for engaging him but not as legitimate in their own right.

The patient emphasized his need for response, involvement, and acceptance. When he returned to see Dr. R., the patient was "deeply gratified by how much I remember about him," Dr. R. wrote, now much more tenderly, revealing their previously concealed mutual warmth. The patient had considerable difficulty with asking his wife or analyst for what he needed; he wanted the other to share in mutual wanting and asking. He felt considerable shame, humiliation, and rage in asking another person for what he needed, as if he were helplessly submitting to the other. At the beginning of the treatment, the patient had felt depressed and uncared for, craving what he pictured someone else was getting. This pathological jealousy was reported against the backdrop of the mother caring for the sick sister, while the mean maternal grandmother cared for the patient.

The centerpiece of Dr. R.'s presentation was his "countertransference error" of unexpectedly encouraging his patient. Dr. R. was "puzzled about my joining in the euphoria," troubled that he had neglected to talk about the patient's projection of conflict onto his wife and to inquire why it was so important for the patient to have his wife "first show him that she wanted sex as much as he did." In this session, the patient was hypomanic, with excited tone and slightly pressured speech. When the patient said he "wished that he could clear up his sex problem," Dr. R. surprised himself by his enthusiastic response to his patient. Dr. R. told us he "was hyperalert and excited by the hope that at last maybe the patient could soon terminate." He described his patient in that session as "euphoric . . . filled with enthusiasm and resolve . . . strongly engaged throughout the hour not only with his own associations but with me." Dr. R. told us how different this Monday was from so many other Mondays when the patient was depressed, "almost always affectively withdrawn . . . It was as though I wasn't there . . . I gradually felt a sense of futility about his monotonous litany." The analyst would become sleepy, even briefly fall asleep, on such Mondays. In this session, routine and excited images clashed, and wishes for intense mutual involvement were clear. The patient wanted his wife to want him and he treasured the analyst's enthusiasm for him. I saw patient and analyst each wanting to "join in the euphoria," so as to feel more substantially engaged with the other. Such intense temptation to share emotional connectedness seemed to keep the analyst from being able to step back to ask the patient about his hypomanic excitement.

The patient fell asleep as his wife was preparing to have sex with him. She invited him to *ask* her when he was ready. He dreamt about his friend Y. having a vagina with semen, pubic hair, and slicked back black hair. Y. and the patient had been a team that together could tackle anything. But Y. never grew up and was now "begging" the patient for a job. We heard references to hideous teeth and insatiable appetites, with rapid shifts between male and female images. Having to ask for what he wanted felt humiliating. Dr. R. felt disappointed that his patient did not react visibly to his interpretation of the patient's projection of his sadism onto his wife. Then he told about his memories of dozing off in Monday sessions. I imagined a link between Dr. R.'s reporting his current and past disappointments, and his memories of feeling sleepy and dozing off on the patient. I felt surprised that Dr. R. didn't tell more about how they worked with these Monday feelings that each was not there for the other, that Dr. R. didn't reveal *something* of his "personal feelings."

So, when Dr. R. focused on his patient's avoidance of acknowledging that Dr. R. had fallen asleep on him, I wanted to focus on both partners, on what had been going on between the two of them that had led the analyst to fall asleep, *as well as* how the patient felt about the disruption between them *and* the analyst's sleeping. I imagined that focusing on the disruption between the analytic couple would take both of them back to their difficulty with Mondays, to how each partner felt that the other was not there for him. Then I imagined they could understand more clearly how the patient's Monday depression and affective withdrawal related to the weekend separation from the analyst and to his hesitation to allow himself to again *ask* for what he needed from the analyst without some acknowledgment of this difficulty from the analyst. I imagined that they hadn't addressed *directly* their mutual dissatisfaction on Mondays.

Dr. R. believes that the analyst needs to do self-analysis of his sleepiness in sessions but that it does not need to be jointly examined, even when this has been a regular phenomenon that has intruded on the analytic process. We disagree. I believe when there has been a disruption in the analytic work that involves both partners, that they need to address together what has gone wrong. Without acknowledgment and exploration of how both partners have contributed to the disruption, it may often be impossible to get beyond it. I thought of the two references in this session to something being out of view, including a mirror image of the patient being out of view. I picture the patient trying to signal the analyst about something they were not looking at: perhaps what the patient wanted from the analyst, what he wanted the analyst to want from him, and what the analyst did want from him. In addition to the patient's hesitation to defeat his friend Y. and the analyst, I thought of his fears of terminating the analysis and of being "a team" with the analyst. So, I might have said,

"We've both been having trouble connecting with each other on Mondays. We've both been hesitant to acknowledge that we've been disappointed that the other one hasn't been more emotionally available. I haven't been with you on weekends and then you haven't been with me on Mondays."

Although the second reported session was on a Monday, both partners were now up. The patient was euphoric, enthusiastic, strongly engaged emotionally with himself and with Dr. R. He would not let his wife force her wishes on him; she should accept him as he was, she should want sex as he did. Dr. R. describes being drawn into the patient's euphoria. Besides offering encouragement, he interpreted the patient's fear of his sadism towards his wife, did not interpret the patient's (sadistic) transference wishes, and wondered why he didn't ask why the wife had to *show him* that she wanted sex as much as he did (my emphasis). Here I imagined that Dr. R. may have been alluding to feelings not being addressed between them, not only sadistic ones, but perhaps especially wishes that the analyst, like the wife, *show* that he wanted the patient.

In the third session, the excitement of the prior day was gone; the patient was depressed and dejected. Sex with his wife was routine; his penis felt anesthetic, dead. Dr. R. focused on the patient's fear and wish to disappoint the analyst, excited at the prospect of the patient's success. In the fourth session, the patient clarified that he'd left the Monday session excited and encouraged, watching for Dr. R.'s car. Then he suddenly shifted from longings to be with Dr. R. to love of his own new car. When he'd been excited telling Dr. R. about his new car, he had felt that Dr. R. had put him down by asking about his excitement. He returned rapidly to his Monday excitement of Dr. R. encouraging him. Now he could terminate, except that he failed in bed with his wife. Dr. R. interpreted the patient's fear and wish to hurt and defeat the analyst/pal. Several months later, the patient was able to help his wife resist their son's provocations; they succeeded at sex. Dr. R. *playfully* interpreted, "It sounds like a lucky thing that at least that time I didn't tell you before you had sex how well you were doing." Laughing, the patient thought of his sister: "He hadn't ever seen her this way before. She really looked pretty." I imagined that the patient's enthusiastic response about his sister, following Dr. R.'s playful interpretation, may have referred, besides oedipal rivalry, to his pleasure in Dr. R.'s acknowledgment that he needed not to get in the patient's way, as he had been doing. Had I caught this, I would have wanted to say, "Just like your sister, I look better to you when I'm encouraging and don't get in your way, as I have been."

I would have wanted to explore the patient's feelings of humiliation at needing and asking for what he wanted, with his wife and with his analyst. Dr. R. referred to the patient's transference fantasy of the analyst as narcissistically needing the treatment success for himself rather than allowing the patient to keep it. But we didn't get to hear how they opened this up. I would have wanted to talk more about the patient's angry hunger for encouragement, fathering, parenting. I imagined that although both analytic partners had wanted a more intense affective engagement with each other, this had been difficult for them to fully acknowledge together. Now that their mutual tenderness was more available following the patient's return, the patient's conflicted longings for the analyst as parent could be focused more centrally in the treatment.

My goal is not primarily for the therapist to provide his patient with love but to use his own struggles in staying close to his patient in order to help his patient work out his related conflicts. I contend that to do so, the therapist needs to allow himself access to his own wishes, needs, and defenses in the room with his patient. Otherwise, he will miss much of what is playing out between them. As I describe in Chapter 8, all of us therapists have to miss some of what is being lived out between our patients and ourselves, so that clinical discussants can expand our perspectives, if they seek to do so constructively. So, I had two intentions in my discussion of Dr. R.'s clinical case. I wanted to try to bring into view some of what he seemed not to have seen. And I wanted to use this clinical example to argue the advantages of the therapist's seeking access to his own wishes, needs, and defenses in order to be in the position to be able to help his patients most effectively.

5

Perverse Defenses in
Neurotic Patients

INTRODUCTION: PERVERSE AND NARCISSISTIC
ASPECTS OF DEFENSE IN NEUROTIC PATIENTS

As I reviewed my struggles to determine whether my two patients described in Chapter 2, Professor A. and Mr. B., couldn't or wouldn't do better in holding still long enough to face and attempt to resolve their conflicts more satisfactorily, I realized that colleagues who have listened to this material (in a peer supervision study group and at public presentations) similarly have kept changing their minds about my patients' treatability. Here I focus on the meanings of the fact that patient, therapist, and others who have listened to the process material have had such difficulty pinning down what the patient can and cannot do. This shifting of therapeutic judgment about the patient differs substantially from what I and my colleagues experience with more typical patients with whom we are usually more confident in our assessment of what they can accomplish in treatment.

My two patients had affect intolerance, periods of regression during analysis in which they were unable to function collaboratively so that they needed to be sustained by me, and intense clinging to infantile modes of relating. In addition, it now seems clearer to me that they also did indeed keep shifting their ability *and* willingness to confront what is wrong, drawing predominantly on a type of defense akin to disavowal. Such disavowal contrasts with a willingness to address painful affect, conflict, and limitations sufficiently and consistently over time so as to be able to resolve these conflicts more satisfactorily. My patients' disavowal can be described as an attitude of not caring, dismissal, or indifference that is achieved by distracting themselves, *tuning out* what is wrong. They focused instead on excitement—from sadomasochistic object relating, and for Professor A. also sexual excitement—and narcissistic self-aggrandizement. Although such efforts to distract oneself do not actually result in dissociation or an altered state of consciousness, such analogies are useful. As I discussed in Chapter 2, I needed to change my either/or attitude toward analyzability, that patients were clearly either analyzable or not analyzable, into a view that such patients oscillate between engagement and acknowledgment of conflict and retreat and disavowal.

My two patients showed a perverse refusal to accept reality (Grossman, 1992, 1993, 1996) as well as their own needs, feelings, and authentic relations with others. Instead, they attempted to create an illusory world of their own in which pain and need were expunged by excitement and braggadocio and genuine loving relationships were replaced by interchangeable connection with anonymous, unvalued people. I shall use the term "perverse defense," to refer to such cultivation of states of excitement, distraction, and pomposity, as well as sadomasochistic relations with others, that attempt to protect against the unbearable: intense affects, painful ideas, and loving, committed need of a valued, distinct person.

When we call someone perverse, we describe the provocative stance of a person who refuses to be reasonable and behave like everyone else together with our own attacking, judgmental counterresponse. Perverse attitudes refer to qualities that are provocative, vengeful, obstinate, peevish, grandiose, dismissive, and distracting. Professor A. tried to maintain the excited illusion with anonymous women, with his woman partner, and with me in the transference/countertransference that he possessed us and could do what he wanted with us. He would seek to induce me and his partner to look forward to his availability, physically and emotionally, so as to frustrate and disappoint us, emphasizing his sadistic omnipotent control over helpless need of the other—that she and I were now to feel. Not only was he repeating his mother's torturing style of relating, but he was also attempting to manage his own unbearable response to the unavailability of the other person, especially his sadness, loss, and murderous rage. I connect the perverse aspects of my patients' defenses with their affect intolerance, therapeutic disability, and therapeutic impasse.

Although I focus here on perverse defense, the reader should bear in mind the multiple other perspectives (beyond affect intolerance and difficulty with affect regulation) from which I have addressed these treatments: for example, terror of loss and separation, especially of the therapist, as termination began to feel more imminent and real; identification with the pathological parent as aggressor; terrors of intimacy, especially involving fears of disappointment, subjugation, and merger (disorganization); and terrors of destructiveness in self and other.[1]

Perverse and narcissistic aspects of defense against feelings, needs, and painful reality were complementary in my two neurotic patients, who did not have obligatory perversion. I refer especially to the cultivation of states of altered awareness as protection against those feelings and needs that seem unbearable to the patient. My two patients sought to *tune out* intolerable feelings and needs by efforts at self-aggrandizement, arrogance, grandiosity, and demeaning others *and* by efforts to feel excited, powerful, and sadistic in teasing and tempting others with the possibility of genuine relatedness, only to enjoy frustrating such hope in the other. My two patients preferred relations with anonymous, interchangeable persons to genuine relations with separate and distinct people.

---

[1]Discussions by Michael S. Porder, M. D. and Irving Steingart, Ph.D. showed me that I had not been sufficiently clear about these other analytic perspectives.

Narcissistic and perverse mechanisms in my two patients especially intersected at two points: first, at attempts to distract oneself from what is wrong by filling oneself up with antithetical feelings that are both grandiose and exciting, so as to achieve an altered state of awareness; and second, at the refusal to rely on, need, and love others. With my two patients, interpretation of the narcissistic aspects of defense, although necessary, was ultimately less useful for the progress of their analyses than was focus on their perverse defenses. Each of my patients would attempt to dismiss what was wrong by attempting to elevate himself above his contempt for ordinary human concerns and ordinary human beings. My patients' narcissistic efforts to tune out reality, needs of others, and whatever else was wrong within, also had the perverse quality of a peevish child who refuses to pay attention. They would become excited as they provocatively refused to be reasonable like everyone else, drawing others into fighting with them.

My two patients' perverse relatedness involved perverse sadomasochistic object relations in which the other person is not accorded the status of a valued, needed, loved, separate person. The perverse excitement of provoking and dismissing others (and reality and one's own conflicts) helped the patient feel grandiose and omnipotent, thereby elevating self-esteem. My patients felt relieved to be contained, held, and challenged in their sadomasochistic object relating; then they did not have to feel separate and alone with their own intolerable feelings and needs. Profound oscillations in their therapeutic availability reflected shifts between narcissistic and perverse self-sufficiency with rejection of the need for others and terror of being separate and alone. This terror then led back to wishes for closeness, containment, and protection by the other. Dread of intimacy (disappointment, subjugation, merger/disorganization) activated perverse and narcissistic defenses against need.

I emphasize the *excitement*, in one's grandiosity and in one's omnipotent ability to provoke others, as especially differentiating perverse from narcissistic defenses. When we think about narcissistic defenses, we ordinarily think about self-esteem enhancement so as to avoid whatever is painful and dangerous, including needs of others. The other person tends to feel excluded, alone, insignificant, unwanted, and may feel tempted to intrude on the narcissist. But we don't ordinarily emphasize the narcissist's excited wish to provoke the other person into jumping into his drama. We certainly could focus, for one obvious example, on the narcissist seeking, in his exhibitionism, to elicit in the other person envy, self-denigration, and sadomasochistic wishes to surrender to the awe-inspiring exhibitionist. When we focus on such (sexually) exciting wishes to engage, possess, and torture the other person as a helpless participant in the patient's scenes, this sadomasochistic object relations aspect of narcissistic defense is, I believe, more evocatively grasped from the viewpoint of perverse defense. Such differentiation, although helpful, is, of course, arbitrary. Excited provocation of others, as viewed from within the object relations of the narcissist, certainly could be considered an aspect of narcissistic defense.

Therapists tend to get caught in perverse sadomasochistic traps from which they self-righteously tend to force their patients to acknowledge the demands of reality and of the treatment. Here, therapists pressure patients to be different from who they are when therapists cannot tolerate feeling helpless and resentful in response to patients' sadomasochistic torturing of them. My patients would seem to offer the promise of acknowledging their needs and conflicts, especially now with me in the transference, only to sadistically disappoint me. In order to address our perverse sadomasochistic relatedness, I had to grasp my own identification with the role of torturer before I could show my patients how such torturing protected them from their human need of me.

We are now accustomed to considering our patients' narcissistic defenses and our own countertransference responses of feeling disregarded, insignificant, and alone (e.g., see Joseph 1993, Schafer 1997). But we have not attended to perverse aspects of defense and our countertransference responses in neurotic patients who do not have perversions. Perverse defenses evoke perverse countertransferences in therapists—the opprobrium accorded to perversion—in which we relish being sadistically judgmental, dominating, attacking. Therapists' sadistic pleasure in such perverse countertransference attitudes is more difficult for us to bear than is our countertransference response of feeling excluded, alone, and insignificant in response to patients' narcissistic defenses. We could approach, but not quite capture, similar countertransference feelings without the concept of perverse defense by focusing on the mutual sadism between therapist and narcissistic patient. We need to acknowledge the perverse and antagonistic affective force-field we are drawn into by perverse patients who refuse to be reasonable. Then we can shift our focus away from pinning down sexual perverts toward more constructive understanding of perverse mechanisms in neurosis.

PERVERSE DEFENSE IN NEUROTIC PATIENTS

To apply the concept of perverse defense to neurotic patients, we need to separate perverse defense from our traditional views of perversion. The patients under consideration do not have obligatory perversion that requires a specific behavior for sexual satisfaction. Perversion and neurosis have been too sharply and schematically differentiated in psychoanalysis. It is time to integrate perverse with neurotic defenses. To do so, we need to move from an assumed requisite sexual function in perverse defenses toward a broader view of how perverse defenses also provide vital aid with key nonsexual tasks of affect management, self-esteem regulation, and object relations.

CLINICAL VIGNETTES

By considering my patient, Professor A., to have a sexual addiction rather than a perversion in Chapter 2, I did not focus sharply enough on his efforts to stay distracted, to tune out reality and need through sexual excitement with interchangeable partners. I moved quickly to his addictive hunger, especially as a substitute for me in the analytic transference. Earlier in the treatment, when his hunger for a parent was easier for him to tolerate with me in the transference, we were fine. It should be clear from Chapter 2 that this had been a very productive, passionate treatment, satisfying for both of us. Professor A. was intensely engaged; he could need me, love me, hate me, compete with me, and want to destroy me. We had had little trouble working with the displaced transference meanings of his sexual actions. I became the longed for heterosexual and homosexual object of his intense maternal and paternal transference desires.

Once, however, termination came within sight, the treatment situation changed dramatically, as his defenses against needing me (and his partner) suddenly escalated. Not only did he step up finding substitutes for us, but he seemed to take a more insistent turn away from real relationships with distinctive, valued people (me as therapist and his partner) toward illusory relationships with anonymous, interchangeable people. From this perspective, although my patient did not have an obligatory perversion, it became more useful to think of him as having perverse relationships rather than primarily as having an addictive need for others.

Professor A. used sexual stimulation with anonymous, interchangeable women[2] to take himself away emotionally from his need for L. (his partner) and for me as his therapist. Especially when he felt loving and loved with either of us, he would seem to extinguish such loving feelings by the claim that neither of us was the one he wanted, as he pursued some anonymous substitute. In his protracted sexual excitement, he could tune out reality, his needs of specific people (especially his partner and me), and his pain and rage at the limitations,

---

[2]To protect my patient's confidentiality, I omit details of his sexual behaviors. Although I cannot convey in depth the fantasies my patient was enacting with his women, I can show a somewhat symmetical perverse enactment with me in the transference.

delays, and absence in his relationship with us. Some days on the analytic couch, by picturing his sexual substitutes, he could wipe out all other feelings, especially awareness of need for me. Professor A. would pretend that his excited connection with a sexual substitute would continue forever, while she willingly provided him whatever he wanted.

He could acknowledge how much he did not want to have a real relationship with L. and with me but to shift between bits of loving relatedness and retreat into exciting, illusory relationships with anonymous women. He emphasized his intense fears of loss and disappointment, repetition of his childhood experiences with both parents, if he continued to stay in close loving relatedness with either of us. Especially in the face of separation, he would refuse to value me as someone good who had helped him and whom he still needed (and hated). Instead, he would dismiss me from his mind and turn to a sexual substitute, so that he would not miss me, feel hurt, disappointed, sad, lonely, and enraged with me.

Professor A. would induce me to become more optimistic that he would again take part in the therapeutic work, come to the sessions consistently, stay closer and more available, only to frustrate and disappoint me by then immediately skipping sessions, turning more to his sexual substitutes, talking about ending the treatment because I could not help him further, and staying remote from me emotionally. We had repeated sequences in which he and I would work well together in a series of sessions, he would feel appreciative that I had helped him to change, express optimism about further change, leave the session warmly "promising" that he would try to work on what we had just discussed and would see me the following day, even though he had originally been unsure of his availability. Instead, he would miss the next session or couple of sessions, having returned to his sexual substitutes and his unwillingness to relinquish his childlike claim to continual indulgence.

Professor A. seemed to want to put me in the position in which he had felt with his mother. She would arouse expectation in him only to disappoint and frustrate him with her emotional unavailability. Similarly, he would carp about L. not being as slim and pretty as his first love; then he would stay away from her, focus his attention on other women, and not allow her (or me) to take her place with him for granted. With termination in sight, Professor A. kept me uncertain about his committment to further treatment; he was repeatedly ready to end the treatment, to come less frequently, to predict that academic and publishing pressures would lead him to miss so many sessions that we might as well stop, and to induce both of us to feel hopeless that further treatment could be of any use. He would contend that my interpretations had become stale and repetitive, that he simply needed to go out on his own and do what we had already talked about so much.

For example, on a Monday he reported a dream in which he hesitates to get off an exit of the highway on which he is driving. He changes lanes reluctantly, accidentally bumping the back of a small truck that has speeded up, so that he misses the exit. At the next exit, he goes up a steep uphill ramp, then drives off a bridge spanning a river. He jumps out of the car, feeling as if the earth is spinning away from him, so that he is lost in space. He associates this to feeling he is not ready to terminate his analysis, although he believes strongly that he should be able to manage on his own. The exit signs at which he felt reluctant to get off remind him of places where he felt remote and lonely; he fears losing connection with the world. Later in the week, he will speak about his own angry "jumping off the face of the earth." We talk about his hesitation to feel and work with his transference attachment to me, his fear and wish that he will never leave me, so that he can have a chance to work out his terrors of closeness and separateness.

He then steps up his sexual activities considerably, more than ever before he claims, even including one that was risky. He suggests that his behavior keeps him tied to me in a perverse way. Since he's never used that phrase before, I wonder what he means. He presents himself as a failure to me, showing me that he cannot manage himself on his own, he responds, so that we will both fail and stay together. Professor A. suggests that by spoiling what he and I are doing together, he doesn't need to miss me and want to be with me so much. Instead, he can focus on ending his treatment. I interpret his wish to provoke me into stopping and rescuing him, as he demonstrates his inability to function competently without me, unable to be alone, to be reasonable with others, to tolerate frustration, limitations, delays, or to care for himself.

We certainly had talked a great deal about Professor A.'s hesitation to manage himself competently on his own without me, as he can do during my summer vacation. Professor A. had wanted me to rescue him when he got into trouble, when he felt unable to motivate himself, to be his caring parent in so many ways. During the analysis, he had become strikingly less passive and dependent, much better able to enjoy and use his considerable abilities and aggression. On Friday, he is dramatically different, much more concerned about himself, appreciating his connection with me, looking forward to seeing me again soon. Referring to his recent dream, he says, "I've been going through falling off the face of the earth this week, cutting myself off from you and from L." As he leaves he says, "I was thinking I'd see you tomorrow, that it's Thursday." I respond warmly, "So, it's a wish, perhaps one you can hold onto." With a big smile he says, "I'll try."

Only later do I feel I've been set up to look forward to his coming closer to me so that he can frustrate me rather than continue to feel his wishes toward me. It is too much of a relief for me to feel that we are again connected meaningfully rather than to feel tortured and dismissed by his threats to terminate the analysis or by the web of pessimism and hopelessness he spins around us, in which I can also become trapped. I can feel myself angrily wanting to break through and take away his torturing and unsettling me in my position as a constructive analyst, to force him to feel his attachment to me and to L. From my wish to dominate and force Professor A. so I can escape from feeling unsettled with him, I can identify with his dominating and forcing me so that he can avoid feeling how much he needs me. Then I can interpret more comfortably how our perverse relatedness protects him from needing me more fully and directly.

It is now clear to me, but was not then, that I had become caught up in, and unable to get fully outside of, the perverse transference/countertransference, even as I worked to interpret it. Thus, to the degree that I felt angry pressure to force Professor A. to acknowledge his flight-from attachment to L. and to me, I *temporarily* lost my empathic perspective on his terror of intimacy with both of us. Once I could more fully extract myself from the affective force-field between us, I could then interpret, more empathically, that the primary motivation for his perverse relatedness with L. and with me was his terror of feeling close and loving. So, even while I had discovered something new between us, a perverse way of relating, I had remained too caught up in angry tensions between us to be able to grasp more clearly that he had to flee. I emphasize this point because I believe such countertransference is not unique to me. When we become caught up with our analysands in intense affective tensions, we may need several steps to extract ourselves and to understand what has transpired between us. It should be no surprise that there is always another perspective from which to understand therapeutic interaction. Instead of primarily criticizing ourselves for where we have become caught up and what else we have been unable to see, better that we tolerate and integrate such limitations, so that we can be more aware of them in the future. Then we can stay focused on helping our patients move forward.

The following week, Professor A. recognizes that he shifted from feeling competent and appreciative to feeling irresponsible. In the Monday session, he used my help to get out of feeling enraged and hopeless about getting a colleague's assistance, while Wednesday he stays in bed, cancels his appointments, and doesn't come to his session. I interpret that instead of allowing himself to feel appreciative and loving with me and his partner, he tortures us with promises that he won't keep so that he can pretend he has godlike control and power over ordinary human need. He adds, "I turn to stone a lot. I ought to let my blood warm up and hug people more because they need it, just as much as I need it. It's a lot easier said than done." I remind him how he runs away from wanting me to hug him, as in a recent dream, to his sexual substitutes. He says he forgets that other people want him to love them; earlier, he had said that when there is continuity in the sessions with me, he can feel I care about him. I say he wants to forget how much *he* cares, how much he wants to hug and be hugged.

In repeated sequences, he delighted in surprising me, either by his absence or his presence, paying me late or very early, keeping me "dangling," as he came to put it. One day, after we speak more about his sadistic control of others, especially me in the transference, he leaves announcing that he would come to his session the following day before traveling to a research center. I respond, too eagerly, enthusiastically, that that would be a first. I again catch myself feeling set up. The following morning he calls to cancel the session since he had not slept that night; he later cancels the next session. In the following session, when he says he didn't want to disappoint me, I say that he also did want to disappoint me. He talks about wanting to turn the tables on me, to leave me when I'm here, as I leave him for my summer vacation. He connects his fantasy that he possesses his sexual substitutes, who willingly allow him to do whatever he wants with them, with similar wishes toward me and L. He can now feel his pleasure in keeping me dangling, in pretending to own me. Then, more sadly, Professor A. talks about how when he dehumanizes me, he respects neither me nor himself, although then he doesn't have to feel anxious about committing himself to needing me (or L.). He sees how exciting, powerful, and safe he feels in repeating his mother's behavior with him.

In another sequence, he felt terrified about beginning a new project at which he didn't feel fully proficient. He felt resentful that he had to tackle this project and that it would occupy so much of his time, taking him away from more satisfying activities, including being with L. He felt terrified that he could neither begin the project nor complete it, that he'd remain stuck as he now felt. In two sessions at the end of the previous week, he had felt much closer to me, as he often did in Thursday and Friday sessions, able to talk again about wanting me to be the father who hugs him, able to bring his longings from his sexual substitutes to me in the transference. But now he felt very anxious and depressed; perhaps he needed medication. He insisted that I could not help him with this. Indeed, what I said to him didn't seem to help much. He insisted that he was stuck and that I was useless. He seemed more regressed, not open to my influence. I felt as helpless as he seemed to feel.

He spoke of his envy of his mother who did not have to work; she would curl up on the couch, depressed, intoxicated, and watch tv. He wanted to curl up on the couch like her, not have to work, have a woman care for him totally forever. He expressed this not as a wish but as a fate that would just befall him, from which he would never recover. Then I caught on and was able to interpret to my patient, that in my feeling helpless, I was to curl up with him on the couch, so that we would remain together forever. He would not need to move forward, terminate his treatment, and leave me. Now we were both able to get out of the regressive sadomasochistic trap in which we had both gotten stuck. Now again he was my analytic patient; we could address his regressive shift interpretively, that is, talk about what had just happened between us.

He shifted from surrender to helpless depression to talking about his *wishes* to fail, to hold onto me forever as his depressed mother, and then to his rage at his mother's failures with him, and to his hatred of her disability. We returned to his wishes from the previous week to turn me into the father who hugged and encouraged him to acknowledge the poverty of his relationship with his mother, so that he could separate from her, and take his own place in the world. Now he could say, with less terror, that he would never want to leave me, would want to regress further, have me care for him completely, lose himself in me. He could tolerate and step out of his merger wishes toward me as the depressed mother when he rediscovered that he could also connect to me as a constructive father who would help him individuate further.

My other patient, Mr. B., described in Chapter 2, similarly ran away from needing his partner and me, but not directly into sexual excitement, although his sadomasochism certainly was (sexually) exciting. Mr. B. used his arrogance and grandiosity to demean the rest of us and his needs of us, to keep himself aloof. What I want to emphasize here, however, are not his narcissistic defenses, self-absorption and self-aggrandizement, but his perverse ability to tune out reality and his needs of others through the excitement of his sadomasochistic provocativeness and illusions of omnipotent control. Like my sexualizing patient, this man could also preserve a state of distractedness in which nothing mattered over very long periods of time. He did not need to think about what was wrong; nothing was wrong; he was right and the world would listen to him. He would work himself up into an excited state as he emphasized his superiority and contempt, his refusal to be reasonable, provoking me sadomasochistically to pursue him, argue with him, show my concern for him, and contain him. Indeed, he would sob when I would interpret his wish to remain with me forever in such therapeutic stalemate.

Mr. B. and his mother had shared this kind of perverse attitude toward reality and need, emphasizing a magical quality to their togetherness that was to protect both of them from the dangers they put into the outside world and then attempted to avoid. Each could and would tune out what was wrong within and between them. Approaching Mr. B.'s unwillingness to be an ordinary patient by analyzing his narcissistic defenses against need and pain did not get us very far. Nor did exploration of his profound envy, spoiling, rage, and self-hatred allow him to engage more in the treatment and diminish my feelings of helplessness and anger with him. He was so intolerant of acknowledging his pleasure in torturing me, or his aggression more generally, that it was difficult to gain a foothold in analyzing the sadomasochism between us. It was much easier for us to talk about his narcissistic defenses in his dealings with me than about his perverse sadomasochism.

I could feel resentful, helpless, and frustrated with Mr. B. and want to bully him into interrupting what often seemed like meaningless chatter in which he made no acknowledgment of any problem or need or reference to any issue of the treatment. I kept wanting him to do *some* therapeutic work, make some genuine connections, be different from how he was. I had to become convinced that my resentment with Mr. B. made sense in the context of his sadomasochistic delight in tormenting me with my inability to affect him. No matter what we accomplished in one session, until the very end of this treatment, Mr. B. would be back the next day seemingly untouched, unconnected, unconcerned; I would feel toyed with, dismissed, and diminished. As with Professor A., I needed to use my wishes to dominate and force Mr. B. in order to identify with his need to do so with me, so that I could work with him on his terror of acknowledging what else he wanted from me.

It became clearer how much he had grown up feeling dominated by his mother's needs, feelings, and beliefs, so that he felt that only one person could be important while the other one had to be degraded. His envy of me became much more focused on my being the know-it-all who makes pronouncements and interpretations while he·has to be my lackey who parrots back what I've said. Now both sides of his sadomasochism became more available, including his willingness to surrender to me as the dominating mother in order to preserve our relationship free from the dangers of separateness and destructive hatred. But then he felt terrified of losing his separate identity. We had to work to get underneath his pleasure and excitement in being either master or slave toward his underlying rage, disappointment, and hurt with his mother and with me.

WHAT IS PERVERSE?

Many have felt that the designation "perverse" should be abandoned as overly judgmental and condemnatory, as we struggled earlier about the designations "narcissistic" or "borderline." However, it is precisely this provocative tone that I find useful. One immediately thinks of a person, especially a child, behaving peevishly, obstinately, doing what he should not do, so as to arouse and excite the other into anger and outrage. A. K. Richards (1996) tried to define perverse behavior by the fact of its calling forth "social opprobrium." The analyst needs to be prepared that he will be tempted, whether or not he acknowledges this to himself and to his "perverse" patient, to feel irritated, impatient, angry, to take the patient in hand to make him behave better. But that is where the patient is stuck—at trying to get someone else to remain responsible for stopping, controlling, criticizing, containing him, because of his fears of having to be responsible for his own internal contents. In these terms, the patient's quasi-delusion of his omnipotent power—in his vindictiveness, refusal to accept reality and the limitations of adulthood, rejection of others, perverse attempts to dominate, tease, and torture others—collapses into the perverse play of a child who tries to keep the other involved with him, despite his clamor that he does not need anyone.

Here, perverse, rather than a definition of sexual deviance, becomes a useful, apt description of someone's attitudes, not only towards reality, but also towards others, his own needs, and himself. It implies that the author of the term is, to a degree, caught up in antagonistic feeling toward the other whom he is condemning. It describes the provocative stance of the one who refuses to be reasonable and behave like everyone else together with the antagonistic counterresponse of his audience. Part of the dictionary (New Shorter O.E.D., 1993) definition of perversion involves "turning aside from truth or right." Now that we can more easily acknowledge the difficulty or impossibility of knowing what is true or right, it may be easier for us to accept a playful, perverse, stance toward perverse attitudes, from which we acknowledge and seek to understand why we wish to condemn the other.

HOW DO PERVERSE DEFENSES WORK?

My two patients' "perverse" refusal to accept the common limitations of adulthood reflected chronic rage and vindictiveness and a bitter refusal to live in the present. Instead they emphasized what was still missing and wrong, clinging to the role of neglected child. They tuned out their awareness of the inappropriateness of their impossible wishes with excitement, distraction, activity, narcissistic self-aggrandizement, anything that would shift their focus away from recognition of what was wrong within. They just did not pay attention. Bach (1977) described the "narcissistic state of consciousness" as attempting "through selective alterations of reflective awareness...to establish or recapture an ego state of physical and mental wholeness, well-being and self-esteem, either alone or with the help of some object used primarily for this purpose." Additionally, each of my patients drew upon narcissistic specialness and grandeur as protection. Each used the excitement of torturing and teasing the needed one to avoid what was wrong. Professor A.'s (sexual) excitement helped to validate his illusion that he actually could possess others.

Excitement here seems like an enhancement of this more global style of tuning out unpleasant reality rather than primarily serving to sustain a perversion. This is akin to sexualization in that excitement is used to defend against painful affect and need (Coen 1981). In addition, the excitement helps the patient preserve a distracted state of mind, an altered state of awareness, in which he can ignore the discrepancies between his wishes and reality. A sense of entitlement allows for superego corruption (Coen 1988) in such perverse disregard of reality.

The refusal to really need others was a hallmark of the sadomasochistic object relations of my two patients. This refusal was covert, teasing, and provocative, unlike that of the more decidedly schizoid patient with whom one knows where one stands. Each patient kept trying to entice the other with the possibility of genuine relatedness only to enjoy frustrating such hope in the other, to keep the other guessing, to retain power, control, and domination over the other's need for the patient, as if the patient could be the only one who does not need others.

PERVERSE COUNTERTRANSFERENCE

It should be no surprise that we will be drawn into patients' affective force-fields, whether they are perverse or anything else. Perverse attitudes in patients will tend to draw out perverse attitudes in therapists. The therapist is to be drawn into fighting with the patient, showing the patient over and over again the therapist's concern, angry frustration, and inability to stay outside of the patient's emotional orbit. Although the patient craves the therapist's care and concern, he will soon eradicate such awareness and desire, which threaten him. He wants the other to want him so that he does not need to bear such desire in himself (cf. Joseph 1975, 1982, 1983, Steiner 1993). Therapist and patient can easily become embroiled in sadomasochistic battles over the unreasonableness and impossibility of the patient's perverse attitudes toward reality and toward others. Such sado-masochistic struggle in the therapeutic situation merely helps to keep the patient where he is rather than affording him the possibility of moving forward. The therapist has to extract himself from the temptation to force change on the patient.

I had felt tempted to escape my angry and helpless feelings with each of my patients by pressuring them to be different, more like ordinary analysands. I needed to recognize that I was overly eager to achieve a more reliable sense of connectedness with each patient that avoided his need to torture me with his unavailability and to keep himself emotionally uncommitted. I had felt unsure of my position with each man as he had felt with his mother.

From my wishes to dominate and force each of my two patients, I was able to identify with each man's pleasure in torturing me. I could then feel and interpret how this torture protected him from his intense need of me. I would feel frustrated that each man could acknowledge his intense dependent neediness but then had to keep running away from needing me in the therapeutic transference. I often could not tell where I stood with a patient who could shift abruptly from being attached, available, and collaborative to being dismissive, rejecting, and remote. I would have to shift from wanting to pin down each man with his dependent hunger to tolerating his terror of this need and his perverse defenses against it. Only then could I help him work with his pattern of oscillating between his intense need and his omnipotent, perverse, exciting control of his needed object, now me in the transference.

With the possibility of termination in sight, my patients' ongoing refusal to feel appreciative and grateful with me and their partners became louder, as they kept finding fault with each of us, running from involvement with us to their distractions. On the other hand, each patient, at times, was able to feel sad and mourn what he had missed, even acknowledge the good things he had received from his parents, relatives, partner, and me. Hence, I could believe that he was finally ready to accept limits and limitations. But just as these new expectations came into view, he would return to a much more one-sided insistence on what he had not gotten as a child and was now not getting from his partner and from me.

My two patients presented themselves as if they were incapable of loving others, inviting me and others to critically affirm this (defensive) view of themselves. I found myself feeling that each patient wanted me to agree with his view of himself as uncaring rather than as shifting between being caring and uncaring. My patients were more comfortable feeling that they could not get close emotionally to others, that they merely needed somebody, anybody, not a particular person. I needed to extricate myself from the countertransference trap of indicting each patient as incapable of loving, when I would feel resentful and want to condemn him as irresponsible, uncaring, selfish, extractive, and destructive. Neither these ugly character traits nor the severity of my patients' psychopathology prevented them from loving, unlike what certain theoretical positions predict.

FROM PERVERSE TOWARD
LOVING RELATEDNESS

Once we could acknowledge that my patients could love and be loved, they feared that the intensity of their need for the other would lead to unbearable disappointment, hurt, loss, and rage on the one hand, and surrender, subjugation, and merger, on the other. Each man was very dependent, not schizoid, but needed to keep oscillating between his attachment to important others and to himself, his internalized maternal imago, and a perverse state of distractedness in which he did not need real, separate people but could play at living in the perverse, illusory world he created.

At some point, I had to shift from only feeling empathic with each patient's terror of relying on and loving others to address his *refusal* to preserve an ongoing loving relatedness with his partner and with me. That is, each patient wanted me to continue to agree with him that his childhood sense that others were not reliable precluded his ability to love me and his partner. To help each man get outside of his perverse way of relating, I had to help him acknowledge that he was capable of sustained appreciation and love of others, especially now with me in the therapeutic transference.

Schafer (1996) also suggests that patients who have reached the depressive position protect themselves against acknowledgment of goodness in themselves and in others primarily to avoid intense longings for the other that could lead to disappointment based on childhood experience. Schafer follows the contemporary Kleinians in the belief that patients in the paranoid–schizoid position tend to present "false goodness" that is involved with narcissistic need, rage, demandingness, fantasied omnipotence, undoing, and so on. I prefer a less schematic division of capacity for concern, especially with those patients who seem to fluctuate in their willingness and ability to preserve their loving relatedness and commitment to others. I am now painfully aware that trying to pin down a fixed assessment of my patients' emotional capacities tended to trap me in only one pole of their vacillating willingness and ability to share a common world, tolerate their feelings, and love others.

My patients were capable of such loving relatedness although they were terrified to remain aware of such feelings for prolonged periods. In his perverse way, each man would distract himself from generous and appreciative feelings toward himself and the other, by filling himself with feelings, fantasies, and longings about someone or something else. He retreated to the safe illusion of not needing others; these others could be regarded as unreliable, disappointing parents rather than as new and good objects. Fearing that his monstrous greed, envy, and rage could destroy good objects, each man clung to viewing his objects as bad—unsatisfying and dispensable. Each patient had to be helped to gain the confidence that therapist/partner and he, himself, unlike his needy and vulnerable parents and child self, could now withstand and even enjoy his passions.

THERAPEUTIC DISABILITY AND THERAPEUTIC IMPASSE

The paths that I and the colleagues who have listened to this material have followed in trying to assess the treatability of my two patients included the following. I first tried to understand the problem as my/our refusal to acknowledge sufficiently the degree of the patient's illness or health. Then I imagined what was wrong was that I was not tolerating sufficiently my patients' regressive need to have me accept, affirm, and hold them without interpretive comment. Then I believed that I needed to tolerate shifting back and forth more flexibly between an interpretive stance and a containing one. I criticized myself (and other traditional analysts) for trying to define whether a patient in analysis was or was not analyzable. Instead, I believed that I needed to tolerate my uncertainty over very long periods during which I needed to keep shifting my treatment approach.

Now I do not believe that it is possible to escape the dilemma of being unable to determine such patients' therapeutic capacities. Unlike Grossman (1992, 1993, 1996) and the Novicks (1996), I believe that the patient's pleasure in the quasi-delusion of omnipotence in his perverse attitude is only one factor, not necessarily the key determinant, in his attempts to manage his internal world. Interpretation of such perverse attitudes may not be sufficient to help such patients change. Extracting himself from the trap of sadomasochistic struggle with the patient, the therapist would have to be able to show the patient the multiple meanings of the patient's unwillingness to test himself, his beliefs, and his expectations of others. Such meanings include the patient's fear that he cannot manage certain affects, wishes, needs, ideas, or perceptions separately on his own apart from the therapist, who is assigned the task of managing what the patient dreads within himself. Then the patient cannot separate from the therapist and the internalized pathological parent. The patient's ongoing fear that he cannot manage what is inside of him tends to preclude his being able to relinquish his perverse defenses, to change, adapt to reality, and terminate his analysis. Thus analyzing the patient's perverse defenses also requires analyzing his affect intolerance, terror of separateness, of destructiveness, and whatever else he fears in managing himself on his own apart from the therapist.

TOWARD RESOLVING THE PERVERSION/ NEUROSIS DICHOTOMY

Freud's elaboration of disavowal was connected with his view of perversion (fetishism), although he drew on analogies to those who are not perverse. Thus Freud allowed for some similarities between perversion and neurosis, as he did between psychosis and neurosis. Like the child whose father has died but still imagines that father will return at dinnertime, neurotics attempt to modify painful reality by the substitution of wishful fantasy (Freud 1911, 1924, 1927). Neurotics and children can use disavowal; splitting of the ego can "apply to other states more like the neuroses and, finally, to the neuroses themselves" (Freud 1940a, p. 202). However, neurotics, unlike perverts, *repress* (Freud 1940a) one of their contradictory attitudes toward reality. Morris (1993) emphasizes Freud's (1940a, p. 204) claim that "disavowal is always supplemented by an acknowledgment." Morris proposes that during oscillation between disavowal and acknowledgment, disavowal helps to narcissistically affirm the capacities of the narrating self.

Lee Grossman (1992, 1993, 1996) has recently described a "perverse" attitude toward reality in patients who do not have a perversion. This designation applies to patients, not all sexually perverse, who dismiss certain painful aspects of reality through widespread disavowal of troubling perceptions of reality. Obligatory sexual perversion then, in effect, becomes only one, much smaller subset of all those patients who have perverse attitudes toward reality. Grossman emphasizes the dishonest conscience that allows such patients not to have to differentiate fantasy from reality but to act instead as if they were incapable of such differentiation. He insists that his patients were fully capable of such acknowledgment of reality but chose, as one of their predominant attitudes, not to do so.

Grossman (1992, 1993, 1996) follows Freud (1940b) in separating perversion from neurosis, perverse from neurotic defense, and wish from perception of reality. In this view, neurosis defends against dangerous wishes while perversion preserves the wish and defends against dangerous reality. Although we may now acknowledge such sharp differentiation between neurosis and perversion as arbitrary and inaccurate, it has been difficult for psychoanalysts to relinquish. Grossman links perversion and neurosis in showing that they can share certain common ("perverse") attitudes toward reality, while he preserves this sharp differentiation between the defensive aims of perversion and neurosis.

Rather than an either/or position that the patient is capable or incapable of acknowledging reality, my patients seemed to have shifting ability and willingness to accept and address reality. My patients, like Grossman's, certainly did know the difference between fantasy and reality, although they could choose to ignore such difference when they needed or wanted to. So they would oscillate between acknowledgment and disavowal of painful reality (cf. Morris 1993). Although both patients knew they could not always be the center of attention with others, much of the time they would tune out such awareness of limitations and insist on continual indulgence. Mr. B. knew that he could not really foretell business trends but he would act, to his detriment, as if his predictions must determine the fate of the economy. Professor A. knew that his central fantasy of owning his women and me in the transference, so that he was free to do as he pleased with us, was an impossible illusion. However, working up his own excited state helped Professor A. (and Mr. B.) to make this illusion feel more vivid, more real, so that excited illusion virtually became reality (cf. Nydes 1950 on masturbation fantasy).

What seems *perverse* to me is such patients' attitudes toward reality; they act as if they, unlike the rest of us, do not have to test their beliefs. The ordinary neurotic will repress his more contradictory attitude toward reality (Freud 1940a), having determined that his fantasy is unrealistic, so that wish and reality *tend not to* cross each other. In his perverse mode, the patient tends to preserve both contradictory attitudes in consciousness while trying, during excited arousal, to affirm the validity of his more unrealistic attitude. In this perverse mode, more than the ordinary neurotic, he refuses to accept the limitations of reality.

Perverse, defensive use of the therapist and the treatment in so-called transference perversion has been variously described as destroying therapeutic meaning, humiliating the therapist, and rendering him helpless, while preserving the illusion of unity between patient and therapist (Etchegoyen 1978); turning the therapist into a fetishistic object who can be controlled and used (Renik 1992); avoidance of looking at the terrifying female genital (Reed 1993). Reed described therapeutic impasses where both patient and therapist seemed hesitant to look at *something* wrong between them, which Reed understood as referring exclusively to the female therapist's missing phallus. The process material emphasized the patient's hesitation to fully see and acknowledge her hopeless, quasi-delusional conviction that she could not obtain what she needed from the deficient therapist/mother. If the patient viewed the therapist as deficient, then it made sense that she would desperately try to grab something for herself from the therapist (Coen 1993). A broader therapeutic focus on what the patient saw as missing in her female therapist might then be more useful than exclusive emphasis on the latter's missing phallus. Indeed, Reed's published paper (1997) does look beyond the missing phallus.

In our current postmodern questioning of the assumptions of our theories (c.f., Chessick 1995, S. Cooper 1996, Mayer 1996), we are less comfortable than our predecessors with theoretical differentiation that we cannot document clinically. In an earlier era, clinicians could derive comfort from avowed theoretical certainty and the insistence that selected patients were different from all the rest of us. They, not we, were crazy, narcissistic, perverse, borderline, homosexual, pregenital, developmentally arrested, and so on. Clinicians have slowly come to participate in the contemporary questioning of our motivations for preserving such a demeaning stance toward those we regard as different. Gender theorists have challenged society's insistence on a sharp binary division of gender and sexual roles (e.g., Butler 1990, 1993, Butler and Scott 1992, Castle 1993, De Lauretis 1994, Fuss 1991, Garber 1995). Psychoanalysts and everyone else have struggled with the power and politics of categories of labelling and diagnosis (see especially the historian, Scott 1988, 1991, 1992).

Hence, in examining perverse defenses in neurotic patients, we need to be wary of condemning such patients, now newly labelled "perverse," as different and pathological. Instead, it is better that we integrate perverse mechanisms with the other, ordinary ways we all have of managing ourselves. I do not believe that perversity is differentiated by whether a person desires others of the same sex, the opposite sex, or otherwise. In retrospect, it seems to me that many analysts turned to perversion as an arena in which to study issues that classical analysts then would not emphasize with ordinary neurotic patients: childhood trauma, especially vicissitudes of parent/child relationships, and more generally how what really happened became integrated with wish, fantasy, conflict, and defense; object relations more generally; preoedipal need and conflict; intense aggression; superego conflict; the use of sexuality for defense. In her essay, Greenacre (1967) lamented the difficulty of getting other traditional analysts to talk with her about the role of infantile trauma, aspects of the mother/child relationship, preoedipal need and conflict, issues of narcissistic vulnerability, and so on. Some of this could be *smuggled* into perversion by talking about physical, bodily trauma or about weakness of genital integrity rather than about narcissistic vulnerability. Unfortunately, gay men and lesbian women were used as examples of perversion to find what we did not want to acknowledge in the rest of us.

This sharp differentiation between perversion and neurosis has already been somewhat eroded by emphasizing similarities between people. Arlow (1971) described character perversion in a non-pervert as involving defensive disavowal akin to that of the fetishist. Some writing about female perversion softens the definition of perversion from something obligatory for sexual gratification to something merely exciting and pleasurable (L. Kaplan 1991a, b, Richards 1996). Stoller (1975, 1979) placed hostility at the center of sexual arousal for everyone, perverse and nonperverse alike, providing another link between perversion and neurosis. In my book essay on perversion (Coen 1985), I could still emphasize the novelty of regarding perversion as a "solution to intrapsychic conflict" rather than as merely repetition to master infantile trauma or as the expression of a partial pregenital impulse in collusion with a poorly functioning superego.

But if perversion represented an attempt to manage intrapsychic conflict, conflict that was now understandable and analyzable, how different was it really from neurosis? Yet perverts seemed different from neurotics! I (1992) described perverse object relations, including in dependent patients who were not perverts, "as involving exploitation, extractiveness, and destructiveness with the partner, whose own separate needs and identity are obliterated in the service of the patient's own urgent defensive requirements" (see also Kernberg 1992). Sadomasochistic object relations has been described as remarkably similar to perversion or at least to perverse object relations (Coen 1992, Novick 1990, 1996, Novick & Novick 1996). I described a "looser" view of perversion that regarded "bits of perverse behavior" that serve important defensive requirements, whether or not they are obligatory for the patient's sexual functioning, to be the equivalent of perversion. I was ambivalent about whether to link or to separate perversion and neurosis.

We clinicians have too long used the perverse defense of averting our gaze from those we would dismiss as perverse, fixing our sight instead on their difference from all the rest of us. It is time for us to see much more clearly that we are all both perverse and not perverse. We can no longer rid ourselves of what we find objectionable by insisting that it belongs only to others. It is time to integrate perversion and neurosis, as it is time to emphasize similarities instead of primarily differences among people.

6

The Wish to Regress in Patient and Therapist

What we want from our patients has been very difficult for us to talk about. We have permitted ourselves only certain very few "unobjectionable," "legitimate" wishes with our patients. It seems as if, in the treatment situation, only patients, not therapists, have felt safe and free enough to have wishes. We allow ourselves the wish to help our patients change and grow, so long as it remains reasonably sublimated and doesn't mushroom into more driven need. But any further acknowledgment of therapists' needs and wishes with their patients continues to engender considerable resistance as dangerous. Many traditional analysts continue to fear that any acknowledgment of wishes, desires, and feelings toward our patients will leave us teetering atop the "slippery slope" of uncontrolled action. Of course, our goal is to help patients achieve maximum autonomy from their internal conflicts and from us, their therapists. And certainly our focus is on their needs and wishes rather than our own. But it would be psychoanalytically naive to assume that once we enter the treatment situation, we can purge ourselves of all wishes, now stirred by the presence of our patients.

My aim here is to expand the subjective domain of therapists' awareness to include more of what we want from our patients, so that we can manage ourselves and our patients therapeutically, for the sake of their growth. The therapist's wish to regress is used as a paradigm of this "forbidden" topic of what therapists want from their patients. I am indebted to Rosemary Balsam's discussion (1997; see Chapter 2) for the suggestion that I had lost my therapeutic perspective because I had joined my patient in mutual regression. Here I want to explore instances of mutual regression between my patients and me in terms of my temptation to join them in regressive relatedness, thereby *temporarily* ceding my role as constructive therapist who contains and interprets.

By now you should be clear that I do not believe that such regressive wishes are merely my own idiosyncrasy. On the contrary, I again offer my own example to help other clinicians find similar wishes in themselves. I believe that we all have the potential, in varying degrees, to want to return to and become stuck in some form of regressive relatedness that promises relief from conflict. Beware the temptation to reject such regressive wishes as pathological, or to shift attention elsewhere, perhaps by explaining them away as defense against rage, separateness, or love.

I have been struck by how few colleagues who have heard me present this material have shared similar concerns about their own avoidance of experiencing regressive wishes with patients. One discussant even insisted he never experienced regressive wishes with his patients. Emphasis on defense is valid but shifts the focus away from acknowledging the power of our regressive temptations. So I emphasize primarily, and want my readers to consider, the wish to regress in my patients and in myself toward a pathological object relationship opposed to separateness and competence, rather than its defensive functions. But I will suggest that the context for our mutual regression largely involved feelings of hopeless despair that became unbearable for both of us; fears of separateness and rage contributed, much more for my patient than for me.

THE PATIENT'S WISH TO REGRESS AND
THE THERAPIST'S RESPONSE

Given Dr. S.'s (Coen 1992) history of depression and considerable regressive potential, I felt uneasy when he quickly indicated that he wanted an analysis. In effect, he put himself on my couch. He soon began to talk in an anxious, depressed way about not wanting to go to work, not wanting to face the problems of life, and wanting to stay in bed, which he began to enact. I feared Dr. S. would regress further and disorganize; I thought I should not have let him get on my couch. In what felt like a heroic attempt to stem his regressive behavior, I interpreted it as if it were motivated by a driven wish: to be cared for as a child by me as a parent. To my surprise, this made sense to Dr. S., and to a considerable degree he was able to shift to the level of talking about his regressive wishes rather than living them out. I felt reassured that by continuing to explore his regressive longings, we would help to strengthen rather than disorganize him. I was intrigued that interpreting the wish to regress had so dramatically shifted Dr. S. from seriously regressive behavior that had threatened to disrupt his treatment and his life, to the possibility of analyzing his regressive wishes.

I do not think that I contributed to Dr. S.'s regressive threats early in his treatment. From his history and current behavior, I had ample reason to be concerned that analysis might lead to his undoing. I was substantially reassured by his response to my interpretation of his wish to regress. This intervention opened up a very fruitful exploration of his powerfully regressive, dependent wishes. I certainly did not lose my therapeutic footing here. On the contrary, I learned the importance of therapeutic containment and interpretation of regressive wishes.

Ms. B. began her session terrified that she was going crazy and needed to be hospitalized. Feeling unable to manage her work and her life, she proceeded to give me examples of how poorly she was functioning. Feeling panicky, depressed, and hopeless, she insisted she could not cope with the exigencies of life; she needed a hospital. By the end of the session, we had moved to Ms. B.'s being able to own her wishes to go crazy, regress, and have me care for her full-time. The more she got into her rage-filled demand that I care for her totally, the more she was able to feel and connect her current wishes to regress with her bitter feelings of deprivation, neglect, and misuse by her parents. As this session progressed, she and I were able to get hold of her sadomasochistic desires to torment me with her failure and falling apart, to blame me and make me responsible for her and for her difficulties. The more crazy and suicidal she became, the more she would cause her parents and me to suffer. She talked about giving up her job and managing on her savings. The last four days she hadn't bothered to shower. Should she let herself regress further and insist that I fully take over her care? She mused that some believe it's therapeutic for patients to regress as fully as possible.

Now she felt much better, as she owned her wishes to regress further in order to torture her parents and me. She was no longer terrified of going crazy and requiring hospitalization. She wanted me to accept her just as she was without any interpretation of defense, so she would not have to experience me as a dissatisfied, critical parent relentlessly insisting she do more in the treatment. She enjoyed feeling dependent on me, wanting me to care for her and love her so much more. Ms. B. ended the session pleased with how much she had been able to let herself go, indulging her wishes to regress, attack, and torture me. This contrasted with her panicky conviction earlier in the session that she was *actually* going crazy. Ms. B.'s wish to go crazy and be hospitalized made her feel less anxiously responsible for her desires that I care for her. She felt "creepy" with me and thought I would misuse her sexually; she feared feeling intense desire toward me. Her regressive presentation of herself as defective and incapable abated more often as she became more comfortable with wanting closeness and caring from me, which included loving and sexual desire.

With Ms. B., as far as I can tell, I did not get drawn into mutual regression. I had little difficulty interpreting her wishes to regress, go crazy, and be hospitalized. I could easily interpret the sadomasochistic torture in her threats and attacks. I enjoyed working with her dependent wishes toward me in the transference, her self-presentation as deficient, and her fears of loving relatedness between us. Despite her fearfulness that I would exploit her sexually, Ms. B. was more comfortable with preserving loving feelings between us than were my other three patients. I did not feel rattled by her anxiety that she would regress forever. Despite how anxious, angry, and negativistic she could be, something remained basically positive between us.

Here I continue with Professor A. from Chapters 2 and 5. I elaborate Balsam's (1997) suggestion that he and I had, at times, become caught up in mutual regression to a depressed mother/child dyad. For prolonged periods, he seemed to need me to contain his regression, without our being able to talk about (interpret) what he was needing and wanting from me. Now he seemed to run from his intense attachment to me in the transference to the safety of sexual excitement with anonymous women. Whereas earlier in this treatment, we could easily link his excited wishes for these women with his longings toward me in the transference, now he and I could no longer connect so intimately. Now, in contrast to the situation earlier, his perverse behavior served to obliterate his desires for loving closeness with me in the transference. Contending that his anxiety and depression had impaired his ability to function competently at his academic, research, and writing projects, he infected me with his worry. When I could get myself out of this shared anxiety, it became clear that Professor A. needed to hold on to me, because he feared losing me in terminating, by demonstrating his inability to function on his own.

When I told Professor A. that he was too panicky to terminate his analysis anytime soon and that he was terrified of allowing himself to feel close and loving with me in the transference, he became less panicky and came out of his regressive display of dysfunction. Calming down, he allowed himself more connectedness with me until he again became threatened by feeling close and loving with me, whereupon he pulled himself away. This clearly was a repetitive pattern.

As should be clear by now, before termination came into view, I had enjoyed and in fact had had little difficulty working with Professor A.'s regressive wishes; his treatment had been deeply productive and satisfying for both of us. It was absolutely not the case, as some have speculated, that early on we had been superficially engaged, only later to get beyond a conjoint defensive avoidance. I was surprised when my interpretations of his regressive wishes *suddenly* became ineffective. Then I had difficulty tolerating his regressive and defensive disengagement from me via his almost exclusive emphasis on experiencing continual sexual excitement with his anonymous women, in and out of our sessions. Although he spoke of his envy of his mother, who could curl up on the couch when she felt depressed, not caring for their home or for him, he now kept himself and his maternal wishes remote from me. I could get caught up in his hopelessness and his panicky feeling that he would disorganize and become unable to function as he did actually deteriorate. He and I became locked into a depressed maternal transference, from which for a time neither of us could find our way out again. Only at those times that I could become aware of my temptation to join Professor A. as depressed mother or child by responding to his unconscious invitation that I feel hopeless and curl up with him on the analytic couch could I extract myself from our mutual regression. I had *temporarily* lost my place as a constructive therapist helping Professor A. Instead, I joined him in feeling helpless and hopeless. He would never get better; we would remain together forever. Clinging to an idealization of dependent relatedness, we could *temporarily* feel unable to function as responsible adults. At those times when I could become aware of my wishes to join Professor A. in his childlike hopelessness and disability, I could extricate myself from the panic he sought to have us share as a way to keep us together, yet safely distanced from close, loving feelings and from his rage. At that point I could again want to be, and feel like, a hopeful, helpful therapist. In retrospect, I see that some of the pressure I had felt to talk about his enactments, rather than simply contain them, involved my discomfort with our being stuck in this mutual regression. I had wanted to have him change magically back into the patient who could talk with me about his wishes rather than lose himself in them. But once outside of and unthreatened by his regression, I no longer needed to dislodge him from it. Then I could contain his regression while interpreting, much more comfortably and patiently, how we had both become stuck.

Professor A.'s terror of losing me in terminating seemed the key factor in his regression. As he faced the prospect of eventual termination, I *became* his uncaring parent (mother and father), who wanted him to remain remote and not burden me with his needs, sadness, and resentment. Sexual titillation with anonymous women protected him against unbearable feelings of sadness and rage with me as the parent who promised but failed to deliver and kept him away from me, as he imagined I wanted. His severe regression toward union with the depressed mother was understandable in the context of his unbearable transference hopelessness that I could really be concerned about him. I can imagine now that his earlier anxiety and hopelessness that I could not help to stem his disorganization—in his mind I was now the ineffective, uncaring parent—had become too real and unbearable, as it had for me also. It was as if a caring, capable parent no longer existed, tempting me to to want to share his regressive union. Reassured by his much improved functioning, and now outside of his regression, I could capture and interpret his transference hopelessness, unbearable to him but no longer to me.

Mr. N. (for negativistic, also see Chapter 3), an angry schizoid/narcissistic man who had never had a loving relationship, was convinced he was stupid, deficient, and unappealing. As the incapable one, he had to surrender to me as the bright, thoughtful one. But he could defeat me by devaluing and forgetting what I provided him. This had been the pattern of his relating with his explosive, narcissistic father. His mother had been very depressed, withdrawn, and negativistic. He would be touched by my concern for him, feel grateful, want more, only to immediately erase what had just touched him. Terrified of feeling close, appreciative, and loving, he would arrogantly attack, criticize, and reject me in the transference, as he did the women he dated. He had changed therapists and girlfriends repeatedly, as he so often threatened to do with me; someone else would help and appreciate him. He felt free, superior, and triumphant when he ended a relationship. Otherwise, he feared he would be trapped forever in a helpless, dependent relationship in which he would be misused. More so than any other patient I have treated, Mr. N. preserved virtually no positive sense of our work and our relationship. Other negativistic patients at least showed a clear ambivalence, even as they rejected, dismissed, and destroyed the treatment, so that we could preserve a sense of something good between us. Mr. N. wanted to keep me under the gun. He felt I was concerned with him only because the treatment was in jeopardy; I would not care for him otherwise. He would parrot interpretations I had made, only to demonstrate how, despite his reciting them like mantras, he still had not changed. We talked about his omnipotent stance as the rejecter of all human need; him as the rejecting parent to me as the helpless, needy child; his terror of staying close and loving. Eventually, he felt pained that he rejected what was good from me and others. He asked if he was all evil, describing himself as Darth Vader destroying the forces of good. Tearfully, Mr. N. acknowledged how frightened he felt to shed his rejecting negativism—it would be like giving up the person he had always been, his protective skin. If he preserved caring feelings between us, he said he felt terrified that despite how consistent I had been, I would somehow disappoint him.

Mr. N.'s ongoing rejection and elimination of the value of our work and our relationship kept him, and *at times* me, from being able to preserve what was good between us. Feeling angry, dismissed, and unappreciated, I would want to attack him as hopeless and get rid of him. In the face of his insistent and persuasive negativism, I would at times miss the point that he was inducing in me what he had felt as a child with his rejecting and demeaning father. Under his ferocious, rejecting attacks I could temporarily regress from my therapeutic capacity into actually feeling like the rejected, demeaned child or the rejecting, demeaning father. Identified with his father's cruel and arrogant attacks, he attempted to demolish my interpretive position. Alternatively, he would seek to provoke me into becoming the father who would put him down and keep him down. Just as he had succumbed to listening to the insistent, know-it-all father, I too would be regressively tempted to give in to his negativistic, dogmatic certainty. When I could recognize how safe and powerful he and I could both feel under an omnipotent rejecter/destroyer, or as the rejecter/destroyer, I could interpret and get us both out of this trap. I had to feel my own regressive willingness to surrender my autonomy if I was to help my patient feel similar wishes in himself and then want to move forward.

I disagree with comments that Mr. N. suffered from an "inability to regress." Mr. N. readily regressed to the pathological sadomasochistic relatedness that was familiar to him. His opening up wishes for more positive, caring relatedness, getting beyond his negativism and sadomasochism, was progressive rather than regressive. The wish to be admired and loved by me as a good parent was mostly new for Mr. N.

PATIENT AND THERAPIST IN REGRESSION: DEFINING THE TERMS

I want to explore how patients' wishes to regress and remain regressed lead to therapeutic stalemate and to consider the difficulties patient and therapist must face if they are to extricate themselves from such traps. Although I was used to carefully considering my countertransference feelings, I had not been prepared to consider that I might join nonpsychotic patients in mutual regression. I now believe that the concept of mutual regression can help therapists appreciate how they can at times lose the ability to understand, contain, and interpret treatment process. For example, I have a much milder *potential* than has my patient, Professor A., to feel superego pressure to restore an anxious, depressed parent or, failing that, to join the parent in mutual regression. Although I certainly know this very well about myself, I do have *some potential* to be drawn into such traps, from which I then need to extricate myself. When my patients become stuck in regressive states in which I lose my therapeutic footing, I now take for granted that I need to investigate whether my participation in their regression has prevented me from being able to work with it. When I can catch my receptivity to a patient's invitation to join in mutual regression, I can then regain my position as containing and interpreting therapist.

Regression is defined as a defensive return to an earlier, more immature mode of functioning (Laplanche and Pontalis, 1973, Moore and Fine 1990). By the wish to regress, I refer to wishes to return to more infantile modes of relatedness to the other, experienced as a vitally needed parental object. However, I am referring specifically to *yearnings for a pathological object relationship opposed to healthy competence, growth, and individuation.* I regard as progressive, despite their infantile nature, any childlike longings for an object relationship in which one can further develop oneself. By mutual regression I refer only to instances in which the therapeutic couple *seeks to share a pathological object relationship that precludes separateness.* It is crucial that we differentiate wishes for an object relationship that aims to destroy separateness and competence from one that seeks to promote them. Regressive wishes for a destructive relationship lead to crippling and stagnation, within the treatment and outside it. In the treatment, we get stalemate, preservation of the familiar, terror of change, and interminability. My patients wished to return to a pathological parent/ child relationship they imagined would provide them protection, comfort, and caring. This regressive longing obscured their feelings of rage, disappointment, and dissatisfaction with the deficient parent.

Wishes to participate in a parent/child relationship opposed to separateness and competence may take familiar sadomasochistic forms, in which neither partner feels capable of autonomous functioning. I believe that mutual regression between the therapeutic couple involves more than the therapist's willing acceptance of the patient's projective identification. Certainly, therapists can temporarily be disrupted by willingly taking on roles that patients assign them and induce in them. I want to emphasize how the therapist's wishes to join patients in regressive relatedness disrupt the treatment situation.

So long as the therapist joins the patient in living out a pathological relationship *opposed to competence and separateness,* both therapeutic partners forcelose the prospect of growth and love. Of course, we therapists will get caught up in countertransference enactments, no matter how much treatment we have had. Better then that we be prepared to know our vulnerabilities and temptations, here our regressive wishes. Do not regard such preparedness as the vestige of an outmoded ego psychology that imprisons us through its insistence on vigilance and control. On the contrary, therapist and patient regain freedom by acknowledging their mutual willingness to relinquish it, not by changing their psychoanalytic theory. I believe strongly, for the patient's growth and our own, that we therapists must remain responsible for our regressive, self-defeating wishes.

I do not find it helpful to regard as an "inability to regress" the fear of needs, wishes, and feelings found in rigid characters— obsessional, sadomasochistic, paranoid, schizoid (Coen 1992, Shapiro 1981). In point of fact, their intolerance of affect and need is broader than their fear of regression. I believe, in agreeement with Inderbitzin and Levy (2000), that the concept of regression does not clarify such fears of needing and feeling. Similarly, I do not find it helpful to invoke the therapist's regression in the service of the patient to explain allowing ourselves to feel need and affect toward our patient. I will therefore not emphasize the useful aspects of the therapist's regression but will focus instead on how the therapist's wishes to join patients in mutual regression derail constructive treatment process. I prefer to think of helping rigid characters develop a tolerance for what previously had seemed intolerable (Coen 1997, Chapter 2, Krystal 1975, 1978a, b).

COUNTERTRANSFERENCE AND THE THERAPIST'S WISHES TO REGRESS

The therapist's temptation to join in mutual regression with the patient can be considered an aspect of the therapist's countertransference.

Although mutual regression between patient and therapist stands on a continuum with other countertransference phenomena, it occupies that pole with the greatest potential for disrupting the treatment process. I acknowledge that all countertransference involves the therapist's participation, willing and unwilling, no matter how much the therapist might feel forced into it by the patient. However, in mutual regression between the therapeutic couple, the therapist's wishful participation warrants special emphasis. We can consider as regression any wishful movement of the therapist out of the position of thoughtful, focused attention on the patient's needs and conflicts to a less differentiated relatedness, much more determined by the therapist's needs and conflicts. I would not regard the therapist as regressed so long as he or she seeks to examine those needs and conflicts for the sake of the patient's treatment. As we therapists struggle with our countertransference feelings, it is not often that we lose our therapeutic position for very long, even if *temporarily* we cannot understand these feelings. We are still able to recognize that we have been moved by countertransference feelings that have temporarily disrupted us. We preserve the perspective that we need to process and understand our feelings more fully in order to assist our patient. We remain in the position of the concerned, reflective therapist, struggling to make sense both of the patient's feelings and our own. By contrast, sometimes what we feel so disrupts us that we lose our position as therapists and enter into enactments with the patient. I assume that by the time that we are able to identify an episode of this sort as an enactment, we have also regained our therapeutic position. Although we may have been tempted to join the patient in mutually gratifying and protective behavior, we have been able to extricate ourselves sufficiently to examine more objectively, and for the sake of advancing the patient's treatment, what has occurred between the therapeutic pair.

Katz (1998) has argued that alongside what is spoken between patient and analyst there exists a dimension of the treatment process that is enacted between them. Smith (see Opatow 1996) has suggested that enactments, rather than being exceptional events, are the continuous background of the treatment. Katz defined enactment as that aspect of the dynamic, continuous unconscious treatment process that is expressed in action. Even what is expressed verbally between the therapeutic couple can be regarded as a spoken action not delimited by the meanings of the words spoken. Sound, rhyme, rhythm, flow, interruption, and incomprehensibility also matter as do the visual, olfactory, kinesthetic, and affective accompaniments of the utterance (see Mahony 1989b). Speech is but one mode of action between the therapeutic couple; it is not to be privileged over other modes of communication or interaction. When our countertransference feelings do not remain within our thoughtful therapeutic purview but succeed in driving us toward a less differentiated relatedness to the patient and to our own feelings, we have been forced out of our role as therapist. But we have not *chosen* to abandon our therapeutic position. Intolerable feelings, needs for defense, and regressive wishes can intersect to create a countertransference disruption as therapists seek regressive, wishful relief from unbearable conflict.

I regard mutual regression between patient and therapist not as a necessary or expectable phenomenon of joint regulation of affect and mental state, which is to be regarded as a healthy adaptive process (see Aron and Bushra 1998) but as an abdication of the analyzing function in favor of a more infantile relatedness with the patient and with the therapist's internal objects. Although such interference in the therapist's functioning is usually *temporary*, it can be prolonged; to be overcome, it demands the therapist's attention. Our current optimistic view is that countertransference tends usually to be briefer, less derailing of the treatment process, and more amenable to the therapist's introspection than is the kind of mutual regression between the therapeutic couple, in which the therapist actually *wants* to relinquish the role of therapist to join the other in a pathological object relationship that seeks to destroy separateness and competence. We have come to regard countertransference as expectable, even inevitable, and as offering the positive potential for learning something new about the patient. We hope to catch our countertransference feelings and wishes while they are still contained within our mind, before we enact them. I cannot find, in the therapist's wish to join a patient in mutual regression, anything comparably optimistic or useful as regards the progress of an intensive treatment. Through my wishes to join patients in mutual regression, we learned nothing new about their early parental relationships. Our mutual regression occurred, it seems, when we both found unbearable the fact that I had become the uncaring, ineffective parent in the transference–countertransference and a more constructive imago was unavailable. I do not share the optimistic view that many colleagues prefer, that our mutual regression was inevitable and useful in the sense of suddenly revealing what previously had been unavailable. I can say that when I had extricated myself from our mutual regression, I could again help my patient explore and bear the unbearable through my own recovered capacity to capture for both of us the feelings contained in his remoteness. Would I now be able to preserve an optimism that our mutual regression might be a path forward? If not overwhelmed with the hopelessness being repeated between us, I could use it to help my patient integrate feelings that had once been experienced as life threatening, as I have been able to do with patients I did not join in mutual regression.

In Chapter 1, I described the role of mutually constructed and preserved negative feelings, especially sadomasochistic engagement, as a barrier to loving relatedness between patient and therapist. Vignettes from other therapists and from my own work indicated that therapists and patients unconsciously unite to avoid loving feelings between them by emphasizing what is wrong rather than what is good between them. Angry, dissatisfied, antagonistic feelings can be safer for both patient and therapist than the openness and vulnerability of feeling close and loving. In each clinical example, therapists needed to extricate themselves from such safe, negative barriers in order to be able to open up loving feelings between the therapeutic couple. From my current perspective, therapist and patient can here be viewed as sharing a regressive relatedness, hostile and often sadomasochistic, as a defense against loving feelings between them as differentiated, separate people.

Therapists certainly need time to process what has transpired during a session, what has and has not been worked with and why, in order to proceed with the work of the treatment. Such processing of the therapist's experience is very different from the therapist's wish to move out of the position of therapist into regressive relatedness with the patient, *primarily* for the therapist's needs. For example, Ms. T.'s session focused on her wishes to have me, as an admiring and desiring father, love her. She was feeling much better about herself, much more capable and desirable, but was also frightened I would misuse my power with her as others had done. I was struck throughout this very productive session by her hesitation to work with a dream in which she pulls from the ground two tuber-like root vegetables described offhandedly as phallic. Because of the dirt on these vegetables, she is initially reluctant to eat them. When she finally bites into one, it tastes wonderful; she feels ecstatic but is concerned that she may not have enough to eat. Although she was easily able to connect this dream with her hunger toward me in the transference, she avoided, despite my interventions, the images of pulling out, biting, and swallowing.

After the session, I wondered whether it might be best to follow her lead in slowly engaging her hungry wishes toward me. Her castrative wishes did not make me anxious. During and after the session, I found myself thinking of Arlow's (1986) example of a supervisee who does not interpret her patient's clearly castrative wishes because she thought the patient had not yet gotten close enough to the material. Arlow advised her to interpret both the defense and the wish, as the patient could not do so for herself. Arlow is not explicit about whether the analyst felt uneasy with castrative wishes. My conscious concern was that my patient would become more frightened by the aggression in her desires if I persisted in interpreting her defenses against them. In the next session, however, I found a connection to this dream and interpreted my patient's wish to pull out, bite, and swallow the power of my genitals. I was then surprised that my interpretation seemed to have little effect.

A few sessions later, as we worked with another dream in which the patient runs away from involvement with capable men, I learned that she had felt criticized by my interpretation of her castrative wishes. She linked the interpretation to her experience with a previous analyst, whom she regarded as critical and domineering, and with whom she had felt highly submissive. Ms. T. had felt that she should not have her "bad" castrative wishes; that she should somehow just be content with herself as a woman; and that I was angry with her for wanting to challenge my power and authority. She had blocked out her envy and rivalry with her father, brothers, husband, and me in the transference, and more generally her rage at her childhood deprivation, her profound insecurity, and her willingness to surrender to others' needs of her. Now she began to feel more comfortable with challenging my power and authority and wanting to rob me of them.

Ordinarily, as we work, we are able to shift flexibly back and forth between sharing in our patient's inner world and getting sufficiently outside it so as to be able to contain and interpret the patient's needs and conflicts. We should also be able, for the sake of the patient's treatment, to shift easily back and forth between immersion in our own feelings and needs and taking a therapeutic perspective on them. We can be said to have regressed from our therapeutic position only when we have lost our ability to function as therapist for the sake of the patient's needs, which requires that we understand both the patient's needs and our own. So long as we can shift flexibly back and forth between sampling the inner world of the patient and oneself, and our position as therapist, we have not regressed. Thompson (1980) emphasized the need of analysts, as they analyze, for objective assessment of both the patient's productions and their own. We must preserve the treatment frame for both patient and therapist so that each is free to fantasize and feel. Unless we are secure in the belief that we will not act on our wishes, here regressive ones, we cannot entertain them fully. A focus on the therapist's willingness to escape the role of therapist in favor of regressive relatedness with the patient must complement the more usual view of the therapist as the *unwilling* victim of the patient's efforts to destroy the therapist's competence. It would be psychoanalytically naive to believe that the therapist's unwilling victimization does not also involve a willing surrender. Consideration of patients' attempted destruction of therapeutic meaning, of the value of the treatment, and of the therapist's ability to understand (Bion 1959, Joseph 1983), remember (Schafer 1997), and interpret (Kernberg 1992a) has been invaluable.

THE THERAPIST'S WISH TO REGRESS: THE LITERATURE

The adaptive value of the therapist's regressive processes for therapeutic work has been noted (Kris 1950, Olinick 1969, 1975, Olinick et al. 1973). Parallel to the patient's regression, the therapist experiences "partial and temporary regression in the service of patient, of psychoanalytic process, of psychoanalytic work ego" (Olinick 1975, p. 150). The processes (empathic, identificatory, introjective, etc.) by which therapists feel their way into the patient's inner life are regarded as regressive from the standpoint of adult interpretive functioning, to which eventually they must return. Avoiding the concept of countertransference, Olinick and colleagues (1973) viewed the varying degrees of therapist's identification with patients as regressive. To nurture one's patient, they held, requires a regressive exchange of roles with the patient. But this sharp differentiation between adult and regressive functioning is, I believe, a relic from a time when we still believed that we could (and indeed should) dissociate ourselves from objectionable needs and wishes in our patients and in ourselves. Today, less judgmental of our countertransference feelings and wishes, we feel less concerned about regression when we feel empathic or nurturing, or when we seek to identify with our patients, unless, of course, we become stuck there.

Regressive wishes for fusion with a depressed maternal introject together with the fears they give rise to have been viewed as stimulating profound negativism in patients, which in turn induces rage, depression, and helplessness in the therapist (Asch 1976, A. Freud 1952, Olinick 1964, 1970, Sterba 1957). More recently, however, a more optimistic view has emerged that regards patients' negativism as adaptive, understandable, and interpretable (M. Bergmann 1998, Limentani 1981, Renik 1991). Negative therapeutic reaction can indicate that the patient is now ready to address something especially painful (Limentani 1981) that had previously been regarded as threatening the repetition of overwhelming childhood trauma (M. Bergmann 1998). Renik (1991) has offered the example of the patient's terror that the therapist is really the dangerously disturbed parent.

In relation to regressed patients' severely pathological transferences, a typical countertransference response is for therapists to regress to their own "defensive character patterns" (Kernberg 1993). Note that none of these authors considers the therapist's wish to join the patient in mutual regression, an omission that encourages therapists to believe that we can manage the severely regressive wishes of our patients without ourselves becoming derailed. Because we cannot, it is better that we prepare ourselves for such difficulties.

Consideration of the therapist's masochistic wishes toward the patient (Balint 1968, Olinick 1964, 1970, Racker 1958, 1968) moves us toward the question of what the therapist wants. The therapist's masochism and concomitant paranoid anxiety lead the guilty therapist to want to fail, to perceive resistance as aggression by the "persecutor" patient, and to focus too exclusively on negative transference and aggression, "hindering . . . perception of the patient's love and what is good in him, which in turn increases the negative transference" (Racker 1958, p. 559). When I wrote about barriers to love between patient and therapist (see Chapter 1), I was not consciously aware that Racker had described so well how sadomasochism can protect against loving feelings between the treatment couple. I had cited Kernberg's acknowledgment (1992b) that sadomasochism between his patient and him had temporarily protected both of them against the desire they felt toward each other. Levy and Inderbitzin (1989) have noted the countertransference surprise of therapists at the hidden positive longings screened by their patients' negativism. Therapists seem to know more about sadomasochism as a protection against dangerous rage and destructiveness between the therapeutic couple than as a protection against love. Similarly, therapists seem to know quite well that an emphasis on loving and caring can protect against rage between the therapeutic couple but are less aware that mutual dissatisfaction can be a protection against love. This is not to emphasize love over aggression, but only to indicate that therapists can fear *both* being hated and loved.

Balint (1968) emphasized that regression is effected both by patient and therapist; the therapist either facilitates or impedes the patient's needed therapeutic regression. A therapist threatened by the patient's regressive needs will strive to avert them. To analyze a patient's regressive longings, the therapist must be comfortable with them. How the therapist responds to these longings tends to determine whether the patient enters a malignant or a benign regression. In the latter, the patient seeks the therapist's recognition; this is constructive, analyzable regression. By contrast, in malignant regression, the patient escalates the demand for gratification, and the treatment spirals out of control. Regression of this sort can no longer be contained and interpreted by the therapist.

Balint pointed out that certain Freudian and Kleinian analytic approaches tend to impinge on patients' regressive needs. He believed that the Freudian stress on interpreting transference tends to overemphasize patients' attachment to their analyst without also cultivating their investment and pleasure in both autonomous functioning and regressive relatedness to that part of their world that exists *between* their objects. Intense dependent attachment to the therapist by fragile, socially isolated patients can lead, as I've unfortunately learned, to delusional relatedness to the all-important therapist. Balint believed also that the Kleinian method of interpreting what patients cannot possibly grasp for themselves exaggerates their sense of deficiency, thereby encouraging submission to and idolization of the seemingly omniscient analyst; this in turn aggravates feelings of aggression, envy, competitiveness, and destructiveness toward the analyst. At two recent panels with eminent Kleinian analysts (see Chapter 8), I thought that their attitudes of contempt, criticism, and apparent omniscience seemed to discourage the patient's autonomous, competent functioning. However, I thought that both of them had become caught up in, and unable to extricate themselves from, one side of their patient's identifications. Balint thought that Kleinian analysts may not always recognize their temptation to act as if omnipotent and omniscient, and thereby to subjugate their analysands. I believe that *all* of us, therapists of every persuasion, need to grasp the temptation we have to overwhelm and immobilize patients by showing them what they cannot see for themselves.

I think it essential that we attend to how we contribute to severe regressive states during treatment. For example, a panel report by Weinshel (1966) describes two patients whose analyst's silence initiated severe regressive responses. The protocol indicates to me that the analyst did not help his two patients understand their sudden terror over new developments in the treatment by interpreting the conflicts that had suddenly led them to feel panicky. Instead, as each patient pleaded in vain for help, he said nothing. Weinshel tactfully commented that an analyst's silence has the potential to contribute to severe regressive states without referring specifically to the presenting analyst.

The regressive needs that therapists feel for patients have been considered in the context of increased vulnerability due to severe illness in the therapist. Lasky (1990) refers to "the analyst's wish to regress" (p. 465) as stimulated by the patient's needs but augmented by the vulnerable analyst's needs for narcissistic supplies from the patient. Lasky openly and persuasively describes the difficulties therapists have in shifting between the sick role, in which they are the primary focus of concern, and greater attention to the patient's concerns, including worries about the therapist's impairment, vulnerability, and self-absorption. But Lasky, one of the few therapists to consider in detail how we are tempted to misuse patients to meet our own needs, considered only the sick therapist, never acknowledging that we are all of us prone to this temptation.

He provides a sensitive critique of the earlier contributions of Dewald (1982), Abend (1982), and Silver (1982), illustrating how illness tends to lead to regression in the therapist's analyzing functions.

When Silver returned to practice, still suffering from a severe illness, she initially worked only with patients she thought might provide her with loving feelings rather than stimulate hatred in her, which she believed she could not then manage. Lasky seems subtly critical of Silver's attitude as regressively narcissistic, rather than realistic or necessary. He reports that he had been unaware that a highly defended patient of his had discovered she could elicit his interest and attention when she spoke about illness or injury, even two years after he had recovered from a serious illness. Despite this sensitivity to illness in the therapist, Lasky, now back at work, seems to have closed off any wishes for his patient's interest, especially as this woman had for so long not cared at all. He confines his poignant description of his regressive wishes to the time when he was acutely ill. The patient complained, in effect, that Lasky was interested only in analytic process, not in her or in her life. She seems to have been signaling the therapist to attend to his need to protect himself from acknowledging their mutual interest in each other.

I take Lasky's article as suggesting that the therapist who has recovered from serious illness seeks to eliminate any longings for closeness with a patient because he continues to fear the intense regressive wishes experienced when ill. I believe that rigid intolerance of wishes and feelings in therapists tends to foreclose access to similar or complementary wishes and feelings in patients.

Kantrowitz (1997) has claimed that therapists, by temporarily providing *containment*, help patients learn to tolerate and regulate intense affects. For her, the power and efficacy of treatment reside in the interaction between patient and therapist, through which *both* are given an opportunity for significant change. Similarly, Aron and Bushra (1998) contend that patient and therapist, mostly out of awareness, mutually regulate each other's mental states (regressive or progressive), with both partners surrendering and being transformed. Therapists aim to modulate their patients' affect states both consciously *and unconsciously*. Aron and Bushra regard this expectable process, in which patient and therapist each contribute to regulating what the other experiences, as "mutual regression." Maroda (1991) had used the term earlier to describe jointly shared experiences of madness and merger. Aron and Bushra maintain that this mutual regulation of affect and mental states begins at birth between parent and child. But if such mutual regulation is a requisite phenomenon between people, including patient and therapist, it would seem to me to be healthy and adaptive rather than regressive, even if it begins in early infancy. This model of the therapeutic couple's mutual regression does not take into account each partner's regressive *wishes*.

Inderbitzin and Levy (2000) have attempted to differentiate regression from expected analytic process and progress, disorganization/psychosis, and threats to the stability of analysis. Arguing that an overly concrete concept of regression has been mis-applied to the treatment situation, they have moved toward discarding the concept altogether, much as Grossman (1986) had earlier discarded the concept of masochism. Now, reified concepts can doubtless obscure our view of a treatment, but I would follow neither Inderbitzin and Levy nor Grossman in discarding either concept, both of which I find useful and evocative clinically in my own thinking and in speaking to patients and colleagues.

WHAT DO THERAPISTS WANT?

Unlike an earlier generation of psychoanalysts and psychotherapists, many of us now believe that we cannot analyze effectively if we remain emotionally remote from our patients. I am referring not to what we say or do but to what we allow ourselves to feel and to want within the therapeutic situation, toward the goal, of course, of helping our patients. I and others (see Chapter 9; Kantrowitz 1997) have observed striking differences, which tend to correlate with the therapist's age, in the degree to which therapist/presenters let us into their affective world. Therapists who have been analyzed, supervised, and trained to expect to work with their own affective resonance with patients seem freer to share their feelings with discussants and an audience than do therapists whose training ended when countertransference was still considered pathological. Even the current shift toward recognizing the potential value of countertransference feelings may not sufficiently have overcome earlier ego ideal constraints and a possible lack of sufficient analysis of certain intense wishes and feelings (especially, but not exclusively, preoedipal ones) in many older therapists. Some of these colleagues may analyze effectively, even outstandingly, but they may be less open to their own inner needs, especially at work. Much of psychoanalytic politics may be a rationalized screen for tension and ambivalence about the therapist's subjectivity and the therapeutic couple's interpersonal experience, covering deeper, more significant concerns about allowing ourselves access to what we want, at varying levels of consciousness, from our patients.

At conferences and in discussion groups, some colleagues seem excessively fearful of opening up "the slippery slope" of therapists' wishes and feelings. This superego-ish attitude seems intended to rein in the rest of us, as if we were at imminent risk of enacting our wishes and feelings with our patients. I have reassured these colleagues that I do not act on my wishes and feelings toward my patients; rather, as I attend to my patients, I continually scan my inner experience for the sake of their treatments. Such reassurance has not calmed these colleagues' concerns about inappropriate action. Yet we share the conviction that our best protection against such action is maximum responsibility for our needs, wishes, desires, and feelings toward our patients. And we agree also that to help our patients achieve maximum autonomy from their inner conflicts and from us as their therapists requires us to manage our contrary impulses. We even agree that, although we should not burden patients with gratuitous disclosure of our feelings, we can at certain times best advance a treatment by telling *something* of our affective experience.

Many of these colleagues would admire Cooper's (1998) thoughtful exploration of the differential impact on a patient of the variety of ways therapists can interpret by disclosing bits of their affective experience. I agree with Cooper's caution that we therapists can use our preferred therapeutic approach in a rigid and defensive manner, and that an exclusive focus on either the interpersonal or the intrapsychic will obscure the other. The anxiety persists, however, that too much attention to therapists' wishes and feelings propels us toward the "slippery slope" of action; it feels safer, therefore, to shift our focus back to intrapsychic defense analysis and away from ourselves. Still, it would be more useful for us to be sufficiently aware of our personal proclivities in analyzing, so that we may catch ourselves in the process of becoming rigidly stuck in any one position, as we interpret or, better yet, as we think. Of course, I use intrapsychic defense analysis when I can; when I cannot, I draw on my own feelings and wishes.

With more negativistic, sadomasochistic patients I rely heavily on what I feel with them. Sometimes my early attempts to interpret the sadomasochism between us are premature, magical efforts to spare myself the torture, as if something better were possible. My getting caught up in such sadomasochism can keep me from seeing the adaptive value of the patient's attempts to sadistically, omnipotently control me in the transference. It is not simply that aspects of parental relationships are being repeated; the patient's negativism also expresses wishes for connection and sadomasochistic loving. Early in the treatment, the patient and I are not to enjoy each other. We are to stay connected through what is wrong between us. I remind myself that I need to survive these efforts at torture and control because that is how the patient needs to relate to me before she can risk wanting something better. I especially attend to those times when I shift into feeling less frustrated, angry, attacked, demeaned, and pushed away, toward feeling more caring, loving, or desiring. When my patient seems more able to tolerate acknowledgment of what is good between us, I will interpret the need to oscillate between negativism, with its safety and control, and caring, with its vulnerability and anxiety (see Olinick 1970).

Even though we seem to agree that we will learn most from talking openly about our difficulties in the treatment situation, it has not been easy for us to do so. It is a major premise of this book that even when we've devoted ourselves to discussing hating and loving feelings between the therapeutic couple, much of the time we've unintentionally shown our discomfort with such passions. I have offered my own struggles with the temptation to regress in order to help readers identify similar wishes in themselves that impede the treatment process. I encourage readers to share their difficulties in the treatment situation more *openly,* so that we can all learn more about our common dilemmas and move psychoanalysis and intensive psychotherapy forward (see Chapter 9). My patients can seek to destroy my value, usefulness, and competence in order to preserve their own omnipotence, self-sufficiency, and detachment. But I believe that their destructiveness is unable to undermine my analyzing function if I am not willing, even *temporarily,* to relinquish my role as therapist in favor of a more regressive relatedness with them. The issue is less my avoidance of acknowledging patients' destructiveness toward my analytic functioning, than allowing them to dislodge me from my role as therapist so that we can share a regressive relatedness in which neither of us is free to be competent, separate, and loving. Much earlier in my career, as a psychiatrist with disturbed patients, I expected that to reach and help them I had to consider my temptations to join them in their craziness. To make genuine contact with very disturbed patients seemed to require a willingness to live *temporarily* in their world. In my book (1992) about highly dependent transferences, I emphasized my comfort with sharing dependent feelings with my patients, without recognizing our mutual regression. I think I had made an unconscious either/or distinction (Akhtar 1996) between very disturbed patients, with whom I would be tempted to regress, and more analyzable patients, with whom I would not. With the latter, I seemed to expect that I should be able to move easily in and out of their world. With the patients described here, however, I felt that when we got into trouble, I was being shut out of authentic emotional contact.

I did not readily grasp that indeed each patient was barring loving relatedness, but only so that we might connect with each other in a more negative, regressive way. My feeling dissatisfied with my patients' negativism, rejection, and remoteness obscured my own willingness to share in this regressive relatedness. That is, each of us could feel safer feeling angry, critical, and dissatisfied with the other, rather than feeling warmly accepting and loving. I do not feel concerned about sharing childlike longings with patients, which feels progressive, unless we become stuck in them. They then become regressive wishes to share a pathological parent–child relationship that opposes separateness, competence, and love. When unconsciously we jointly idealize regressive relatedness, we retreat from relishing angry wishes to destroy the deficient parent and proclaim our own abilities. Unless we can feel our own willingness to remain stuck in negative, regressive relatedness, we cannot offer our patients the potential to become unstuck and to move forward with us toward something more separate, differentiated, and loving.

7

How Much Does the Therapist at Work Need to Feel?

INTRODUCTION: LET'S TALK ABOUT OUR FEELINGS AT WORK

This chapter was stimulated by controversy at a recent panel (1999), "What in the world is the relationship?" among Lisa Weinstein, Jody Davies, Fred Busch, Michael Miletic, and Michelle Price about Davies' use of her own feelings. Weinstein and Busch were highly critical of Davies' emphasis on her own affective experience with her patient, as if it were diversion from the patient's internal conflicts. They objected to Davies' prominent focus on trying to understand her patient through her own feelings toward him *and* to her disclosing some of her feelings to the audience and, at times, to the patient. They objected that such emphasis on the therapist's affects obscures the treatment situation, hindering close examination of the patient's defensive efforts to protect against conflict. Miletic, Price, and Davies responded vigorously to this attack on Davies' therapeutic approach.

The debate was highly politicized as traditional analysts defending the faith by focusing on the intrapsychic against relational/

interpersonal analysts who were muddying the analytic field with overemphasis on their own feelings. I felt provoked that this controversy was stifling constructive consideration of how best to use our own feelings toward the goal of helping our patients. In my view, Davies had been unfairly, severely rebuked for what seemed to me an excellent model of an analyst's access to and use of her own affective experience. I thought that excessive critical focus on disclosure of the analyst's affects, as in another example I cite later with Renik, had interfered with the task of assessing the values and potential pitfalls in Davies' emphasis on the use of her own feelings at work.

Yes, of course, there are risks of disclosing the therapist's affects to patients, although that is not my focus here. I'm more concerned that censure of the therapist's public disclosure of her affects to other therapists interferes with our ability to learn from each other how to work best with our most difficult patients. Earlier, we were not to talk about our countertransference in public (Sandler and Sandler 1998). Public disclosure of the therapist's affects may seem like shameful, dangerous exhibitionism, threatening to lead the audience into forbidden temptation. I believe that our collective fearfulness has inhibited public discussion of our affects, wishes, and needs with our patients (see Chapters 6, 8 and 9). Many colleagues have told me that attention to our own feelings with patients makes them anxious *they* will approach the "slippery slope" of loss of control and enactment.

This chapter seeks to consider how much the therapist at work needs to feel.[1] For me, this is not a political debate between traditional and relational analysts, both of whose work I value and use, but my ongoing wish that we talk openly in public about our common difficulties, especially with tolerating those feelings, wishes, and needs that are unbearable for our patients and then, to some degree, *for ourselves*. I certainly do not intend to convey that traditional analysts allow themselves to feel less than do relational analysts or

---

[1]My consideration of the intensity of the analyst's affects is descriptive, without considering whether they can be quantified (see Rapaport 1960).

that traditional psychoanalytic clinical theory aims to constrict the analyst's affects at work. I believe strongly that it is not our theory but our own inner constraints that compromise therapists' comfort with our affects at work. By now it should be clear that I am a traditional analyst who tries to integrate the helpful clinical contributions of colleagues' relational, interpersonal, Kleinian, and attachment theory perspectives.

I want to try to cut through competitive psychoanalytic politics so that we can focus instead on our common difficulties with tolerating the most painful feelings stirred by our patients and learn from each other through our differences. We can break down the sharp division between traditional and relational psychoanalytic perspectives by focusing on what each position may help its adherents to avoid. My intention is not primarily to criticize either group but to emphasize how any psychoanalytic approach may help us to manage ourselves more comfortably (Basch, 1981, Carvajal unpublished, Coen 1981), especially by avoidance of what threatens us. Rigid focus on either the intrapsychic or the interpersonal, without the capacity to shift flexibly between these perspectives (cf. Cooper 1998, see Chapter 6), may speak to the therapist's anxiety about his own affective experience at work, managed by a rigidly compulsive need to constrict what he feels. I believe that the unthreatened therapist at work should have little difficulty integrating intrapsychic and interpersonal *and* valuable aspects of both traditional and relational approaches to psychotherapeutic process. Therapists' refusal to consider colleagues' different ways of working therapeutically forecloses the chance to learn something new.

So, I want to examine how our own psychoanalytic approach, whether traditional, relational, or other, can serve to protect us. As at this recent panel, much of the ongoing, angry debate over therapists' focus on our own feeling responses toward patients has been framed in terms of psychoanalytic politics. More traditional psychoanalysts contend that excessive attention to the relationship between the therapeutic dyad may obscure and avoid patients' conflicts by external focus on the therapeutic couple and the patient's life outside the treatment. Excessive focus on interaction between the therapeutic couple, the argument states, may speak to the therapist's intolerance of his patient as a separate person with needs and conflicts in which the therapist, *sometimes,* may have no role. Overemphasis on the therapist's importance to the relationship can be intrusive to patients who feel vulnerable about their separateness and autonomy (Racker 1968, Olinick 1970), especially when they had felt impinged upon by a parent's own needs.

Therapists can protect against patients' conflicts that endanger them by shifting their gaze toward less dangerous, more reassuring aspects of the therapeutic couple's interaction. Or, traditional analysts argue that certain relational analysts, such as Renik[2] and Hoffman, give up on the possibility of catching the therapist's countertransference by introspection while it is still within the therapist's psyche, before it is enacted (Wasserman, 1999). They argue that too easy acceptance of the inevitability of enactment between the therapeutic couple discourages therapists' careful attention to their own feelings, wishes, and needs, so as to monitor the affective force-field between the therapeutic couple. They contend that certain relationalists discourage patients' regressive experience, thereby limiting the depth of therapeutic exploration. These arguments could be extended to suggest that therapists' avoidance of careful self-monitoring *can* protect therapists from responsible ownership of dangerous feelings and wishes, including regressive longings, in both patient and therapist.

More relational analysts counter that traditional analysts do not pay sufficient attention to patients' conflicts as these are expressed

---

[2]Note that in this chapter, Renik, viewed as both traditional and relational psychoanalyst, becomes a model analyst who seeks constructive integration of both perspectives. This is not to say that I do not disagree with some of his emphases, as noted, only that I applaud the attempt to integrate divergent views. Otherwise, his image here would assume epic proportions, more than either of us should bear!

within the analytic dyad. These relationalists argue that more traditional analysts tend to leave themselves out affectively of what transpires between the treatment couple. The traditional analyst can avoid what his patient needs to involve him in by restricting his focus, so that the analyst himself remains outside of the patient's conflictual field. This argument could be extended, similarly, to the point of contending that certain traditional analysts may need to protect themselves from experiencing their own dangerous wishes and feelings that are being evoked within the treatment situation by some patients.

Certain relationalists (e.g., Buechler 1999) encourage therapists to draw on their own passions to help and inspire patients, especially with depressive hopelessness. Buechler, championing passion, aims to help therapists tolerate and use, more comfortably, their own affective responses to patients. She does not consider how much therapists need to feel in order to enable patients to confront, tolerate, and manage the latter's unbearable feelings. More traditional analysts certainly agree that therapists need to engage patients about their avoidance of what is wrong, while simultaneously analyzing patients' reactions to efforts to engage them (Bader 1994, 1995, Coen, 1992, Mayer 1994, Renik 1995, 1998, unpublished).

The history of psychoanalysis as treatment has played out around our contradictory attitudes toward emphasis on cognitive understanding and interpretation as against the central role of affective experience. Despite our common belief that both understanding and affective experience are key components of any effective psychoanalysis, we may differ in our emphasis. But when we have become wary that the clinicians's affects and desires in the treatment situation may lead him astray, then we have needed to overemphasize understanding, mastery, restraint. The current version of this controversy is between treatment as understanding and mastery versus treatment as an affective experience within a new object relationship that aims to repair what has gone wrong before. Most of us object to polarizing the goals of treatment, seeking instead to integrate understanding, mastery, and affective experience within a new relationship. This chapter will focus on our current attitudes toward the therapist's affects, especially with those patients who are most difficult for us to treat because of their affect intolerance.

Is it sufficient for us therapists to feel a little of what our patients find unbearable or do we need to feel much more deeply to help them with their affect intolerance? How much pain do we therapists have to feel to help our most difficult patients? Do we actually have to take in, contain, and process, for and with our patients, what they have been unable to feel for themselves? How deeply do we have to go in our empathic resonance and identificatory experience with our patients and their internal objects? Here I extend my earlier (Chapter 2) views of how to help patients to bear unbearable affects by contending that the therapist does indeed need to assist the patient *by experiencing with and for the patient* what the patient has been unable to tolerate feeling on his own.

With our most difficult patients, we therapists do indeed need to feel deeply, contain, and metabolize what they have heretofore found unbearable. Only by our capacity to persist with feeling and containing what such patients repudiate can we eventually hope to find creative ways to help them face their own internal horrors, as we show them what we have had to process together. We should not comfort ourselves with the illusion that we only need to feel *bits or moments* of empathic resonance with our most difficult patients. Some, not all, of these patients have been traumatized, in some sense, during childhood. I raise the issue of childhood trauma because psychoanalytic writing about the treatment of those who have been traumatized comes closest to my present position (e.g., Bromberg 2000, Davies 1994, 1996, 1999, unpublished, Davies and Frawley 1994, Russell 1998).

Of course, excessive focus on the clinician's affects, as on anything else, can serve defensive functions, taking us away from whatever threatens us in the treatment situation. This chapter will consider defensive uses of the therapist's attention to his own affective experience. I note especially the therapist's narcissistic self-enhancement through overvaluing his capacity to feel as well as his undue pressure to stay connected emotionally with more difficult patients, who need to disrupt such connectedness between the therapeutic couple so as to preserve their distance and protect against threatening affects. But here I emphasize instead the opposite: our own difficulties with tolerating intensely painful affects with our patients and our own abundant rationalizations for sparing ourselves such discomfort. So, reader, before you object to what I have *not* considered, try to stay with my argument and with the difficulties, my own and colleagues', I will share with you.

SOME CLINICAL BACKGROUND

Numerous colleagues pressed me to tell what was transpiring in Professor A.'s analysis at the point where I joined him in mutual regression (see Chapter 6). I argued that I wanted to focus on my own wish to regress with my patient in a depressed maternal transference rather than on its defensive functions for both of us. I contended that a defensive focus would divert colleagues from acknowledging similar regressive wishes in themselves, wishes that indeed most colleagues disclaimed. I was pained that highly capable colleagues insisted to me that they just didn't experience regressive wishes. My aim, to use the therapist's wish to regress as a paradigm for addressing our discomfort with acknowledging our more general wishes and needs with patients, had been thwarted.

I eventually did respond to colleagues' challenge, deciding that indeed Professor A. and I had both become unable to tolerate his intense depressive hopelessness, which he repeated and enacted in the transference with me. His depressive hopelessness became too real, infecting me so that I could not preserve my more confident, optimistic perspective on what was transpiring between us. Then his sudden dysfunction became too threatening for me. When I could stand to feel his hopelessness for both of us without it overwhelming me, then I could help him face the horror that he had felt as a child, which he was now reexperiencing in the transference with me. His sense that I could not and did not want to help him with his feelings was horrifying. I could talk with Professor A. about his notion that I wanted him to remain emotionally remote from me, to find ways to distract himself, including sexual excitement with his anonymous women, so that he would not burden me with his needs and feelings.

But first, I needed to feel what he could not bear to feel, his childhood depressive hopelessness that there would ever be a parent capable of helping him, that he would be alone forever. He needed to distract himself from the horrors of this bleak prospect. And I needed to be able to feel, for both of us, the extent of the hopelessness between us, before I could help him to bear this hopelessness, when he was able to interrupt his distractions. Then, of course, we had the space in which to open up his rage and sadness with me as the parent/therapist who would not and could not help him. But even when I was convinced that I could tolerate Professor A.'s unbearable feelings, he still needed to run away from them, so that his emotional availability and connectedness continued to oscillate. My ability to contain what he could not tolerate was a necessary but insufficient condition for him to do so. Professor A. felt safer with the illusion that he lived in a world of his own, in which he controlled all his relationships. He feared preserving caring feelings toward his partner and me, so that he fought against missing and valuing us. Instead he would erase us from his mind, replace us with anonymous others, encouraging all of us to give up on the prospect of mutual caring. Now, I could interrupt Professor A.'s stirring up hopelessness between us as protection against fears of loving relatedness.

Davies (1994, 1996, 1999, unpublished, Davies and Frawley 1994) has eloquently described her own emotional resonance with traumatized patients, highlighting the resonance of her own vulnerable child–self with that of her patient. Davies (1999) makes highly effective use of her own vulnerable responses so as to help her traumatized patient, Daniel, address his vulnerabilities. Her easy openness about her responses offers both patient and reader a model toward which to strive for tolerance of what is overwhelming.[3] Davies also shows us

---

[3]Here is another epic model of the therapist at work to expand our affective range by empathic identification.

that her patient can respond with rage and sadism to her offerings, when they are experienced as seductive, excessive, intrusive, or motivated too much by the therapist's own needs. For example, Davies poignantly describes how, in a quasi-somnambulistic state, she covered Daniel with a blanket as he reexperienced terrifying coldness from when he had been forced by his father to remain naked on an ice-cold wintry porch. Davies acknowledges her patient's recognition that she knew first-hand what he'd experienced.

Daniel was very touched, only to return the following day sadistically enraged, attacking the therapist for her own self-serving unconcern. Davies elaborates her patients' shift from appreciative caring to sadistic attack, understandable as transference repetition with reversal (the vulnerable are attacked); fearfulness of remaining open, needy, and vulnerable; fear and rage in seeing the vulnerable child's needs in the therapist, as she literally moved so far out of her usual therapeutic position (in her chair). Davies makes clear that she did not *choose* to get out of her chair in order to cover her patient; she was barely conscious of her action. I admire Davies' lack of defensiveness with patient and reader about her own affective experience. She seems comfortable exploring her patient's and her own feelings.

I am persuaded that Davies, as therapist, needed to resonate with her own vulnerable child–self in order to help her traumatized patient. I imagine that all of us as therapist would have needed similar access to our own vulnerable child–self, which, to varying degrees, we all have, to help this patient bear his terrifying vulnerability. My concern is that many or most of us, unable to tolerate such emotional resonance, would have needed to restrict our own and this patient's access to the unbearable. In such a state of emotional constriction, we would not have been able to help this very traumatized patient. Or, Davies (1996) describes her entering deeply into the inner world of abused Amanda. After Amanda intrudes into Davies' closed office in the therapist's absence, Davies reveals her own helpless confusion, doubt, denial, and powerful sense that she was not to speak about feeling violated by Amanda's intrusion into the therapist's space. By struggling with her own affective experience, Davies can speak the unspeakable with Amanda.

I refer the reader to my description of Mr. R. my very rejecting patient, in Chapter 3. I struggled to preserve my sense that we could work with his rage, now suddenly louder and clearer, in the face of his destruction of the treatment. He dropped an hour, barely came at all, rarely called when he wasn't coming. All this coming from under his former sadomasochistic compliance, there seemed as if there might be more potential for engaging his rage and destructiveness. And yet he came less and less. For some time, I was able to persist with feeling what I imagined he could not bear to feel—how enraged, desperate, and hopeless he had felt as a child in the face of massive rejection by both parents—rejection that he now induced in me. I felt I needed to contain these unbearable feelings for him while trying to metabolize them and return them to him in more palatable form. My pride and pleasure in my ability to contain what Mr. R. could not tolerate helped me to deny my sense that he was no longer a patient. I struggled between feeling that I needed to sustain this treatment when he could not, and feeling that I was deluding myself, that he had insufficient motivation to work with his masochism, that he was content to remain stuck in the misery he made of his life and his relationships.

Just when I was finally prepared to accept that Mr. R. did not wish to continue this treatment, he seemed to turn around a bit. I describe more of my dilemma in Chapter 3, but I want readers of the present chapter to resonate with my struggle to feel and contain in myself what my patient found so unbearable. My awareness of his fear, that feeling his rage and hopeless despair would return him to the horrors of his childhood experiences, helped me to endure his disengagement from the treatment. My emphasis, when I did interpret rather than contain these feelings, was that Mr. R.'s fear of feeling enraged, desperate, and hopeless made sense in relation to what he had lived through as a child with both parents, neither of whom could help him with such feelings.

I was struck by how painful I found a single consultation with Ms. T. who had repeated with her therapist her previous childhood experience of caring, seduction, and abuse with a parent. I could feel her pressure to idealize and seduce me as specially caring with her. Even her seduction and abuse, with both parent and therapist, had, in part, felt caring, special, intense, involved, so different from the remoteness with her other parent. Knowing that I would see this patient only once, I found myself imagining the pain of having to endure her hurt, disappointment, and outrage directly in the transference, once she had relinquished her idealization of me. Would I have been able to bear and contain her despair, so that she could ultimately work her way through her horrors? I felt absolutely convinced that her intensive treatment would require the therapist's ability to tolerate and metabolize her pain.

THE THERAPIST'S AFFECTIVE ROLE IN HELPING PATIENTS BEAR THE UNBEARABLE

Some clinicians have moved in the direction of suggesting, *without explicitly saying so,* that to treat *traumatized* patients, therapists need to be capable of bearing for the patient the overwhelming affects these patients have needed to sequester. Such walled-off, frightening affects will now need to be enacted with the therapist as disruptions and disturbances between patient and therapist, a very difficult prospect indeed for both therapeutic partners. Therapists who cannot tolerate the very painful affects in such enactment will tend to close off their, and their patient's, affective experience. Or, affects that the therapeutic couple cannot tolerate together will result in these severe disruptions of the treatment process (M. Hurwitz, unpublished). However, the enactment of disrupting the treatment process can serve as a *marker* of failure of affective regulation by the therapeutic couple. This chapter emphasizes the optimistic *potential* in this model, that the difficulty now disrupting the treatment can become the pathway toward integration of previously intolerable affect by patient and therapist. Such progress requires that the therapist now be capable of bearing for himself, and for his patient, what had heretofore been, for whatever reason, intolerable.

From a traditional perspective, Shengold (1991) views primitive, traumatic affect as involving the combination of omnipotent feeling with murderous intent. The "terrible intensity" ("too muchness") and delusional expectation of total destruction of other and oneself become unbearable. Defensive narcissistic retreat from unbearable affect intensifies omnipotence together with the sense of destructiveness, leading in a a terrible spiral to greater retreat. Violence and hatred need to be balanced by a newly developed ability to love the analyst as a separate person whom the patient does not want to destroy (Shengold 1999). How to accomplish this very difficult task is the art of analysis.

Epstein (1977, 1979, 1981, 1984, 1987, 1999) has described the clinician's need to bear his own "bad" feelings as deficient therapist/ parent in order to enable his patient to express her unbearable, long-stifled rage, a task the parents had been unable to fulfil. Living out the role of bad parent can be so difficult for many clinicians to tolerate, Epstein shows, that they eagerly counterattack their patients, as had the parents previously. Epstein draws on Winnicott's (1968) view that the therapist needs to bear the full extent of both his patient's destructiveness toward him and his own counterhatred toward his patient. Of course, not all "bad therapist" feelings should be attributed to the patient's parental transferences. At times, the therapist needs to acknowledge, for himself, sometimes for his patient, that, for however long, he has not functioned optimally. When the patient actually induces and indicts our failure as "bad therapist/parent," we need to accept it, often to acknowledge it to the patient as the parent could not do, before we can talk about transference repetition.

Heiman (1950) wrote that the analyst needs to *"sustain* the feelings that are stirred up in him, as opposed to discharging them (as does the patient), in order to *subordinate* them to the analytic task in which he functions as the patient's mirror reflection." Sandler and Sandler (1998) credit Heiman with the first explicit statement that countertransference can be used constructively. Tähkä (1993) suggested that the view of countertransference (of Heiman and subsequent Kleinians such as Rosenfeld, Racker, and Grinberg) as an aspect of the patient's personality forced into the analyst through projective identification be seen as a young child's view, before the establishment of self and object constancy, that he fully possesses and magically controls others. Boesky (2000) contends that viewing the analyst as the passive recipient of the patient's projective identification omits the analyst's active contribution to the shape of transference and resistance. Tähkä (1993) emphasizes the interplay of the object relational needs of each therapeutic partner toward the other.

The contemporary Kleinians (e.g., Joseph 1983) view the analyst's task with patients in the paranoid-schizoid position as needing to contain what the patient cannot tolerate: separateness, autonomy, internal conflict, and external reality. The patient communicates to the therapist by projective identification what the patient cannot bear in himself. The therapist contains and processes for the patient what is unbearable, metabolizing and transforming it, so that *at some later point*, the therapist can find creative ways to return it to the patient (Bion 1962, 1967, Coltart 1986, Joseph 1975, 1982, 1983, 1987, Steiner 1993). Maternal reverie, for Bion (1962, 1967), is an openness to the reception and acceptance of the infant's affects, helping him to feel that he, his needs, and feelings are tolerable to the mother, and hence ultimately to himself. Ogden (1997c) has shown in lovely detail his use of reverie for processing his patients' projections.

This Kleinian model is complemented by the application to adult treatment of research on infant-mother interaction (e.g., Aron and Bushra 1998, Beebe unpublished, Beebe and Lachmann 1998, Coates 1998, Eagle 1995, Fonagy 1991, Fonagy and Target 1996, Fonagy et al. 1993, Fonagy et al. 1995, Kiersky and Beebe 1994, Lachmann and Beebe 1996, Schore 1994, Stern 1990), highlighting the mother's vital role in helping infants manage their feelings through her empathic responsiveness, calming, containing, and transforming function, and by her ability to help repair breaches in their relationship. The traumatic effect of the mother's inability to assist her young infant to manage his level of arousal, his proto-affects, is emphasized. Fonagy and his collaborators posit the mother's need to "mentalize" her own and her child's affective experience so that the child can learn to think about his own and the other's mental state and so as to protect the child from impingement by the mother's "unmentalized" trauma. They show that mothers who can think about their own trauma tend not to attribute negative images of self and other to their children, helping to foster secure attachment with them. Krystal's (1978a) view that children need mothers to calm and regulate them before they feel overwhelmed by their feelings has now been extended to earliest infancy. Beebe's (Beebe and Lachmann 1994, Beebe, Lachmann, and Jaffee 1997, Beebe and Lachmann 1998, Beebe unpublished, see Chapter 10) videotapes show young children being helped through interactive regulation with the mother to develop the beginnings of affect tolerance and management. Aron and Bushra's (1998) extension of this mother/infant model to adult treatment views each therapeutic partner as contributing, mostly out of awareness, to regulating his own and the other's mental and affect states.

Even if we are skeptical about the applicability of mother/ infant models to adult treatment, such models help to clarify the therapist's vital (maternal) role in helping the patient to regulate her affects when she cannot do so on her own, so that she can develop comfort and confidence in her affective capacities. Thus the need for the therapist as an "affect-regulator" becomes a crucial function of attachment to the therapist (Silverman 1998). The therapist's generative role as facilitator of the patient's uncompleted development has been integrated within traditional psychoanalysis (e.g., Settlage 1994, Tähkä 1993). The patient needs to feel sufficiently held and affirmed by the therapist —legitimate analytic functions—before the therapist can interpret (Akhtar 1994, Killingmo 1989). Or from a Bionian perspective, the therapist needs to contain the affect and action of part–object transference in contrast to interpreting the spoken fantasy of whole–object transference (LaFarge 2000).

Elaborating from Krystal (1975, 1978a, b) and the attachment researchers, patients' vigorous attempts to control affect and need can be regarded as protection against the terror of feeling overwhelmed in the expectation of traumatic repetition of early childhood affective experiences. Such patients lack the confidence that the therapist, unlike the earlier mother, will be able to intervene effectively. Hence, such patients dread drowning in feelings and needs once these are opened a bit. More familiar is the therapist's need to explore patients' fantasied fears of the dangers of specific affects, such as hatred and love.

BEYOND TRAUMA

Some, not all, patients with severe affect intolerance have been traumatized, in some sense. The literature about analysis of traumatized patients comes closest to the position that the therapist needs to join the patient in metabolizing the affective horrors of the patient's childhood trauma (see especially Davies 1994, 1996, 1999, unpublished, Davies and Frawley 1994, Russell 1998). Perhaps with patients who have been *overtly* traumatized, sexually, physically, or emotionally, therapists have been compelled to feel and to *talk and write* about the painful affects they have experienced during the treatment encounter. Clinicians may have felt that it was legitimate or necessary to share in their traumatized patients' overwhelming affects.

Russell (1998) suggested that trauma produces unbearable affects, leading to repetitive enactments, until these feelings can be processed. Unbearable affects from early trauma will be expressed and defended against as severe disruptions in the treatment, as impasses, severe regressions, psychotic episodes, especially as painful disturbances in the transference/countertransference field. Therapists' resistance to experiencing their traumatized patients' feelings forecloses the possibility that these patients will become able to integrate their unbearable feelings. "The therapist knows the [patient's] trauma by the way she feels," Russell wrote (1998, p. 31). Leavy (1998) clarified Russell's view that therapists of traumatized patients need to *feel and live through* versions of earlier trauma that are expressed during treatment as some crisis threatening to "overwhelm the relationship" (p. 140). Russell died prematurely, before he could clarify in writing how much he thought the therapist needs to process affectively in order to help his traumatized patient.

Davies (1994, 1996, 1999, unpublished, Davies and Frawley 1994) similarly contends that patients cannot process their traumatically overwhelming affective experiences alone. Patient and therapist need to create a safe enough situation within which they can both tolerate affect and need, in oneself and in the other. Although Davies beautifully describes her own affective resonance with her patient's trauma as necessary within the interaction between the therapeutic couple, she too does not state *explicitly* how much she believes the therapist needs to feel in order to help her traumatized patient. But Davies' clinical reports are congruent with the thesis of this chapter that it is the therapist's task to help her traumatized patient bear the unbearable (we even use the same wording) by doing so with and for her patient. The therapist must "*fully* enter into the dissociative world of the (sexually abused) patient" (Davies and Frawley 1994, p. 152, my emphasis). The therapist needs to show her patient that she "can *bear the unbearable*; that she can tolerate, contain, process, and ultimately, make explicit the profound neglect the patient suffered as a child" (Davies and Frawley 1994, p. 169, my emphasis). To the degree that a sexually abused patient has not been able to put and preserve her trauma in words, she will need to enact these traumatic role relationships with the therapist, who must bear them. Although Davies focuses on the therapist's need to feel the patient's intolerable role relationships, while I emphasize somewhat more the terrifying affects in these relationships, clearly we're writing about similar therapeutic tasks. Thus our literature may convey an artificial division between what is necessary with those who have been traumatized as against the rest of our patients who cannot bear their own painful feelings. I don't think that we should separate traumatized patients' unbearable affects from other patients' unbearable affects. I suggest more broadly that to help patients who are terrified to feel their own affective experiences—not all of whom have been overtly traumatized—therapists may need to assist by containing, metabolizing, and then, *at some point,* returning the unbearable affects to the patient. Focus on disclosure of the therapist's affects may distract our attention from the therapist's creative attempts to engage the patient so as to address painful conflict. At Renik's (unpublished) recent evocative presentation, I thought there was too much concern about what Renik told his patient rather than about the need to engage his patient about what was wrong, given that this patient was threatening to derail his third analysis. Better that we focus instead on how the therapist uses his own painful feelings to assist his patient to confront what he flees. Many of us now believe the therapist's pressure to act his feelings, by disclosure or enactment, can be relieved by the capacity to tolerate his feelings, for the sake of his patient's treatment.

TOWARD PERSPECTIVE ON THE THERAPIST'S AFFECTS

Although this chapter is focused on the therapist's resonance with the patient's disowned negative affects, the therapist's affects need to be framed within a broader context. Of course, therapists need to feel more than just these repudiated negative affects. Akhtar[4] (unpublished) suggests a trifold division of the therapist's affects: feeling empathically *with* the patient's felt experience; *for* the patient what he rejects or repudiates; *towards* the patient, generative affects like tenderness, concern, and love. Tähkä (1993), drawing on H. Deutsch (1926), Racker (1957), and Sandler (1976), divides the therapist's affects into "object-seeking," including empathy, and "object-responding," including complementary responses to the patient's internal objects.

---

[4]I gratefully acknowledge Salman Akhtar's help as discussant, colleague, and friend. Other discussions by Morton Aronson and by Kay McKenzie also helped me clarify my arguments.

Countertransference involves both. The therapist needs to be free to enjoy (generative concern) his patient's growth, which, in his role as a new developmental object, he facilitates.

Akhtar would also have me include the therapist's need to contain the patient's positive affects, which he is afraid to preserve inside himself. I certainly agree with this, although it is much easier for me to contain the positive than the very negative. Patients who are fearful of closeness will project what is good in them, and between them and the therapist, into the therapist who needs to contain these affects and find ways to return them eventually to the patient (Akhtar 1995, Hamilton 1986, Klein, 1946, Schafer, unpublished). Hamilton described therapists' need to affirm patients' capacity for relatedness, which they communicate to the therapist via positive projective identification. Especially for those who expect hurt, disappointment, and rejection, negativism with its safety and control is much safer than caring with its vulnerability and anxiety, (cf. Coen 1994a, Chapter 5, Joseph 1975, 1982, 1983, Olinick 1970, Schafer unpublished, Steiner 1993).

The therapist's comfort with his affects will, of course, vary with his own psychological development, with his comfort and confidence in his ability to manage his affects and to use them effectively with his patients. Thus Coltart (1986, 1991, 1992a, b, 1996) describes her greater comfort with using her feelings and intentions, especially humor and fury, later in her career. Objecting that colleagues refer to her case as "when Dr. Coltart shouted at a patient," Coltart (1991), like Maroda (1999), laments that therapists so rarely describe their feelings. Of course, therapists will respond differently to what threatens them most with certain aspects of patients, especially during crises, as with deep regression, psychotic episodes, stalemates, threatened termination, or erotized or malignant hate-filled transference (Gabbard 1991). Akhtar (unpublished) pointed out cultural variations in therapist's affective expression, from restraint to exuberance, the pole at which he puts "too spicy Indian analysts".

HOW MUCH DOES THE THERAPIST HAVE TO FEEL?

What is at issue here is what and how much the therapist needs to tolerate feeling in order to assist patients to address feelings they had previously needed to avoid. How deeply do we need to feel what's inside our patients, affects, wishes, needs and defenses in order to help them? Is it sufficient for us to know where our patients need to go, to sample just *a bit* of what they need to feel in order to help them? Or, do we really have to feel much more deeply for ourselves what is inside of our patients? How much do we need to live affectively with our patients, their roles, and their parents'? When is our inability to *easily* shake off affective identification with our patients and their internal objects excessive, pathological countertransference? Or, is such intense affective involvement between the therapeutic couple requisite for helping certain patients newly manage what they have previously been unable to tolerate?

Much of our literature (e.g., Racker, Bird, Kernberg, Shengold) has emphasized the *negative* side of therapists' emotional experience, the danger that therapists' inability to tolerate the full intensity of their patients hating and loving feelings will interfere with full analysis of patients' conflicts. But we have not sufficiently considered the *positive* side of therapists' emotional experience, our need to resonate deeply with the unbearable in our patients in order to help them to do so. My concern here is with patients who become stuck in treatment because they cannot tolerate some feelings, needs, and wishes. *Now*, I would emphasize the therapist's need to assist his stuck patient by the therapist's ability to persist with feeling what the patient cannot feel. Through the therapist's capacity to feel with and for his patient, how and why these feelings, needs, and wishes became intolerable, gradually, over time, the therapist can help his patient share the therapist's empathy for the patient's previously unbearable childhood experience. However, even when the therapist is able to feel, contain, and metabolize what the patient cannot face, this certainly does not mean that the patient will, soon or ever, become able to share the therapist's success. The frustrated, angry therapist becomes tempted to judge the patient as untreatable, insufficiently motivated for change (cf. Rothstein 1998) rather than persist with sharing the patient's terror.

I would argue that effective therapists need to be able to feel with their patients and with themselves, continually shifting their cognitive and affective focus so as to attend to what is most central in the treatment. Sometimes, this will be primarily inside the patient, sometimes it will be inside the therapist, sometimes it will be *somewhere* between them. Sometimes, even if what is most pressing is inside the therapist, the patient still cannot bear to hear this, so the therapist continually needs to assess what to do with his affects during sessions, what to contain and process further, and what to draw on in talking with his patient. My concern is with any position that encourages us to close off our own affective experience rather than to use our feelings so as to help our patients. When the patient is out of touch with his terror, as when his protections are working overtime, say with action defenses, like perversion (see Chapter 5), it may be especially difficult for the therapist to remain empathic with what terrifies his patient. Such action defenses can easily obscure, for patient and therapist, collaborative focus on what the patient is fleeing. Indeed, I've been struck by our conjoint difficulty with preserving our focus, when the patient has needed defensively to keep shifting our focus to avoid what he could not bear to face. I now take for granted that when a patient and I cannot maintain a therapeutic focus, I need to preserve my empathic resonance with what my patient cannot tolerate over a prolonged time before my patient will be able to do so. I also assume that my patient's fears of emotional engagement with me contribute to our difficulty in finding each other. I have to respect his need to flee while I wait for appropriate opportunities to talk with him about his fear of allowing me to see his deepest concerns.

Empathic therapists cannot somehow, magically, jump into the closed-off world of patients with severe affect intolerance to then restore their capacity to feel. The therapist may come up with the wrong feelings at the wrong time, when the patient does not want to engage with him about what's wrong. The empathic therapist's efforts to engage his closed-off patient will not somehow lead her, with loving appreciation, to open herself up, as the therapist wishes, even when his interpretation is correct. To the degree that she fears close contact with her feelings and needs, including for the therapist, she must avoid such engagement. There is nothing magical in the therapist's need to contain and process what he and his patient feel as they struggle to make and avoid contact, so that at some point, when they both feel safer, they can try to talk together about what they've both been through.

So, how much do we therapists need to feel? Whatever it takes to help our patients be able to feel what they cannot bear to feel. Especially with more difficult patients, some of whom may have been traumatized, the therapist needs to feel intensely painful feelings, wishes, and needs. With our more difficult patients, I do not believe it is sufficient that we merely sample a bit of their feelings. Here, I extend my view of what we therapists at work need access to within ourselves to include our own capacity to bear in their full force, with and for all of our patients, especially for those who have felt overwhelmed by their childhood experiences and feelings, what they cannot bear for themselves. This can be very painful for the therapist, whether the patient is directly expressing her pain or signalling that she cannot tolerate facing it by avoidant or disruptive processes. If the therapist can persist over time with feeling what the patient cannot tolerate, it becomes possible to find creative ways to help his patient to do so too.

I have not argued previously that where there is major difficulty in an intensive treatment, the therapeutic couple may be contending with feelings that neither of them can stand. We need to be prepared that we will impinge and intrude upon patients who experienced this as children by enacting the temptation to trample them by interpretation that makes them responsible for *our* feelings (cf. Balint 1968, Coen Chapter 6, Olinick 1970, Racker 1968). Far better that we be able to talk openly with them about how we have become caught up in repeating destructive invasion and undermining of the other rather than rationalize such interpretive enactment as therapeutic.

THERAPISTS' MISUSE OF AFFECT

Of course, there is risk that therapists' efforts to assist patients with traumatically overwhelming affects may derive from therapists' masochistic or guilty needs to mire themselves in their patients' pain. Therapists, like patients, need to struggle with contradictory temptations to live regressively inside past painful affect *as well as* to integrate it, relinquishing the past so as to live in the present. So long as the therapist has access to both sides of these contrary temptations, he can assist his patients to do the same. I believe the greater risk is that fear of temptation to surrender to our own past pain leads to closing ourselves off emotionally from patients who most need our affective resonance and openness. Criticizing therapists' consciously pressured efforts to empathize concordantly with the surface of patients' affective presentation, Bolognini (1997, unpublished) contrasts forced contact ("empathism") with more spontaneous and genuine empathy. Bolognini would have therapists examine our pressured need to stay connected with patients because of our difficulties with separateness and our patients' hidden, threatening affects.

Of course, not all of the therapist's affects are relevant to the immediate therapeutic encounter or enhance rather than obscure his grasp of it. Attention to the therapist's affects requires *responsible* assessment and management of them for the sake of the patient's treatment. Wild, destructive treatment (Schafer 1985) results from the entitlement to interpret the therapist's affects as all helpful countertransference (Boesky 2000, Sandler 1976). The implied criticism of Kleinian analysts' use of the concept of projective identification applies only when the therapist defensively insists his affects come from the patient, without having processed them responsibly.

Focus on the therapist's affects may hinder his ability to attend to the patient's immediate need or conflict, which may differ from his own. Emphasis on containment may avoid persistent focus on conflict overripe for interpretation or realistic assessment of treatment failure. Exhibiting our affective capacities with patients like Mr. R., as we used to exhibit our cognitive and interpretive prowess, can be a narcissistic enhancement. Pride in the capacity to tolerate and contain terrible feelings with the most difficult patients, a manic defense, can help to bear uncertainty, helplessness, and hopelessness. Even if we don't succeed, at least we've been able to survive being in the trenches with them. We need to preserve our balance between optimism and despair to assess accurately what our patients can and cannot address. The concept of containment is not intended to immobilize the therapist into passivity. Containment does not obviate interpretation of the patient's defensive destruction of the treatment—understanding, meaning, memory, value, appreciation, caring, love.

CODA

This chapter began with my angry reaction to a panel at which a very capable therapist was attacked for sharing her affective experiences with her patient *openly and publicly* with colleagues. Of course, we will disagree on how to conduct intensive treatment, including on how to use ourselves in the process. But I want us to be able to consider together how we all tend to run away from what is most painful with our patients without using psychoanalytic politics to cover our common difficulties. I believe that we can learn most from each other how we can be the most effective clinicians, given our talents and limitations, by such open and public sharing of our work, especially of our difficulties at work, as revealed through what we feel and want with our patients. Hence, we need not to focus on censuring each other for differences in clinical theory and technique, as occurred at the panel that led to this chapter. Rather, we need to learn from each other how to help those patients with whom we have the most difficulty working.

When we differ in our therapeutic approach, we can study and compare our techniques so as to assess which techniques are most useful for which patients and for which clinicians. Our therapeutic approach should acknowledge that we all need to protect ourselves, to varying degrees, from what we regard as unbearable by restricting our focus and constricting access to our feelings, wishes, and needs. As a result, *open and public* sharing of our difficulties at work affords us the chance to learn through colleagues' eyes, by becoming *newly* able to see and feel, some of what we had been unable, or not allowed ourselves, to experience (Coen Chapter 8, Tuckett 1993). But we cannot do so when we aim to attack each other for our differences, rather than seek to learn from each other through them.

Part III

Helping Therapists' Affect Tolerance through Talking and Writing About our Work

8

Discussing Colleagues' Therapeutic Work

A lthough therapists often discuss their colleagues' case presentations in public, there is virtually no literature about the therapist as discussant. This chapter will consider the discussant's tasks, opportunities, and difficulties. Many distinguished colleagues have confided to me and to others that when invited to present their own treatment process material in a public forum, they refuse to do so. They have on previous occasions been so humiliated by discussants' attacks on them and their work that they have vowed never again to expose their work publicly, orally, or even in writing. Other, less experienced clinical authors have divulged that discussants' critical attacks have deterred them from further writing. Recall how few colleagues responded to a request (see, Tuckett 1991) for clinical cases that could be published for the rest of us to study.

This chapter aims to promote constructive collaboration in clinical work between therapist/presenters and discussants, in contrast to attitudes that are primarily destructively antagonistic or dismissive. A more constructive atmosphere might make it easier for us to gather colleagues' therapeutic case material so that we might learn how they work therapeutically and how the therapeutic process unfolds with their patients. We might even be able to learn about differences in treatment process based on frequency of sessions, or whether or how far we can differentiate psychoanalysis from psychotherapy. A constructive atmosphere in which we seek to learn what is most effective with our most difficult patients would contrast sharply with our previous attitudes of certainty, superiority, and arrogance. Once upon a time, psychoanalysts, in contrast to patients and other clinicians, were presumed to know. It is time for us to all try to learn together what we do not know.

It would be naive to assume that therapist/authors can simply describe their therapeutic work to colleagues without the intrusion of various aims and needs in and out of their awareness. Rather than being regarded as factual reports, clinical case descriptions can be viewed more broadly as written documents having various combinations of expressive and communicative functions. As readers of clinical documents, we aim, just as with literary texts, not to psychoanalyze the author or the work but to inform the text by resonating with it as fully as possible. Often, we fail, as we succumb to the irresistible urge to assail both author and work with interpretive spears. I recommend that clinical discussants draw on the methodology of both intensive clinical work and psychoanalytic literary criticism. I know of no previous attempts to apply the latter methodology to the understanding of contemporary clinical writing. It seems surprising that we have not sought to elaborate how we might use our clinical skills as discussants, critics, or readers of treatment process material. Perhaps we have been wary of intruding on colleagues were we to make explicit how to do perceptive readings of their written cases.

Rather than attempt to pin down the actual therapeutic encounter, clinical discussants can focus instead on the *presentation process*, on what comes alive for them as they read and listen to the therapist/author's case report. This presentation process is not identical to the actual therapeutic encounter. What comes alive for the discussant certainly may not be the same as what has grabbed the author. But by focusing on the presentation process, discussants can maximally engage the therapist/author's attempts to convey (or avoid) those aspects of the treatment process that are most vital to the author. Although the goal is certainly not supervision, the analogy is apt that more can be learned about authors' clinical work by trying to follow their presentation than by a more tenacious effort to determine what really happened.

I suggest that clinical discussants are most effective when they confine themselves to an intermediate realm between their imaginary processing of the written clinical text and the actual therapeutic encounter. Discussants and authors can then meet in a protected, borderland space, apart from the actual therapeutic situation, a place where discussants use their reveries of the *presentation process* to find an imagined author and an imagined therapeutic scene. Clinical discussants would then be under less pressure to understand and interpret actual treatment process, and so would be somewhat less concerned with helping, harming, or educating the therapist/author.

My notion of discussants playing with colleagues' clinical material includes opening oneself up to passionate imagination; then containing, processing, and transforming such imaginative products; and finally delivering some of these ideas in a manner that allows maximum access. It should be some small comfort to clinical authors to grasp that discussants are imagining the process of their clinical texts rather than judging the competence of their clinical work. Clinical authors might then more easily accept that they have allowed the discussant to see and then to show them what they did not fully know they knew. Like Tuckett (1993), I believe that the potential for collaboration between therapist/author and discussant resides in the fact that treating therapists, even skilled ones doing good work, reveal more than they can fully grasp and that discussants can help them catch some of what is not fully conscious. Hence, the experience of writing about a case and presenting it, together with the audience's response, may clarify unrecognized aspects of the therapeutic interaction. This offers the possibility that the relationship between author and discussant can become constructively collaborative rather than deleterious.

Discussants, once removed from the immediate therapeutic situation, may be more capable than either therapist or patient of recognizing the affective force-field in which they have become caught up. Discussants may thus be able to extricate themselves from such an affective trap and to describe it more fully to the treating therapist. Do not misunderstand me to contend that discussants have privileged access to objective assessment of the author's clinical limitations. Discussants will be unable to grasp much of what the treating therapist knows, much of which he or she does not reveal. Discussants are not wiser than treating therapists. In our postmodern world, we seek not objective certainty but subjective perspectives that usefully inform us. It is not simply that participation in the treatment process limits the therapist's attention or that we each find our own perspective, so that outside others can find so much else to observe (Bromberg 1984). That discussants and authors will have different perspectives, that they will see differently, is true but not useful unless this difference can open something new for authors.

It is a psychoanalytic premise that we all have limitations in what we can tolerate, in ourselves and in others, limitations that blind us some of the time. Discussants and clinical authors, looking together, can see more than either can see alone. Even good treatments become stuck as the therapeutic couple lose their way. Presenting clinical work allows others to help a treating therapist to regain therapeutic perspective and see what is being enacted and has remained, however long, outside of the therapeutic couple's awareness.

To my mind, what is at issue is not theory (relational versus Freudian, objectivist versus subjectivist) but our comfort and our willingness to use ourselves to understand rather than usurp another. I do not believe that it is our theory that primarily determines our capacity to use affective experiences in the service of helping our patients or colleagues. We may argue vigorously for constructivism and yet discuss, supervise, or analyze with authoritarian dogmatism. It would be psychoanalytically naive to assume that discussants' acceptance of a constructivist perspective, though helpful, is sufficient to enable them to provide helpful commentary. This is not a matter of civility, tact, or manners. For us as discussants, self-observation, self-understanding, and self-analysis are our most powerful tools. Self-analysis of our reactions as discussants can help us grasp the patient/therapist interaction.

Nor do I believe that differences in theoretical orientation between presenter and discussant necessarily interfere with their constructive collaboration. On the contrary, if negative forces do not interfere, presenter and discussant can eagerly compare and learn from differences in their approaches. It is a major premise of this chapter and of this book that most therapists today want to improve their skills by learning how their colleagues work differently. I will argue, in my clinical examples, that when Freudian and developmental therapists competitively criticize Kleinian therapists, theoretical differences are but the manifest content or pretext. When I sat down after presenting a clinical case some years ago, the chairperson, a self psychologist, angrily whispered to me, "What got in the way of your work was how angry you were at your patient!" I was aware neither of feeling angry with my patient nor that something was in my way; I had minimal concern about how caring I felt toward her (see Chapter 1). This colleague claimed he was attacking my object relations technique as insufficiently empathic; in one clinical segment, in order to focus my patient's angry hunger, I had remained somewhat more silent than I had been. I was certainly not silently withholding with this very needy patient. That's just not my style. On the contrary, I was actively drawing out her hunger into intense transference attachment toward me, so that she felt cared for and contained. But at this point I thought she could tolerate, some of the time, our working with her angry, demanding feelings. Indeed, she needed to oscillate between feeling that I was actually providing her the loving care she felt she had missed as a child and working with her conflicted longings. This colleague's unwarranted attack on me was not primarily about theoretical differences; rather it arose out of narcissistic, competitive factors. Contrast this response with the potential for constructive consideration of what indeed my patient needed from me and could and could not tolerate at that point in her treatment. Self psychologists, contemporary Kleinians, or other Freudians might well question whether my patient was ready to become responsible for her internal conflict. Here we would be drawing on and transcending theoretical differences so as to try to determine how best to work with my patient. This is help I would gladly receive.

As I have intimated, discussants of treatment process material tend to be drawn into whatever affective force-field patient and therapist have constructed. By affective force-field, I refer to a combination of wishes, needs, affects, and defenses in which the therapeutic couple have become caught up in the transference–countertransference, where they remain stuck, and from which they need to be extricated. Loewald (1970, 1975) wrote about a transference force-field between patient and therapist, that, in reenacting the past, offers the potential for change. As clinician, reader, discussant, and writer, I have drawn on the concept of affective force-field as I attempt to feel my way passionately into what transpires between me and my patients and between me and literary or clinical texts. Thus, my recent clinical writing has focused on mutual problems between my patients and me regarding feelings and wishes.

I cannot say that I first developed this way of working with patients and then "applied" it to literary and clinical texts. Rather, my way of working, in which I strive to feel my way into an affective force-field between me and the other, has developed simultaneously in my roles as clinician, reader, and discussant. In retrospect, it seems it was in my psychoanalytic literary criticism that I first described this use of myself, earlier (1982a) than in my clinical papers. Since then, I have become freer to draw on difficulties between my patients and me in order to understand and then describe the therapeutic situation between us. This freedom derives, of course, both from internal and external factors. I have been influenced not only by an intersubjective focus, but also (and especially) by a broader shift within our field toward a more accepting attitude and concern for our difficulties as clinicians. Ogden (1994, 1997c, d), in particular, has described his use of his reverie experiences in the clinical situation.

Throughout this chapter there will be tension and slippage between the contrasting positions of clinical discussants' focus on their imaginings of what the author is conveying and their attempts to inform the author about the actual therapeutic process. What is at issue is not theory (e.g. tension between subjectivist and objectivist perspectives), but pragmatic concern about how discussants can make their reactions most accessible to presenters. Indeed, discussants need to be aware that it will be difficult for them to remain fancifully playful and to resist the temptation to supervise. I encourage discussants to restrain themselves from imposing what they have gleaned on presenters. Discussants and presenters collaborate best when discussants don't force presenters to acknowledge their hidden countertransference, as revealed by the discussant's parallel reactions. Better that discussants describe in part how they have responded to a presentation, allowing the presenter room in which to move toward or away from their reactions. Remember that the presenter is not in treatment or supervision with the discussant. Even when the discussant has keenly grasped the presenter's interfering countertransference, needs and conflicts in presenter and discussant may still impede their ability to collaborate in a way that allows the presenter to accept what the discussant has shown. To be truly helpful to the presenting clinician, discussants need to embrace, contain, and process whatever feelings they experience as they read and listen, so that they can draw on such feelings to inform them about the presentation. Competitive, destructive, and critical feelings can be used to understand their reactions to the case, the colleague, and the task of discussion. I am by no means advocating a reaction formation approach that would have discussants be merely kind, not to say bland and dull. Sometimes it is necessary to let presenters know what is wrong with their work, even to discourage them from further writing. For discussants to provide passionate, constructive commentary, they need full access to all of their wishes to do otherwise. To avoid contending with a colleague's material may appear to the audience as hostile and dismissive of the clinician/author. This chapter points to an ideal educational model for discussants, one worth striving toward, though it may often be beyond us.

I was motivated to write this paper after I began to make sense out of my own reactions as clinical discussant of a distinguished colleague's discussion of another distinguished colleague's treatment process material. I struggled to tolerate that I too was caught up in feelings similar to those of the discussant, the therapist, and the patient. I then realized that understanding what I was feeling could be the way out of this trap toward writing a reasonably toned commentary relatively untainted by the feelings of superiority and contempt in which we had all become caught up. I hoped my struggle would help clarify some of what discussant, therapist, and patient could not get far enough outside of to grasp fully. Even as I struggled with feelings of superiority, contempt, and competitiveness, I was still much too eager to show the others what I was grasping more fully than they were. Today I would try not to force interpretations on the others but to offer playful readings, more lightly, that they would be freer to assimilate or reject.

BACKGROUND

We psychoanalysts have tended not to examine ourselves in the roles of reader, critic, discussant, and educator, though there have been some rare exceptions. Weissman (1962) claimed that analysts like Kris (1952) tended to provide *theoretical* formulations about the critic's role in re-creating the artist's experience. Weissman viewed psycho-analytic critics as having the potential advantage of being "mindful" of their own psychological conflicts, as well as of those of the people they study. But he was not prepared to advise psychoanalytic critics on a methodology for using ourselves. Wyman and Rittenberg (1992) have criticized attempts by psychoanalytic readers to psychoanalyze authors' clinical cases: in effect, to competitively undermine presenting therapists by showing up their failings. They emphasized that authors of clinical case reports can be vulnerable to interpretive attack because they reveal so much of themselves.

The interpersonal field between patient and therapist has been explored through the supervisory experience (e.g., Berman 1997, Bromberg 1982, 1984, Levenson 1982). Candidates' emotional reactions in clinical case seminars have been described as reflecting experiences parallel to those between patient and therapist (Issacharoff 1984). Eigen (1997) provides a lovely example of his use of his painful feelings of exclusion in attempts to assist two supervisees with their need to dissociate themselves from empathic acceptance of their disturbed patients.

Certain authors, both literary critics and psychoanalysts, have described the *processive* reading of texts. Literary critics have advised examining texts for inconsistencies, reversals of direction, unclarity, gaps, traps, areas of indeterminacy and unreadability. Such problems in reading texts become the stuff of interpretation. What is difficult to read is to be understood as bearing on how the text is to be read and on what it means (see, e.g., Barthes 1973, 1979, Fish 1980, Gadamer 1975, Iser 1978, Poulet 1970, Rosenblatt 1938). Psychoanalytic critics have expanded this imaginative reading to include the problem of what readers do with their responses—feelings, wishes, needs, defenses—during the reading process (see, e.g., Bleich 1967, 1975, 1976, 1977, 1978, Gorney 1980, Holland, 1968, 1970, 1973, 1975a, b, 1976, 1978, 1982, Schwartz 1975, 1978, 1980, 1982; Schwartz and Willbern 1982;). Psychoanalytic critics have focused especially on reading as process, during which readers need to contend with the varied problems, especially psychological problems, that texts pose for readers (e.g., see Felman 1977, 1987, Mahony 1977, 1982, 1984a, b, 1986, 1987, 1989, Reed 1982, 1985, Skura 1981). Psychoanalytic readers search for "fault lines," repetition, instinctualization, heightened defense, inconsistent literary style, affect, imagery, symbolism, absence, effects on the reader, and so on (see Loewenberg 1995, Mahony 1982, 1986, 1989).

Psychoanalytic readers have advocated a passionate engagement with the text that leads to an intermixing from which one struggles to extricate oneself through self-observation, self-understanding, and even self-analysis (e.g., Coen 1982a, b, 1984, 1988, 1994a, Loewenberg 1995, Mahony 1982, 1986). This is akin to contemporary clinical writing about the treatment situation in which therapists are encouraged to allow themselves to resonate with intense affect to their patients' feelings, wishes, and needs. Clinicians and psychoanalytic literary critics struggle to differentiate their idiosyncratic reactions from more relevant responses, to patient or text, that they process in order to advance their understanding.

POSSIBILITIES AND PITFALLS
OF CLINICAL DISCUSSIONS

What I mean by playing with texts begins by relinquishing the temptation to pin down what really happened. Psychoanalytic readers, whether literary critics or clinicians, approach their material receptively, responsively, allowing themselves to be moved as fully as possible, to become caught up in feelings, to get lost, and then to find themselves again in creative resonance with their material. They aim not to be too stiff or serious, not overly directed by their own needs or desires, so they can bend and bond with their material, get inside it, be read by it, and read it in light, playful, creative ways. I believe that the best psychoanalytic literary criticism is practiced with a light touch, the critic aiming to illuminate only a little bit, not to burden fiction (or history) with heavy-handed, forced readings (Coen 1994, 1997b). Clinical work too is best done with a light touch, with therapist and patient both playing easily with what transpires in the consulting room. Of course, anxieties in therapist and patient can readily interfere with their comfort and fun in the therapeutic encounter.

My notion of discussants playing with clinical texts draws on Erikson and Winnicott. Erikson (1954, 1955) engaged his patients, readers, and texts in exuberant, highly subjective, imaginative play, as he opened up multiple meanings beyond the obvious, the narrow, or the expected (see Chapter 11). He showed how to transform imaginative passion into creative written interpretation. Winnicott (1971) maintained that creative play is situated in an intermediate, potential space between our own inner experience and our trusting relations with others, with whom we share external reality. Imaginative play with the other's creative product would contrast with the arrogant presumption that one person simply can and should inform the other.

My view of clinical discussants' imaginative play with authors and their texts draws also on my earlier ideas of author—reader interaction (Coen 1994). Rather than seek the flesh-and-blood author and an authentic therapeutic scene, clinical readers elaborate fantasy versions of an imaginary author—compare Booth's (1979) concept of the "implied author"—and imaginary therapeutic scenarios. They do so within an imaginative creative space apart from author and text in response to various literary and psychological needs, unconstrained by the specific reading task at hand. This imaginary space in which readers play exceeds a transitional space (Winnicott, 1967) for connecting with an absent author (see Gorney 1980, Green 1978). It includes the psychic arena in which readers vitalize and give meaning to the text and its imagined author during the reading process. It includes the task of responsibly processing the reader's reveries, surmises, and understandings so as to deliver them effectively to the author.

Discussant readers of clinical texts can try to bring the presentation process to life as vividly as possible, searching for clues in problems in reading that can generate persuasive meanings. Readers search not only within the reported sequence of patient–therapist interaction but within the author's entire text. Authors may reveal more than they are aware not only by what they report of their clinical work but through their entire writing process, by what follows and what doesn't. Material presented in close connection *may* suggest linked or disrupted meaning. A problem posed in one paragraph may be addressed or avoided by what is discussed next. What is vague, unclear, omitted, repetitious, or unsatisfying may reflect something of the text's discomfort. Readers can follow flow, interruption, and shifts in sequence of affective material, wondering about movement toward or away from intense affect. Digression away from the immediacy of the therapeutic scene to earlier times and related feelings in patient or therapist may link the material affectively.

For example, one clinical author (Symposium 1996b) used the word *intruded* in her case report more frequently, so it seemed to me, than any other. I imagined that her feeling intruded on by her patient and his having felt intruded upon by his mother were central affective issues my colleague was highlighting, not fully consciously. Perhaps she wanted help with such disturbing feelings. When I shared my fantasy with my colleague and friend, she acknowledged that although she had not been aware of emphasizing intrusion in her case report, she had indeed felt very much intruded on by her patient. Today, rather than presume that I had grasped actual problems in the treatment situation, I would hope to catch my eager pleasure to join the patient in intruding on my colleague, so that I could describe to her what we were all caught up in.

SAMPLE READINGS OF CLINICAL TEXTS

In discussing a colleague's discussion of another colleague's process material, I found myself (Symposium 1996a) in the trap of wanting to impose my views on the helpless other, discussant and therapist/ author, much as the discussant argued that the therapist was imposing his views on the helpless and demeaned patient. To extricate myself, I tried to explore the position of being the critic/discussant of the therapist's material as we might do in considering parallel process in supervision (e.g., Gediman and Wolkenfeld 1980) or in literary criticism of fiction (Reed 1982, Stimpson 1985). Be aware that both author and discussant are highly competent clinicians though with very different therapeutic perspectives.

The therapist showed how he and his patient moved from their initial difficulty with making empathic emotional contact with each other to the position where they could mutually acknowledge that the patient's childlike needs had been ignored. The therapist said he had become "bogged down" in identifications with the patient's archaic internal objects, from which he had difficulty extricating himself, and that the patient was projecting his conflicts into the therapist. He felt that "the very foundation" of his work "was being called into question." The therapist made clear that he felt dismissed, demeaned, unappreciated, bogged down, irritated, and critical. He showed us how each person dismissed the other. He told us that he felt frustrated and critical of his patient's "clever" ways of extricating himself from acknowledgment of depression and need of the therapist by instead making claims on the therapist for admiration. He pressured his patient to relinquish his defense of manic superiority and his hunger for admiration and acknowledgment, and to get down to the real work of the treatment: admitting his desperation and depression. This led the therapeutic couple deeper into struggle over the legitimate goals of the treatment. That is, the patient wanted the therapist to admire him in order to help him feel better about himself, while the therapist wanted the patient to forego such longings, which the therapist regarded as defensive, and get down to the real work.

The therapist felt pressured to get the patient to acknowledge the therapist's importance to him, which the patient both refused and was afraid to do. When the patient was dismissive of the therapist, the therapist responded by being dismissive of the patient's needs. By pressing the patient to succumb to his desperation and depression, the therapist tried to reverse the situation and become the superior one. The therapist's need for acceptance by the patient was understandable in the context of the patient's mistrust, distance, and superiority. The therapist was not yet able to get far enough outside of the struggle to be able to use his countertransference awareness that he was here bearing the patient's own feeling that his importance to the therapist and to the parents had not been sufficiently acknowledged. In feeling "stuck," the therapist showed his dissatisfaction with the patient, from whom he wanted more.

The patient, because of how forgotten and neglected he had felt as a child with his parents, was hesitant to own for himself how much more he wanted from the therapist. The theme of "the neglected child" appeared clearly in a vignette of the patient taking his daughter horseback riding; he forgot about her and her needs as he fought with the manager and focused on his daughter's regard of him. Skepticism, superiority, contempt, mistrust, aloofness and emotional coldness seemed to have been the patient's attitude toward the child in himself, at times the therapist's attitude toward the patient, and also the parents' attitudes towards the patient's childlike needs and perhaps even their own.

To the degree that the therapist felt like the child who was dismissed and ignored by the superior, cold, aloof parent in the patient, he may have felt reluctant to accept the patient's hunger for admiration from him because the patient would not accord such respect in return. The therapist had to tolerate that he was in a quandary, just like the patient, to be able to feel for himself and for the patient just how horrible it was to expect that there would be no one to understand and accept him. The therapist had to become able to accept that he had temporarily become intolerant of feeling depressed, helpless, and unaccepted. He made clear that he needed to catch himself at being caught up with the patient in fighting "about who was right or wrong," what he described as "coming to my senses." Once he could acknowledge that he was fighting with his patient, he could make sense of their need to fight with each other and could extricate himself from the struggle.

The turning point occurred when the therapist interpreted that the patient feared that the therapist needed to blame him because the therapist could not face his depression over their impasse. He now told the patient that because they had gotten caught up in cruel fighting with each other, they had forgotten the patient's needs as a child. Now the therapeutic couple could work with the patient's childlike needs. The dilemma seemed to be that one person would not acknowledge the emotional importance of the other and the legitimacy of the other's needs. Part of this struggle over whose therapeutic goals were legitimate seemed to represent a more general struggle, between parent and child, within oneself and with the other, over whose needs count.

The discussant suggested that the therapist, identified with the patient's wife and mother, would not allow the patient to feel competent. The discussant saw the therapist enacting this subjugation of the patient by too much pressured explaining to the patient of the defensive meanings of his behavior, while cultivating neither his attempts to function competently in and out of the treatment nor "his admiration and love for the analyst." Author and discussant agreed that therapist and patient had become embroiled in a situation where one knows, confronts, and criticizes the other, who is not valued, empathized with, or understood. However, author and discussant disagreed about why this had happened. Although the discussant also talked about identifications, he suggested that the therapist would analyze much better if he embraced the discussant's developmental perspective, which accords legitimacy to the patient's needs for autonomy, competence, respect, support, and care.

In arguing that the therapist needed to impose less on the patient in order to accord the patient greater respect and autonomy, the discussant contended that a dream interpretation had been hurtful to the patient and served to keep him in the inferior position. The discussant thought that the patient's dream expressed the wish to keep the therapist with him as a sustaining sibling during a separation. I agreed but suggested that to help the patient feel competent as a collaborator he should be asked his associations to the dream. I realized that we had an affective force-field here in which each of us was tempted to impose his ideas on the other. Of course, to some degree that is part of being a therapist, an author, or a discussant. Perhaps the author was now in the role of patient and the discussant had taken the place of the therapist/author. One knows and is competent; the other does not know and is to be criticized.

Had I fully caught on and extricated myself from this trap, or was I repeating the same pattern with the discussant, even as I showed how I tried to deconstruct this pattern? I was still intent, it seems, on demonstrating that I had a better vantage point from which to examine the material than either the discussant or the therapist. Of course, I now had the considerable advantage of viewing the clinical material through the lenses of the author's and the discussant's excellent critiques while I struggled to step outside of their views and the trap in which we had all become bogged down. Through the discussant's eyes, I could *now* see the patient objecting that his wife and therapist discouraged and undermined his efforts on his own behalf. I could see the patient's need to argue with the therapist and others that he was in the right. I could grasp the patient's transference complaints about his "relatively humble role," while others made "the important speeches."

Let us assume that patient and therapist did indeed need to become bogged down in these struggles. Better that we as discussants extricate ourselves from the superior position in which we each claim that this would happen only to this therapist, not to us, or that we would have caught on to the trap much sooner. I imagined the patient was repeating a parental identification in which the parents, because of their own needs, ignored those of the child. If the therapist indeed needed to avoid feeling like "the neglected child," he would have been unable to show the patient how the latter was avoiding such feeling in himself and in his daughter. Patient and therapist seemed to be struggling at cross-purposes, neither seeming able to acknowledge the legitimacy of the other's position. Whether the therapist was in the role of the superior parent or the neglected child or both, he was eventually able to grasp that the angry fighting between patient and therapist had ignored the needy child in the patient. I imagined that when the therapist had been able to feel himself as both rejecting parent and neglected child, he could then help the patient to feel himself in each of these roles. At that point, the child in both patient and therapist seemed to become more legitimate for each of them.

I imagined that when the therapist could show the patient how he had learned to ignore childlike need, in his daughter and in himself, he could begin to grieve that his parents had been so unreceptive to his childhood needs. The therapist became able to interpret both his countertransference as the left-behind lonely one, who grabs hold of the other, and the patient's fear that the therapist would not understand the patient's longing for comfort and warmth but instead would mock him as childish. Now the author could present his material elegantly, as we glimpsed the contrasts between the superior, aloof, cold mother and the needy child and father.

At a presentation by another superb clinician (Panel 1996), I was impressed with how empathic and perceptive the therapist was, yet I wanted to speak out on behalf of the patient. The therapist told us right away about her patient's "chronic sense of being disregarded and of being criticized for not measuring up to a required standard." She then told us that "it is the analyst whom he experiences as not measuring up to what he requires." She thought the patient had reversed roles with her, so that she was now the deficient one. She repeatedly noted her dissatisfaction that her patient was not working better and was *spoiling the therapist's work*. Claiming that the patient was projecting his anger and irritability into her and exerting omnipotent control over her, she interpreted his aggression toward her. She spoke well and poetically for the patient. In the session following her (poetic) interpretation of "coughing out his unwanted self and finding it sweet to become the extremely critical one," he responded, "I wrote a poem." When she twice asked him questions, the first time he responded hesitantly. The second time he said: "I'm surprised you asked me. I'm surprised you want to know." Another time he said, "I didn't expect you to respond. You never do to that kind of thing." When he was critical of seven immigrants on a train, the therapist focused on the seven days until the holidays but not on his implicit criticism of the immigrant therapist, perhaps made so that he might feel more her equal. She complained that he "trimphantly made useless the bit of understanding about himself he had got from me. However, my talking was futile." She regarded his statement that he felt "safe—or very unsafe—or both, I suppose!" as "mocking" rather than reflecting that he both felt safe and unsafe with her.

I wondered how to understand that the therapist felt angry and irritable that the patient was spoiling *her work*. I wanted the therapeutic couple to collaborate. I would have liked to have drawn out much more about his dissatisfaction with the therapist. I felt concerned that the therapist's speaking so well for the patient may have led the patient to feel closely held but also intruded on (a concern shared by Lucy LaFarge as discussant). I wanted her to help him speak for himself. I imagined that he was criticizing the therapist as overpoetic and intrusive, not allowing him to be creative and to contribute understanding. So he spun out his own poetry within his own mind and refused to share it with the therapist. I wondered if he was complaining about the therapist's expectation that he comply with her omniscience. I thought the therapist took over too much, inviting his passivity and compliance, threatening his sense of autonomy and separateness. So while he wanted to feel connected with the therapist, he simultaneously feared being taken over. She seemed annoyed with his need for protection from closeness with her, which she interpreted critically. I felt drawn into an affective force-field of anger, control, and dominance over, and intrusion into, the other's mind. I felt tempted to push back, to insist that the author own more of what she was doing to the patient and to her audience: in short, that she accord all of us greater autonomy, capability, and respect.

There seems to be a difference between American analysts and their British Kleinian colleagues about the usefulness of encouraging collaborative exploration, as in the examples above, in contrast to the analyst's simply interpreting meanings to the patient. Rita Frankiel (Symposium 1996a) suggested that the contemporary Kleinians of London tend not to ask their patients many questions, out of the belief that questioning is ineffective and promotes intellectualization. Grotstein (1996) has remarked that cultural differences between American and British psychoanalysts largely account for this difference.

SOME ADVICE FOR CLINICAL PRESENTERS AND DISCUSSANTS

The discussant is neither a superior arbiter of the therapist/author's work nor a subsidiary commentator on the other's creativity. Discussants can show their talent better by what they do with the presenter's work than by display of their own work. Dismissive attitudes in discussants are usually transparent to an audience, except perhaps to those who share the attitude, either to the presenter personally or to the politics he or she represents, or whose idealization of the discussant clouds their view. I have seen a general trend over the last twenty years away from the bullfight attitude at psychoanalytic presentations, whereby true believers are cheered to gore the heretics. Within our contemporary perspective, we raise questions about what we have heretofore taken for granted. Most of us seek to improve our own clinical work by serious consideration of therapeutic practice that differs from our own.

We want colleagues to show us in detail how and why they make their clinical choices, what their rationales and strategies are. We are dissatisfied when they won't let us see much of how they work and of how they feel and think as they work. We will no longer accept clinical theory, buttressed by arguments against self-disclosure, in place of detailed treatment process material. We will ask presenters repeatedly, in many different ways and in many different situations, to reveal more about their affective experiences, thoughts, and hunches, to share enough of themselves with us that we can get at least somewhat inside the treatment process they are presenting. Clinicians do not need to reveal a great deal of their inner experience for an audience to be able to resonate with them affectively. Presenters who exclude us too fully from the inner struggles of their therapeutic work, no matter how distinguished or capable they are, tend to seem arrogant, closed, and remote. We cannot follow even good clinical work unless the presenter allows us to enter affectively into the treatment situation. That means revealing *something* of the feelings of *both* members of the therapeutic couple.

At two recent examples, my fellow clinicians and I wanted to know what it was like for the therapist to be flooded with highly erotic transference or to be assaulted for long periods by chronic hatred. When the presenting therapists omitted or minimized their affective experience in such presentations, I tried to help them share more of themselves with us. We can easily become competitive and defensive, insisting that our way of working (e.g., traditional Freudian) is better than our colleagues' (e.g., contemporary Kleinian or interpersonal). But I've been impressed in recent years how eager audiences have been to get into the thoughts, feelings, and strategies of colleagues, of whatever school, who are presenting their clinical work. I've noticed this most consistently at the two-day workshops on clinical practice and technique held at the meetings of the American Psychoanalytic Association. Members of the group, including highly skilled and well-regarded colleagues who attend regularly, seem eager to study in depth how other colleagues work differently.

Many presenters need to be encouraged and helped to feel safe enough to share some of themselves with an audience. I refer both to colleagues who avoid presenting because it is too daunting and to those who present but in a manner overly constrained. Such reserve deprives all of us of what we might learn by studying each others' cases in depth. Colleagues' attitudes about presenting their work derive partly from inner conflicts over competence, exhibitionism, envy, competition, success, fear of others' reactions, and so forth; in part from experiences (their own and others') of being attacked; and in part from their having taken on other tasks and obligations. Some highly skilled colleagues choose not to write about their work for mature, nonneurotic reasons, especially to protect their patients' and their own confidentiality (Stein 1988a). Some colleagues tell us more about themselves than we want to know and a few colleagues don't need our help at all. The therapist/writers I know vary considerably in their wishes to contribute to others' creative development. Some, appreciative of help they themselves have received, take considerable pleasure in helping colleagues improve their writing. Other therapist/authors feel that being a discussant is not sufficiently rewarding, to themselves or other authors, to warrant time away from their own writing.

I've been impressed with how useful it has been to assure colleagues, experienced or novice, that their presentation would be assisted rather than attacked. When I've organized and chaired meetings, I've provided such assurance by setting a collegial tone among presenters, discussants, and audience. I've even assured presenters that gratuitously destructive statements would not be tolerated from panelists or audience. I strongly disagree with chairpersons who believe they should not intervene when others viciously attack younger colleagues. I believe that beginning clinical authors need all the help and encouragement they can get, certainly not hostile attack, before they can determine whether their writing can enhance rather than clutter our literature. More seasoned colleagues may welcome spirited controversy aimed to engage rather than dismiss the other.

Complementarity between author and discussant is very different from the situation where authors presume to impress an audience with their work and discussants aim to upstage them, either by presenting their own work or by undermining the presenter's. It is also different from author and discussant indulging (and constraining) themselves in mutual admiration. Narcissistic and competitive struggles between presenters and discussants usually compliment nobody; audiences can easily see how intense needs for acknowledgment and triumph have precluded any contribution by presenter and discussant, to each other or to the audience. But rather than simply stifle competitive, narcissistic, and exhibitionistic desires, presenters and discussants need to be prepared to enjoy them responsibly in public presentation. Audiences seem to be most satisfied when presenters and discussants enhance each other by adding something to the other's understanding. Such mutual enhancement adds to the self-esteem of each participant.

Discussants' acknowledgment that authors help them toward understandings through what is presented, including what is outside an author's full conscious awareness, should temper discussants' attitudes of superiority and criticism and help to lessen authors' narcissistic vulnerabilities. What the discussant constructs has already been provided in some form by the author, who allows the discussant to stand on his or her shoulders. Even when discussants feel certain that a colleague's clinical work is problematic or stuck, the clinician/author has allowed this to be seen, even when unable to fully grasp and so escape such difficulties.

Self-analysis of feeling responses to process material should precede discussants' assuming they are free to talk about such responses. We clinical readers should be especially capable of self-reflection on our intentions as readers (cf. Barratt 1994, Weissman 1962). Responsible clinical discussion requires ownership and processing of discussants' affective responses toward the goal of assisting rather than harming therapist/authors. Schafer (1983) warns us not to expect that we can behave like responsible clinicians outside the consulting room. I suggest that we should expect more of ourselves in the role of discussant. We can use our affective responses to understand and possibly aid the other if we can tolerate our wishes to do otherwise.

I suggest that discussants begin by allowing themselves access to whatever feelings are stimulated by the experience of reading and discussing a colleague's case. Any competitive, destructive, or critical feelings should not be stifled but should instead be drawn on to understand one's reactions to the clinical case, to the author, and to the task at hand. I am impressed with how useful it is to persist at trying to relate one's feelings as discussant to what has been transpiring between the therapeutic couple. When this is done, a discussant can attempt to manage any destructive feelings that do not derive from the presented material so as not to inflict them on the author. I do, however, become worried if my initial drafts of a discussion are calm and dispassionate; something is missing if I have not been caught up in strong feelings by the clinical material. In such cases I would try to understand why I have not been keenly affected by the process material and what this may reflect of the therapeutic engagement (perhaps the avoidance of passionate engagement). I know that if I have been powerfully gripped by a case I will be able to provide interesting readings, but only after I have done considerable work on my own responses. That is as it should be.

Typically I go through several drafts of a discussion, working through what I can recognize of my own inappropriate feelings so as to understand the clinical material better and to produce a more tempered, balanced reading. I attempt to adapt my discussion to the interests, needs, and vulnerabilities of the author. With more problematic clinical material and more vulnerable authors, I keep reworking my discussion to modify my tone and my expectations of what I can succeed in conveying. However, I have seen discussants avoid contending with colleagues' material out of concern that criticism would be unbearable to them. Such avoidance, as I have noted, reveals to the audience both hostility and a disrespect for the therapist/author's capacity to learn and change. Better that discussants encourage a more confident attitude that clinical authors can tolerate respectful questioning of their therapeutic work, from which all of us, author, discussant, and audience, can learn something new. Our psychoanalytic ego ideal includes being open to questioning from others, capable of self-reflection on our difficulties and limitations, and not rigidly defensive or expecting impossible perfection of ourselves. I greatly admire colleagues who have presented stuck or failed cases in which they acknowledged difficulties in their work and listened openly so as to profit from their discussants.

As I've matured as a clinical writer, I've become much more comfortable with looking forward to learning from my discussants. The most satisfying experiences I've had, as presenter or as discussant, have involved situations where each of us has approached the other with respect, concern, and the wish to learn from and contribute to the other. I've been delighted when colleagues have offered suggestions, with tact and consideration, about what might have been interfering between my patients and me especially when I've then been able to use such insight productively with my patients. I've been grateful to colleagues who've shown me limitations in my ways of organizing my clinical material, limitations that had foreclosed a broader perspective toward the complexities of the therapeutic situation. In these cases, it felt like my colleagues both acknowledged my contribution and showed me something I had not quite fully seen on my own. Going beyond simple praise or blame, they addressed my work in order to enhance it. I felt appreciated, understood, and helped toward a new integration. Colleagues have responded similarly when as a discussant I have been able both to be understanding of them and to raise problems respectfully for them to consider. How different this is from my first experience as a clinical presenter, when my distinguished discussant rejected my paper out of hand as insufficiently psychoanalytic. In order to get help with two difficult treatments in a recent clinical paper (see Chapter 2), I deliberately invited my discussants and audience to respond to the problems my patients and I were having in our work. I was grateful for what I learned, just as I had been for the assistance I had received from my peer supervision study group. Discussants, audience, and I all enthusiastically embraced the opportunity to think together constructively about the problems with which my patients and I were contending. My attempt to repeat a similar experience not long afterward with the same group didn't work, perhaps, at least from my own perspective, because, this time unlike the previous occasion, the discussants' were less contributory, and more competitive.

9

Why We Need to Write Openly about Our Clinical Cases

Anumber of colleagues (Galatzer-Levy 1991, Renik 1994, Spence 1981, 1986, 1990, Tuckett 1991, 1993, 1994, Wyman and Rittenberg 1992) have made impassioned pleas to build a library of detailed clinical case descriptions that we can study and research. These colleagues have advised us to write questioning descriptions of treatment process sufficiently open to allow other colleagues access to at least some of the therapeutic couple's inner experience. I will argue that such open case writing needs to engage readers emotionally enough to persuade us of the value and validity of the author's views, rather than simply advancing those views as unsubstantiated claims. That is, open case writing must allow us to remain free to rethink the material creatively on our own, to use it for our own needs. In contrast, closed case writing does not offer us sufficient access to the therapeutic couple's inner experience to allow us to follow what they have done. I argue that we cannot learn from closed case writing because it impairs the reader's or listener's creative freedom to make new use of the clinical material. Readers are not persuaded by authors' assertions without clinical evidence that makes such assertions plausible, evidence that must include something of the therapist/author's affective experience in the therapeutic situation. Then it becomes possible for us to follow the therapist/author's interpretive pathway from experience to understanding to interpretation. Even with the most skilled clinicians (e.g., those at the two-day clinical workshops on psychoanalytic process and technique at the American Psychoanalytic Association meetings), many of us have had to ask how they had reached their clinical conclusions on the case at hand. Invariably, these colleagues succeeded in persuading us only when they had shared a bit of the inner experience from which their understanding followed. Despite the insistence of some of these colleagues that their reasoning should be immediately obvious to us, it was not, until we could follow with them how they had arrived at their view.

This is not an issue of therapeutic perspective, of intrapsychic versus interpersonal orientation, but a requirement for persuading readers of the authenticity and value of the author's ideas. Nor is this primarily a political argument for or against particular clinical groups, except against any style of clinical presentation that does not allow readers and listeners convincing access to the treatment process. Authors whose therapeutic style deemphasizes the therapist's subjectivity cannot persuade their readers, unless they show at least some of their own inner evidence. To move our clinical work forward creatively, we need to become comfortable with open clinical case writing. Not all therapists will agree with my view that therapists need first to be comfortable with working therapeutically in a way sufficiently open as to allow them to process and use their inner experience for the sake of the patient's treatment. But I would hope to persuade readers of this book to join me in the aim of expanding our own domain of responsible subjective awareness so that we might treat our most difficult patients more effectively. Even colleagues with different clinical perspectives need to make their clinical writing convincing by allowing us to follow them, to some degree, in their work.

To learn from each other how to better treat difficult patients, we need to share our difficulties openly. We will learn most from describing our difficulties in the clinical situation, including patients and processes we find difficult, so that all of us can learn together about our common problems—the goal of this book. Other therapists can learn from our open clinical desciptions and help author/therapists (and everyone else) learn more from the clinical material we report. This needs to become an ongoing dialectical process in which authors and readers contribute to each other, so that we learn more about what does and does not work in the therapeutic situation. Note that I do not address the format for case description, whether transcript, case history, or clinical vignette; my aim here is to encourage therapists to share some of their inner affective experience in writing about cases, in whatever format.

Therapist/authors have had many reasons, rational and irrational, to be hesitant about revealing details of what has transpired between themelves and their patients. Our climate of presentation has fostered authors' fears of critical rejection for deviation from accepted technique. In our anxiety about the correctness of our therapeutic technique, we have tended to emphasize form over functional efficacy, as in the privileging of silence and abstinence over engagement (see Lipton 1977). Even when traditional colleagues did work effectively with more disturbed patients, they felt constrained to translate the interventions they needed for engaging these patients into "acceptable" language, omitting or devaluing as ancillary "deviations" from the standard technique of interpretation exclusively. I believe this trend continues, if less vigorously than in the past, and that even now we hesitate to put into print what we actually do, so much do we dread our colleagues' criticism that our practice is no longer acceptable. Such an atmosphere of critical judgment inhibits our ability to explore each other's writing to determine what is and is not most efficacious in our work. Many colleagues (see Chapter 8) have forsworn further presentation or writing after a traumatic experience in which they felt their therapeutic competence (or a colleague's) had been attacked. As a result, I believe, there has been a lag (Gray 1982), a hesitation, in our clinical writing such that we do not describe fully what we actually do in our offices.

Over the past decade, the Program Committee of the American Psychoanalytic Association has encouraged colleagues to present difficult, problem, stalemated, or failed cases in the hope that we will all learn much more from their study than exhibiting our therapeutic prowess and successes. This agenda has helped to modify the climate of presentation at our meetings so that today many of us are more comfortable talking about problem cases. As we've become more willing to investigate our own difficulties at work, especially with more difficult patients, which may be the same thing, it seems to have become somewhat easier to learn from each other. At meetings in recent years, I've been impressed with how eager colleagues have been to study constructively the therapeutic techniques of colleagues from groups other than their own.

Galatzer-Levy (1991) has argued passionately for clinical case writing that allows for the unexpected, that gives readers the freedom to generate new ideas, so that they can think about and reconsider important questions. He considers such writing necessary both for clinical research and for the enhancement of our clinical skills. The study of clinical case reports can complement research on the outcome and efficacy of treatment process. There are many ways, not mutually exclusive, to conduct research in psychoanalysis and intensive psychotherapy. Research study of clinical case reports, for example, might focus on how meanings are constructed by patient, therapist, and readers. Systematic research on treatment process and outcome does not make the study of individual cases obsolete. On the contrary, now that we are so keenly aware of our need to explore how to facilitate change in intensive treatment, we must examine our own work and that of colleagues much more closely. Clinical case reports help us to learn how colleagues work differently, to glean what could be most useful for us and for our patients.

Clinical writers do us greater service by allowing us to inquire with them rather than insisting on what they and/or we already know. Of course, such clinical questioning can be misused as a persuasive rhetorical flourish that in fact stifles inquiry and merely perpetuates received "wisdom." Colleagues who have championed an open sharing of the details of therapeutic experience have bemoaned the fact that most clinical descriptions do not even approach this ideal. On the contrary, they are used by authors primarily as a disingenuous literary device to persuade readers of the merits of whatever thesis is being propounded. That is, clinical material is used to buttress an author's claims, as an appeal to Freud's authority might be, rather than to explore a vexing problem. Some [e.g., T. Shapiro at an editorial board meeting of the *Journal of the American Psychoanalytic Association*] doubt we can learn anything new from clinical reports, which, they argue, merely show what the author wants us to see and little else. I would counter that such pessimism fails to allow for what we can garner despite an author's intentions. Nor does it encourage us to try to change how we write about our cases.

Given that the clinical case report has been a hallmark of our psychotherapeutic literature, it is surprising how little has been published about case writing. We've studied Freud's case reports (Mahony 1982, 1984, 1986, 1996), problems of confidentiality in case reporting (Bollas and Sundelson 1995, Goldberg 1997, Lipton 1991); effects on patients of writing about them and of asking them for permission to do so (Furlong 1998, Stoller 1988), the logic of explanation in clinical cases (Edelson 1986, Lear 1998, Sherwood 1969); discomfort, disinclination, or disinterest with regard to writing about one's work (Stein 1988a, b); concerns about criticism of one's work, especially personal rejection or exclusion for being deemed insufficiently or incorrectly psychoanalytic (Britton 1994, Wyman & Rittenberg 1992); and how to write up cases for institute graduation or psychoanalytic certification. But we've barely considered the problems and tasks of clinical case writing, of what we're after and of how best to achieve it. And we certainly haven't focused on the problems of reading clinical case reports, on what readers are to do with their reading experiences, or on the interaction between writer and reader. Mahony (1993) contends that contemporary clinical authors, unlike Freud, attend only to their interaction with the patient, ignoring their vitally important interaction with the reader. I've used a similar psychoanalytic and literary critical model of interaction among and between author, text, and reader in approaching literature (Coen 1994) and in discussing colleagues' clinical cases (see Chapter 8). More generally, thoughtful psychoanalytic investigation of writing within our field has barely begun. In a review (Coen 1998b) of *Writing in Psychoanalysis* (ed. Piccioli, Rossi, & Semi, 1996), the first volume in a *Rivista di Psicoanalisi* monograph series, I expressed my sense that the contributors' acknowledged feeling of being daunted by their task had become inscribed in their writing. This initial attempt to consider psychoanalytic writing needs to transcend its abstractness, relative lack of focus, and hesitation to pursue specific problems in detail. The rest of us need to join our Italian colleagues in examining psychoanalytic writing.

When authors are primarily invested in joining or promoting a given clinical club, Britton (1994) contends they misuse clinical material for that purpose. Mahony (1982, 1984, 1986, 1996) has convincingly illustrated Freud's effectiveness in persuading patients and readers, in and through his clinical cases, especially that of the Rat Man. We can easily understand Freud's need to promulgate his new ideas by demonstrating, even exaggerating, their therapeutic efficacy. But shouldn't we now be in a very different position, one in which we can question and learn from our clinical experiences rather than insist that we already know? Detailed, convincing exploration of treatment process would be far more persuasive than unsubstantiated claims. Our colleagues in medicine, science, social science, and the humanities would like us to raise questions, as they try to do, rather than merely assert our intellectual authority. We do know that good teaching and good writing raise questions for us to ponder more than they seek to provide us with answers (see Felman 1987).

OPEN VERSUS CLOSED WRITING: CLINICAL EXAMPLES

Closed Writing

I will restrain my temptation to attack closed clinical writing, in the belief that a constructively collaborative approach requires that I process and contain my wishes to do so. Hence, I do not identify the two examples of closed clinical case writing below. I want to emphasize that clinical case writing that shuts out the reader tends not to be persuasive or useful; we cannot learn from it. I aim to challenge our received ideas of how to communicate with each other about our therapeutic work.

I criticize this closed style of therapeutic writing out of my conviction that it arrests the development of our field. When the reader is provided little or no information about the affective force-field between patient and therapist, it becomes impossible to assess the therapist/author's contentions or to creatively imagine alternative views. I cannot conceal my bias against any therapeutic position that does not hold the therapist responsible for processing, for the sake of the patient's growth, any feelings, wishes, and needs experienced toward the patient. More importantly, I believe that therapist/authors, of whatever clinical persuasion, need to engage readers and listeners through at least *some* affective sharing of therapeutic process.

I was pleased to find that in two examples of closed clinical case writing I selected, each author introduced his material or his discussion with a footnote or endnote that seemed to signal (and then dismiss), at least to this reader, an awareness of foreclosure. I point this out not to psychoanalyze the authors but to indicate a playful style of reading clinical cases, even those written up in a closed style.

One author began his discussion by immediately acknowledging that a colleague with whom he had discussed both cases had told him he had not considered how compliant the patients had been with him. The author then argued against his colleague's warning, contending that both patients were able to use the author's interpretations constructively in the service of change. Although this author left himself out of the therapeutic experience, his seeming acknowledgment and disavowal of compliance read to me like the evanescent waving of a red flag, signalling and dismissing *some* problem between patient and therapist. Perhaps the author anticipates and attempts to repel his readers' concerns that he has not described what has transpired affectively between himself and his patients. Such a reading of this clinical case report seeks to establish a collaboration between reader and therapist/author in which each can contribute further to the other. Here the reader can amplify what the author seems to see but not see fully, offering the possibility that the author can now learn from the reader and the reader in turn from the author. If this is done, this formerly closed piece of clinical writing will have been opened up to the therapist's capacity for self-reflection (Barratt 1994) and to dialogue with colleagues.

In this case, the author holds off his warning note until he has presented his clinical material and begins his discussion. Beware the first footnote to clinical material! Remember how Freud (1909, p. 160) begins the Rat Man case with his first footnote, acknowledging Adler's emphasis on the importance of what patients say first. Freud uses the fact that the Rat Man calls his governess by her masculine surname to claim the importance of men's influence on this patient, an aspect of "homosexual object choice." Freud had far better evidence for this contention than the mere fact of the patient referring to his governess as Fräulein Peter. But Freud does not focus on his influence over the Rat Man, even as he proceeds to show us the evidence that the patient turns to other men for support against his conscience. I believe that what is at issue is not that Freud is dealing with "treatment transferences" instead of transference neurosis (Kanzer 1952, Langs 1980, Muslin 1979) or that Freud does not appreciate his patient's contemporary need for him (Zetzel 1966), but rather that Freud is simultaneously acknowledging and disclaiming his influence over his patient. The "Freud" I find in my reading was not prepared to examine further, beyond the signal of a footnote, conflicted needs between patient and analyst. We can read this footnote optimistically and constructively as imagining the therapist/author indicating where he was having trouble and could have used help, had he had his own analyst, supervisor, or collaborative colleague. I'm reminded of a very capable colleague who began a problematic presentation by announcing that a close friend had advised him not to report this case because it would show him at his worst, out of touch with what was wrong. Proceeding against this advice, my colleague seemed to be telling himself and the audience what was wrong, even as he attempted to disavow it. I imagined that, like my "Freud," he too wanted help with the difficulties between him and his patient.

In a footnote from another example of closed clinical case writing, the therapist/author indicates that some might approach the opening phase of treatment with an emphasis other than the patient's capacity for self-reflection on transference experience. Here too I imagine that the author, as he is about to show us his clinical work, may be ambivalently signaling his concern that he is imposing too much on his patients and readers, as he rejects and affirms his contentions. The article concerns problems with the therapeutic engagement of very disturbed patients understood to be defending against fears of ego disintegration. While reporting almost nothing of his own personal experience, he provides ample unconscious determinants of his patients' problems in treatment. Absence of detail about the affective experience of both therapeutic partners makes it impossible, at least for this reader, to follow their therapeutic processes. As reader, I am tempted to see the author's repeated references to the "demand" on patients for self-refection and self-understanding as indicating the therapist's awareness that he may be asking that his patients do what they cannot.

I want to open up this writing toward consideration of the inevitable joint problems both for these fragile patients and for the clinician. In order to help each other with our most difficult patients, we need to show each other something of our difficulties in the therapeutic situation. I'm well aware that a frustrated therapist might be tempted to impose impossible tasks of understanding on fragile patients unprepared to take them on. I've described my own struggles in work with fragile patients to move away from my pressured needs for understanding toward acceptance of the patient's need for something else: for example, containment, contact, acceptance (see Chapters 2, 5, 6). When the patient is less regressed, less terrified, and more tolerant of transference wishes, understanding can indeed become a reasonable therapeutic option.

Rothstein (1998) contends that when a patient terminates treatment unilaterally, as in the second therapist's report, the therapist cannot understand the action because the patient is no longer present to participate in collaborative exploration. Although the clinician may have an excellent hypothesis about why the patient has left abruptly, Rothstein cautions that without the presence of a therapeutic collaborator, there is no treatment. Humility and caution, rather than pretensions to therapeutic omniscience, help us to open up our work with our patients and with each other.

OPEN WRITING

Now I offer examples of much more open clinical writing, for contrast and to consider shifts, even in such open clinical case writing toward more closed expression. A lovely example, one that seems to cry out for such commentary, is Ogden's "On the use of language in psychoanalysis" (1997b). Ogden's essay is an eloquent argument for the priority of the functions, rather than merely the content, of language in writing and in therapeutic dialogue. Because of the directness and clarity of his writing, Ogden's descriptions are eminently accessible to his readers and so are especially suitable for this study. I take for granted that I would find similar shifts in any instance of clinical therapeutic writing, including my own. My remarks should not be construed as a critique of Ogden's writing or clinical skill, both of which I admire.

Ogden would have us clinicians listen to our patients as if we were readers of poetry trying to gauge what is being done to us, focusing on the "experience" of listening. Such attention to problems in our listening experience, Ogden shows, is most useful with more difficult patients, who are indeed difficult for us to listen to. Ogden is here bridging therapeutic practice with reader-response literary criticism that emphasizes attention to problems encountered in the act of reading. Ogden is especially sensitive to times when communication between patient and therapist becomes dead, bogged down, lacking in vitality, imagination, and connectedness for both partners. He is persuasive that we therapists tend to be drawn into our patient's emotional deadness, so that our own speaking becomes deadened. Joseph (1983) tells us that if she feels bored when she interprets to a patient, she takes this as a signal that she is speaking not to her patient but to herself, and so interrupts herself.

Ogden describes his patient, who had been thrown out of two previous treatments, as not talking to him but instead "wrapping herself in the pure sensation sound of words" (p. 228). He felt "utterly useless and without currency for the patient" (p. 229). His later description of his patients' need for sound as "a lifeless, insulating sensory medium" (p. 230) is evocative and convincing. I am therefore struck that he moves immediately from reporting his feeling useless and worthless with this patient to his most abstract, theoretical writing in this otherwise lively, experience-near essay. "I was able to restrict myself," he writes, "to serving as a (potentially) human medium in whose (almost entirely unfelt) presence the patient could engage in relatedness to an 'autistic shape' (the sensation of the sound of her own words (Tustin 1984; see also Ogden 1989a, b). All of the patient's previous experience of relatedness to autistic shapes (for example, painting and listening to music) had been done in isolation" (p. 229). Why at this point in his writing does Ogden refer to Tustin and himself about "autistic shapes"? Why, in this lovely essay that champions the therapist/author's attention to the *effects* of language, does he here not heed himself to refrain from theoretical justification? Perhaps he merely thinks the concept of the autistic-contiguous phase is not sufficiently well known to his readers and needs explication. I wonder, however, whether the therapist/author, feeling useless, worthless, and presumably resentful, might not want to attack the patient as "autistic," and that he needs to justify himself with references to authority, Tustin's and his own. I'm concerned here not with the real flesh-and-blood Ogden but with my own fanciful play as reader with the affective shifts in the writer-Ogden's descriptions (Booth 1979). I hope thereby to alert skilled clinical writers, like Ogden himself, to preserve open clinical description and to ponder their motives when tempted to shift to closed-off writing.

In another moving example from Ogden's writing, "Analyzing forms of aliveness and deadness" (1995), he is exquisitely sensitive to deadness, detachment, distance, and omnipotent control. He provides a lovely description of "Mrs. S." as addicted to him but "not as a personal attachment"; rather she is "powerfully untouchable in her isolation" (p. 55). The centerpiece here is the interaction between patient and therapist after Ogden cancels several sessions because of a death in his family. Mrs. S. is angry that the therapist has been "sadistic" in not telling her precisely who in his family has died. She insists he disclosed this to all his other patients. The therapist feels hurt: "I felt deeply disturbed by a recognition against which I had struggled for most of a decade: it seemed to me that Mrs. S. was unable to feel anything for me as a human being beyond her need to protect herself by means of her efforts to magically enter me and control me from within" (p.59). The therapist thinks back to their telephone talk: "I remembered with great vividness the feeling of attempting to control my voice as I spoke to her in an effort to hold back tears. I wondered whether it was possible that she had heard nothing of that. How could she have not experienced that moment (as I had) as one in which there had been a close connection between the two of us?" Alongside the alienation he feels from Mrs. S., the therapist now also experiences himself as a "spurned lover" (p. 59). This recognition leads him to a further insight: "I could at this point see in retrospect that it was in part my own lack of compassion for Mrs. S. and her wishes to comfort me as *my wife* that had led me to blind myself to the fact that her seeming absence of compassion represented a complex interplay of two powerful, coexisting aspects of her personality. She had been concerned about me and felt despondent that her love was unrecognizable to me (for example, as reflected in my not allowing her to comfort me)" (p. 60).

Again note the shift in tone and style away from the warm connectedness between them: "At the same time there was an important way in which Mrs. S. was unable to come to life as a human being and instead occupied a mechanical, omnipotent world of (1) relatedness to "autistic shapes" and "autistic objects" (Tustin 1980, 1984) (for example, the mechanical, self-sufficiency involved in the sensation-world of exercise and diet) and, (2) paranoid-schizoid fantasies of entering me and parasitically living in me and through me" (p. 60). Soon after this, he is able to write (p. 61): "Mrs. S. had loved me and had felt nothing whatsoever for me at the same time. I had experienced affection for her (which I came to recognize more fully in my experience of feeling like a spurned lover), but could not allow myself to feel warmth or at times even feel compassion for someone who was so clearly inhuman and inhumane (for example, in her treatment of her husband, her children and in her response to me, particularly after my father's death)."

Now therapist and patient speak much more warmly to each other. The therapist tells her he had underestimated both the amount of affection between them and the extent of their unrelatedness. He remarks that "the degree to which it was possible for there to be no human tie between us had diminished" but that it was still a "considerable force to be reckoned with" (p. 61). Mrs. S. responds enthusiastically that he has never spoken that way to her before, that now he doesn't seem as cold as she had been. Although she doesn't sense coldness in him now, she doesn't believe that it had fully disappeared; it just doesn't "dominate everything that occurred between us for the moment" (p. 62). As reader, I feel delighted by this thawing out between the therapeutic couple.

But the author doesn't stay close; he moves back to theoretical understanding, as he writes again about autistic self-sufficiency, omnipotent paranoid-schizoid defensive fantasy, and autistic-contiguous modes of protection. I wonder about the author's attempts to control his voice and his tears with Mrs. S. Why doesn't he want to feel his wishes for her to care about and comfort him? Is he protecting himself from such wishes by imagining that he cannot influence his untouchable patient? She accuses him of sadistic withholding in not sharing more with her and perhaps, more broadly, in not more enthusiastically inviting her to share some closeness with him. Does the therapist persist in getting back at Mrs. S. for her previous rejection of him by not acknowledging the new mutual warmth that exists between them and by pessimistically returning to focus on her autism? This is not to disagree that Mrs. S. both wants to share closeness with the therapist and to remain untouched. But why not, more optimistically, view the patient as needing to oscillate between these two positions because of the dangers of both closeness and distance, rather than regard them as such polar opposites that they can never be integrated? (Remember again that I'm playing fancifully with the written case rather than with the real-life therapist.)

In Chapter 1, I described how my resentment and helplessness at Professor J.'s destruction and devaluation of the treatment and our relationship led me to feel like agreeing with him that his treatment was futile. I kept wanting to conclude that he was incapable of loving, allowing himself to be loved, and of being treated. I was getting back at him and protecting myself as I closed off the treatment and gave up on him, rejecting him and feeling superior to him (as unanalyzable, unlovable, unloving) as he had done to me. I described my difficult struggle to preserve a more consistent interpretive focus on his angrily and defensively trying to push me away, to have me be the angry, disappointed child, so that we would be unable to keep feelings of love and concern open between us. I needed to help him (and myself) to establish, not just preserve, loving feelings between us. I had to learn that analyzing his destructiveness with me was not enough; I had to help him learn how to tolerate a caring relationship through my ability to remain caring even when he attempted to spoil and destroy my concern for him.

I want to note that, unlike many other therapist/authors, Ogden is certainly capable of writing without such shifts away from concerned connectedness with his patient. His moving description of Ms. B., "The woman who couldn't consider" (1997c), shows the therapist helping to open up warm, caring, sensuous connectedness between the therapeutic couple by exploring his reveries of his loss of the loved, deceased J. This clinical vignette has no theoretical distractions, no references to autistic phenomena, to Tustin, or even to Ogden's earlier work. This reader enjoys being able to remain close to the author, Ms. B., and the author's loving memories of J. Nothing intrudes!

Schwaber (1998) has argued against Arlow's (1995) criticism that she (1983, 1995) had neglected her patient's concerns about being hanged while she explored in detail his feeling that she had tried to influence his attending graduate school. Schwaber examined how she and her patient became aware of how pressured he had felt by her subtle clues, which had been unconscious on her part. When patient and therapist were able to discuss what had happened between them, the temporary therapeutic paralysis was undone, the patient felt much better, and the therapeutic couple could see what together they had enacted. Arlow had contended that Schwaber had focused too much on transference–countertransference, thereby missing vital conflictual content in the patient's associations. To my mind, this is an either/or debate that is not ultimately helpful. Therapists need to focus both on conflictual content and on those key transference–countertransference enactments that disrupt the therapeutic couple's ability to attend to current conflict. But Arlow acknowledged his own agenda: to warn contemporary clinicians that we had become too caught up with our countertransferences at the expense of close attention to the expression of conflict in patients' associations. So in fact Arlow was using Schwaber to argue against contemporary emphasis on the therapist's subjectivity. Not to be deterred, Schwaber in turn used Arlow's article to demonstrate the limitations of a clinical approach that downplays the therapist's subjectivity. Neither author used the other profitably, to see something new, but simply argued against the other's position. Because Schwaber used her clinical material polemically, the reader is not free both to join her inside the therapeutic situation and, alternatively, remain outside of it, to decide for oneself. Although Schwaber privileges the therapist's difficulty in grasping the patient's affective experience and point of view, she doesn't acknowledge that her readers encounter similar problems in dealing with a text. She cannot deter the reader's efforts to think with her and for oneself, as one follows her clinical material. When she insists that she is now able to see what she hadn't been able to see before, the reader wants to know more about what had been interfering and what else might be seen now. Readily agreeing with Schwaber how difficult it is to "know" the other's experience, the reader wants to join Schwaber as she explores both her patient and herself, so as to imagine many different possible meanings.

TOWARD OPEN CLINICAL CASE WRITING

Kantrowitz (1997) and I (Chapter 7) have contended that therapists tend to vary, especially by age, in how much they are willing to share their own affective experiences in the therapeutic situation with colleagues, and perhaps even with themselves. This pattern seems related to psychoanalytic training, personal analysis, and supervision. Older colleagues were taught that countertransference is largely pathological, so it is to be overcome in order to maintain technical neutrality and objectivity. The next generation *began* to be taught that countertransference is not only inevitable but useful, offering the potential to expand the range of one's "analyzing instrument" (Isakower 1963). Therapists, rather than feeling they should have fully resolved all their neurotic conflicts, do better to acknowledge what they have and have not been able to resolve. But therapist/authors, both in oral presentations and in writing, have tended to share too little of their inner experience for the rest of us to be able to follow along with them and see how and why they've reached their conclusions. Recently, however, I've been impressed, at clinical and literary workshops, how much we now press colleagues to let us into their affective worlds. Whereas many of our distinguished colleagues have tended to consider their authority sufficient reason for us to accept their ideas, today they are more readily persuaded that the rest of us need some access to their inner experience if we are to follow their reasoning.

But what is it about authors or pesenters sharing their emotional experience that succeeds in persuading us of the affective authenticity or validity of their descriptions? Can't we as readers and listeners be seduced by affect, just as we can be seduced by rhetorical style? Indeed the charisma and charm of some clinical authors can make it hard to resist their arguments, or for certain readers or listeners, to attend to their arguments at all. Stanley Fish (1980), the eminent literary critic, once challenged a small group of us, saying that once he'd presented his interpretation of the poem at hand, we'd never be able to think differently about it. Fish, a very persuasive writer and speaker, believes that persuasion accounts for much of interpretive authority. Indeed, he delivered his interpretation with such forceful insistence that we had difficulty preserving any other view; his became dominant. We certainly can be moved by many different factors in an author's writing: our ready-made transferences to the author or the author's psychoanalytic position; clear, creative, concise evocative writing that highlights a vexing analytic situation (e.g., Joseph 1975, 1982, 1983); resonance and agreement with the author's passionate appeal; or empathic responsiveness to the affective exchanges between therapist and patient. As regards this last, I share with many my admiration for Casement's (1982) description of his deciding whether to hold the hand of a patient who had been seriously burned as a child; for Eigen's (1997) report of his painful feelings of exclusion during supervision; and for the articles by Ogden I have cited. We need to process our reactions—admiration, repulsion, a feeling of being seduced, whatever—as part of our experience of reading descriptions of a therapist/author's inner affective experience. We gauge the affective authenticity of clinical vignettes by our own ability to resonate with them, so that we can feel our way into the therapeutic situation being presented. Clinical writing that falsely and temporarily seduces us can be distinguished from work of enduring value that helps us learn something new about the therapeutic situation.

What I would highlight about *open* clinical writing is not just its affective immediacy, or the author's intention of sharing experience with the reader, but the reader's ability to both resonate with the author's experiences *and* to create new and different readings. If I cannot feel able both to agree with the author's position and to step outside of it, play with it, question it, and construct alternative readings, I feel constrained by the writing. When patients don't allow us the freedom to understand (Bion 1959, Joseph 1983), remember (Schafer 1997), or think creatively (Kernberg 1992a), we feel dissatisfied and try to grasp and eventually interpret why they have needed to constrain us and themselves. I would argue that, to a degree, good clinical writing should resemble any good piece of writing (or of treatment) in that the reader (or listener) isn't blocked at the surface but is moved and able to learn while also free to interpret anew. Some writing, of course (e.g., that of Robbe-Grillet or Calvino), although not open clinical writing, does aim to trap the reader at its surface, forcing the reader to contend with the text's construction (see, e.g., Kermode 1974). Good clinical writing, like all good writing, is worth rereading because the reader can make new use of it. This does not mean that we therapists need to become creative writers, although Mahony (1993, 1996), complaining about the poverty of our clinical case writing compared to Freud's case reports, wishes some could do so. Drawing on Valéry and Einstein, Mahony argues that the pressure on us to write correct, qualified prose makes us poor rhetoricians, dull and unconvincing, unlike Freud. Perhaps we should aim not only to instruct but also to "delight" readers, Holland's (2000) view of the functions of critical writing, so that our writing affords "jouissance," or pleasure (Barthes, 1973), rather than tedium. We clinicians find pleasure in being able to share in, and learn from, our colleagues' intimate therapeutic experiences. Have we, in our contemporary eclectic milieu, forgotten libido? Can't we put the libidinal pleasures of the love and hate among us back into our writing, even as we struggle with each other?

COLLABORATION BETWEEN AUTHORS
AND READERS

We need to allow our readers sufficient access to the details of the emotional climate between the therapeutic couple so that readers can take their place, at least to some degree, both within and without the therapeutic situation. Therapist/authors do not present their work to be supervised or certified but rather to share some idea, experience, or problem with colleagues. For colleagues to collaborate with us, we need to allow them into our minds and experiences sufficiently for them to see what we see, to see what we do not fully know we see, and to see what we do not and cannot see for ourselves. Yes, of course, therapist/authors get burned by such exposure. But we can work to change our expectations of clinical writing and reading toward a model of constructive collaboration in which we try to learn from and contribute to each other.

I agree with Rothstein (1998) that a difficult patient is one who is difficult for a given analyst to treat. This acknowledgment facilitates our investigating the problems encountered by both patient and therapist. By not leaving ourselves out, we allow ourselves to learn more about which patients we potentially can and cannot help. We need to acknowledge our skills and limitations and to recognize the kinds of patients with whom we do well and those with whom we struggle and suffer. We can then be more selective in deciding whom to treat and whom to refer to that colleague who would be most effective with this particular patient. As we continue to learn about our own vulnerabilities, needs, and limitations with certain patients, we can continue our attempts to achieve better resolution of our conflicts.

Not surprisingly, even authors willing to let readers into their affective world vary in emotional availability during their exposition. Of course, some of this is inevitable during writing, as authors step back in their discussions to reflect on what they have just described. But in the course of conveying to the reader the affective immediacy of the therapeutic situation, authors have no such rational reason for emotional retreat from the patient or from the reader. The reader can wonder, as a fantasy in following the flow of the reading process as one might do in following the flow of the therapeutic process, about the irrational reasons for such retreat.

I've tried to explore the point at which clinical writers suddenly turn from clear description of therapeutic process with a patient into something more abstract, didactic, or dogmatic. I have frequently been struck by such shifts in clinical writing from more clearly accessible and convincing interaction for reader or listener to a more heavy-handed imposition on the reader. I had tended to assume that therapist writers, like therapists in the consulting room, tend to impose theory on their clinical material when they feel threatened by what is transpiring between themselves and their patients (Basch 1981, Coen 1987). I've come to believe, however, that it may be more productive to consider such shifts in exposition of therapeutic process, more broadly, in terms of the transference–countertransference affective force-field between patient and therapist (and between writer and reader). That is, for the purpose of understanding a clinical text, it may be fruitful to imagine what the therapist/author may be *doing* with the patient and with the reader. We would need to consider how much of what readers become caught up with in reading a clinical text may possibly parallel the transference–countertransference field and how much may lie outside it in specific affective interaction between or among therapist/author, text, and reader.

10

Is There a Child in the Room? Applications of Child Development Research to Adult Treatment

For this book, I've adapted my discussions of work by two child development researchers as I seek to integrate newer understanding of problems in early development into the intensive treatment of more difficult adult patients.

Susan Coates presented "Gender, trauma, and attachment" to the Association for Psychoanalytic Medicine in 1995. I've admired her pioneering work in understanding and treating gender identity disorders in boys. Here, I discuss Coates's description of gender identity disorder within the context of disrupted attachment. Trauma and gender transformation are to be understood within the imperative need to restore the mother—child relationship. Coates acknowledges that the relationship between gender identity disorder in boys and adult male homosexuality requires much more clarification. Some might object that her work could be used in the political oppression of gay men. I would contend that her work encourages the investigation of conflict in gender identifications, both opposite sex and same sex. There can be conflict in same-sex identifications just as there can be in opposite-sex identifications. It is better that we try to understand such conflict when it does actually exist in anyone, heterosexual, homosexual, bisexual, or otherwise, rather than avoid it. Of course, this is very different from our earlier agenda of attempting to pressure gay men into becoming heterosexual. The 1994 faculty retreat of the Columbia University Center for Psychoanalytic Training and Research was a suitable memorial to the harm psychoanalysts have done to a number of gay and lesbian patients in our misguided efforts to coerce rather than to analyze (see chapter 1). So too was Ralph Roughton's moving plenary address to the American Psychoanalytic Association in May, 2001, about the history of its attitudes toward gay and lesbian colleagues. I encourage the reader to approach Coates's work in this spirit of open exploration.

Within Coates's hierarchy of motivations for gender transformation, she highlights her child patient's (Colin) need to repair his mother, depressed after her abortion, by becoming her female child. Coates shows the intergenerational transmission (from grandmother to mother to child) of the need to repair the mother who becomes depressed after the death of a female child or fetus. We wonder how a 2 1/2-year-old child is able to grasp that his mother wants him to turn into a girl and how the mother transmits to him this pressing need of hers that he become a girl. Coates emphasizes the etiologic role of trauma: the loss of sustaining attachment to the mother through her depression, self-absorption, and the mother's own wishes to connect with and repair her relationship with her own mother, Colin's grandmother; the mother's rage and physical violence toward Colin; the chronic strain trauma of the mother's destructiveness toward her son, with her wishes to invade and usurp his autonomy so as to transform him into her companion, comforter, and appendage.

Coates tells us that Colin's "story" is of unwilling transformation "without any wishful elaboration." Trauma is key. Her interpretation of Colin's "story" *begins* with emphasis on the child's "being taken over from the outside, resulting in a sense of annihilation of the self as Colin is transformed against his will into another" (p. 13). Coates is wary that the role of trauma may be minimized by attention to wish and conflict. But when we emphasize trauma, including the mother's usurpation of the patient's autonomy, in the etiology of Colin's gender identity disorder, how much of his gender identity disorder should we regard as the patient's wishful and defensive attempts to negotiate various needs and conflicts? How much of the gender identity disorder has been perpetrated on the patient, so to speak, and how much has been chosen by the patient? For example, elsewhere (1992, p. 262) Coates writes that "it was *his* invention to become a girl". So I assume there is tension in Coates's efforts to give priority to trauma yet somehow to reconcile trauma with wish, need, and defense. Similarly, therapists and their patients fear that attention to wish, need, and defense may excuse trauma. Not so long ago, rape could be dismissed as if the woman had brought the trauma on herself. Patients who have been traumatized commonly fear that any attention by the therapist to their own wishful motivations makes them vulnerable to repetition of their trauma, now by impingement on them of the therapist's own needs.

We could play out two very different sequences for the development of the child's gender identity disorder. In the first sequence, imagine that: 1) the mother wants to destroy the son's separateness and masculinity; 2) the mother wants the son to be a female/male part of herself; 3) the son denies the mother's destructiveness and instead *wishes* to become female; 4) becoming female becomes sexually exciting for the son. In the second sequence, imagine that: 1) the son wants to become female and to be fused with mother; 2) this feminine transformation becomes pleasurable, soothing, even sensually exciting; 3) the son defends himself partially by believing that his own wish for feminine transformation has been imposed upon him by his mother and that this is her wish rather than his own wish. I suspect that each sequence complements the other and that the therapeutic task is to assess the relative contributions of trauma and conflict to the fantasied gender transformation.

Let me give a literary example from Ernest Hemingway's *The Garden of Eden*[1] (see also Coen 1994a). David, the the novel's central

---

[1]Citations will be from the 1986 Charles Scribners' Sons (New York) edition.

character, is a creative writer who is infatuated by Catherine, his destructive androgynous lover. Catherine wants not only to play at being David's boy twin, as she claims. She relishes dominating him, making him feminine, passive, and submissive, as in her wanting to penetrate him anally. Envying his creativity, she attempts to destroy it by taking him away from his writing, devaluing and humiliating his pleasure in his abilities and accomplishments. She actually burns his writing. Instead of feeling destructive rage toward Catherine, David obliterates his feelings in alcohol or sexual excitement. Hemingway captures very well how intoxication with excitement conceals humiliation, hurt, and rage.

David seems uncertain whether he enjoys Catherine's feminizing him. He seems ambivalent about wishes to surrender to her domination, to have her take him over. However, it is not clear, in his conflicted wish for surrender, that what he primarily *wants* is to be turned into a woman. He seems to patch over this doubt by attempting to persuade himself that he actually *enjoys* and is excited by Catherine's feminine transformation of him. Catherine protests repeatedly that this desire for feminization does not belong only to her, that David also wants to be feminized. But this reads like Catherine's attempt to brainwash him.

At the beginning of *The Garden of Eden*, Catherine announces in a sexualized way her destructive aim toward David; she teases and excites David about what she will do to him. For example: "I'm the destructive type," she said. "And I'm going to destroy you. They'll put a plaque up on the wall of the building outside the room. I'm going to wake up in the night and do something to you that you've never even heard of or imagined. I was going to last night but I was too sleepy." David: "You're too sleepy to be dangerous." Catherine: "Don't lull yourself into any false security. Oh darling let's have it hurry up and be lunch time" (p. 5). Will she harm him or will she please and excite him, as she introduces him to exotic, forbidden pleasures?

In this perverse tension, one defensively insists that he desires what the other will do to him whether he actually wishes it or not. During childhood, such perverse tension recreates the child's helplessness and passivity with a destructive parent; now, however, the parent's destructive intrusion is partly erotized and desired. As a result the child's, and later the patient's, rage can be calmed, at least so long as he remains addicted to such perverse play. Only within the illusion that both partners enjoy the domination, humiliation, and destructive robbery of one of them is the child/patient's rage eased. Since the child/patient's rage continues to endanger the vitally needed relationship with the other [parent/lover/therapist], such exciting perverse transformations become addictive, needing to be endlessly repeated. Of course, the balance between rage and destructiveness in oneself and in the other will vary with each couple considered. But we begin with perverse defense against acknowledgment of rage at the other's [parent's] destructiveness (see Chapter 5). In an intensive treatment, we would then proceed to help our patient move toward full ownership of his rage and destructiveness, without projection and justification because of past trauma.

By perverse use of another person, I (Coen 1992) mean that one engages another sexually so as to provide essential defensive reassurance against certain basic dangers that cannot be managed alone. Perverse object relations involve exploitation, extractiveness, and destructiveness with the partner, whose own separate needs and identity are, to a degree, obliterated in the service of the patient's own urgent defensive requirements. Although I think the term "perverse" captures well the qualities it is used to describe, there is, of course, the risk that "perverse" can be used to condemn rather than to understand (see Chapter 5). Better that we all acknowledge our own perverse aspects rather than try to get rid of them by putting them into others, who we then insist are different from ourselves.

Coates describes a *continuum* in the imitative behavior of boys with gender identity disorder from attempts to understand mother's incomprehensible affects to the full wish to transform oneself into the mother as woman. This is where trauma, wish, and conflict all come together. So we are offered multiple meanings of Colin's imitative identification with his mother: 1) to understand the incomprehensible; 2) to find ways to connect with his needy, vulnerable, depressed, hate-filled mother; 3) to heal her by his becoming her female child; 4) to protect against need, change, loss, and attack by the mother via the illusion that he is now his own mother.

Colin's crossdressing and "making angry eyes" usually occurred in front of a mirror. One of his drawings described a menacing woman reaching out of a mirror to choke another female figure. Did Colin (and other neglected and traumatized children) look at himself (themselves) in the mirror more than the ordinary child? Paulina Kernberg (1984) has described the child's search in the mirror for the mother. I wondered how much of Colin's mirror gazing related to seeking visual (and other) affirmation of himself, affirmation that he could not get sufficiently from his mother. This draws on Winnicott's (1967) notion of "*getting* the mirror to notice and approve."

I believe that mirror play is a creative means throughout life for mastering multiple conflicts via the dynamic tension that the mirror image is both self and other (mother), together with the illusion that one can transform these mirror-images of self and other (Bradlow and Coen 1984, Coen 1981, Coen and Bradlow 1985). Further, pleasurable sensual feeling during mirror play helps to make more vivid and credible these transformations of mirror images. As a result, masturbation, sometimes before a mirror, becomes an arena in which to effect such illusory transformation of dangerous images of self and other. Fantasies of the mother's (or later the therapist's) benign protective presence in the mirror may help to reduce the terror of examining threatening aspects of self and other within the mirror. However, this is exactly what Colin lacks: a comforting and containing mother-in-the-mirror who can help him to process affects and experiences for which he is developmentally unprepared and by which he is traumatically overwhelmed.

We can easily imagine that Colin attempts in his mirror play to provide himself with the mother that he and his own mother lack. In his mirror play, Colin can attempt to change places with the angry destructive aspects of his mother and himself. Bad and good aspects of self and other are easily interchangeable during this mirror play, so that they can seem not to be *permanently* part of self or other. We are told that in her dissociated rage-filled attacks on Colin, the mother stared into his eyes. Into whom was she looking? Many factors contribute to the mother's rage. She can want to murder Colin, who intrudes his own needs into her; or to murder her own mother, who abandoned her and whom she still needs; or to murder her father, who neglected her during her adolescence or who perhaps wanted her to be a boy-girl; or to murder the brother who stole the mother's love; or to murder the other brothers who were catered to; or even to murder the hate-filled, murderous part of herself. Perhaps in Colin's splitting of the mother into idealized and destructive parts and his initial efforts to identify only with the idealized mother, he summons the good mother in the mirror to help manage the bad mother and bad self, for both himself and his mother. In his attempt to rescue and heal his mother, he needs to help contain mother's and his own badness and to persuade her that she is good rather than bad. Coates's clinical material shows Colin's combined efforts at interpersonal repair and intrapsychic defense.

I was struck by Coates's belief that the mother's ability to remember and to integrate her destructive rage at Colin allowed him to diminish his gender transformation and to tolerate his own aggression. Coates suggests that Colin needed his mother to be able to tolerate her destructiveness toward him *and* to acknowledge its effects on him in order to heal the bond between them and to contain Colin's aggression toward her. Once the mother–child bond is restored, the mother needs to regain her role as the constructive container and transformer of the child's unbearable affects. For all these many reasons, as the mother reclaims her mothering role, the child seems less in need of pretending before the mirror that he is his own mother.

Coates understands Colin's "story" as aiming toward fusion with the mother and destruction of her as a separate person. I wonder whether this reading suggests that Colin has grasped his mother's wishes to destroy him as a·separate person, so that he vengefully seeks to do the same to her? Or does he want to become the mother so that she cannot destroy, abandon, neglect, or intrude upon him? Here, through the fantasy of having become the mother and so immune to her destructiveness, he may wish to protect against the many dangerous vicissitudes in the maternal relationship. A very schizoid patient of mine responded, when we explored his fears and wishes for fusion, that if he became his mother or got inside her, he would be safe. Since his mother would not want to hurt herself, she would not hurt him (see Coen 1992).

As Colin began to tolerate his rage and destructiveness toward his mother, he pictured severing a woman's head at the neck. Coates notes that this destructiveness was not fully owned by the child. Indeed, we don't know how successful Colin could become at bearing responsibility for his rage and destructiveness. We can imagine that his attack on a woman's neck reverses the attacks on his neck that his mother actually made. Can we imagine further that wishes to attack and sever a woman's head represent rage-filled, wishful attempts to get rid of what has been wrong in mother's head: her depression, destructiveness toward her child, and misuse of him? Does he now understand how disturbed his mother's head has been? I wonder how much difficulty he will have with mastering his enormous rage at his mother. I wonder how much his relationships, especially with women, will be deformed by his rage and destructiveness and by his rigid needs to contain and transform these dangerous angry feelings.

My schizoid patient who discovered that he wished to get inside his mother to protect himself from her attacks had masturbatory fantasies of strangling women. To his fantasies of strangling women, he associated wishes to shut them up and make them helpless to harm him. Then he could do as he pleased with them, even kill them. He was terrified that he could or would actually destroy his vulnerable mother or me in the transference. Whenever he was very angry with me, he would then try to heal me. He connected his fantasies of strangling women to traumatic experiences with his mother in which he felt taunted, humiliated, sexually excited, and enraged. Painfully, he recalled at age sixteen, mother, drunk, had fought with the entire family, taunting father for not being a man, calling him a "fairy." Removing her blouse and bra, mother had stood, bare-breasted, in front of their home, defying father and patient to stop her, inviting sexual attack from "anyone man enough to handle her." He could feel how much he wanted to go at his mother, to teach her a lesson, to make her behave herself. She should act like a normal mother, who would not humiliate and attack his father or him. He also wanted to possess this wild sexual animal of a mother. He wanted to shut her up, stop her from saying all those horrible things, as he could now feel in his masturbatory fantasies of strangling women by squeezing their necks. He wanted to destroy mother (women) while also enjoying her body as he pleased. So, frightened by the intensity of his sexual sadism, my patient rapidly resumed his defensive posture, feeling anxious, insecure, vulnerable, his aggression again projected onto others.

Coates wonders whether Colin will elaborate wishes to rescue troubled women into sexual scripts, and she wonders what will become of the somatic feelings he experiences in his neck. Here I imagine she is concerned, perhaps not fully consciously, with Colin's future rage and destructiveness. Indeed, what becomes of the rage and destructiveness in the child toward the destructive, intrusive, symbiotic mother and of his vulnerability to and terror of loss and abandonment? How much can the child master his rage and vulnerability to loss and abandonment, rather than continue to transform himself into the mother, or to seek her illusory presence, especially sexually? What allows one to relinquish this driven need for the other, so as instead to rely on oneself, able now to trust one's own internal contents with less terror of one's destructiveness?

What differentiates gender identity disorder from other cases of significant interference with separation-individuation without gender identity disorder? Many boys want to cling to symbiotic attachment with the mother, imitate her, play at being her, feel connected to her, so as to ward off fears of loss and destruction. Or, they emphasize passivity, helplessness, and an unmasculine stance to ward off anger, wishes to separate from mother, competitiveness, and feared retaliation and punishment from both parents. And yet this latter group do not feel strongly that they are feminine, although they are clearly in conflict about being masculine. Perhaps they wish less strongly to be a woman than primarily wish to remain connected with mother. I wonder how much mother and father have to hate and want to destroy their son's masculine identity for gender identity disorder to develop. In Coates's case of Colin, the mother's destructiveness toward the child's masculinity, body, separate self, and separate needs stand out. More than the gender identity disorder, I would emphasize this child's early traumatization and subsequent need to manage traumatically overwhelming affects, especially rage and destructiveness, in mother and in himself. I agree with Coates that the mother's having become capable of responsibly acknowledging her destructiveness toward her son played a crucial role in allowing him to tolerate his rage toward her. Instead of surrendering to his trauma, he could now rage against it, reclaiming himself as a separate person with a separate gender. Now his needs and feelings could become legitimate, even more important than his mother's.

Once the mother could acknowledge that she had violated her son's legitimate needs, usurping the mother–child relationship for her own needs, and destroying her son's separateness and masculinity, he could begin to be freed from their conjoint defensive denial. Now he could liberate himself from the wish to surrender to mother as her female child to rage instead against what had been forced upon him. Or, at least he could rage against what he had felt forced to comply with because of his enormous insecurity in the mother–child relationship. It is so common for traumatized patients to collude in denial with the traumatizing parent; so these patients continue to respond with disbelief to the perception that someone wants to hurt them. Instead, they imagine that the other person's angry critical attack is intended as help or will somehow be magically transformed into something good. Then such traumatized patients, much to their own detriment, keep repeating their early traumatization, since they do not protect themselves against or even cultivate others' destructiveness.

To change, they would have to do what Colin struggled to do, to responsibly bear their perceptions of a parent as destructive together with their concomitant hatred. This entails, for the vulnerable child self, terror of the parent destroying the child or of the child wishing to destroy the hurtful aspect of the parent. For many patients this is too terrifying to imagine, so that instead they preserve their collusion with the parent's denial. It is helpful to encourage traumatized patients to imagine themselves in the role of the destructive parent who wants to attack them. If the patient can have empathy for the destructive parent so as to sample the parent's rage at oneself, then it may become tolerable to feel one's own disappointment, hurt, sadness, and rage toward the destructive parent.

Beatrice Beebe presented "Brief Mother–Infant Treatment Using Psychoanalytically Informed Video Microanalysis: Integrating Procedural and Declarative Processing" to the Association for Psychoanalytic Medicine in 2000. I'm impressed by the power of Beebe's video microanalysis to observe, understand, and treat mother/ infant pairs, to focus maternal impingement, withdrawal, or unresponsiveness. Beebe is persuasive that self- and interactive regulation develop in tandem through each partner's capacities and deficiencies. Beebe and her collaborators (Beebe and Lachmann 1998, Kiersky and Beebe 1994, Lachmann and Beebe 1996) in treating adults, draw heavily on the model that excessive self-soothing occurs when the mother/infant dyad cannot adequately regulate their interaction. They expect more difficult traumatized patients to doubt and mistrust their therapists' abilities to help them manage their feelings. Hence such patients remain withdrawn, detached, distant, insistent on comforting and providing for themselves. Beebe and her collaborators believe that they can engage mistrustful, schizoid patients more effectively by constructing and interpreting model scenes of early maternal failure at affect regulation with the very young child than with our usual later developmental pictures. Such images of maternal impingement, unavailability, or unresponsiveness to the very young child's emotional needs are powerfully evocative. Although I've certainly considered affect intolerance as played out between patients and their parents, I hadn't previously tried to imagine such parental failure to help *very young children* develop their own capacities to regulate themselves affectively (notice the change from Chapters 2, 5, and 6 to Chapter 7). I'd thought of one's sense of omnipotent destructiveness as derived from the difficulties for both older child and parent in tolerating certain dangerous affects, like anger, as the child's sense that the parent is too threatened by the child's anger. *Now* I would imagine the *very young angry child* needs to be calmed/ regulated by the mother before he feels overwhelmed by his feelings (cf. Krystal 1978a for the older child, and Chapter 2) so he doesn't develop a sense of monstrous destructiveness. More broadly, Beebe shows us very young children being helped, through interactive regulation with the mother, to develop beginning confidence and competence in affect tolerance and management.

Beebe emphasizes an optimum range of interaction between mother and infant, neither too much nor too little. Drawing on a dynamic systems model (Sander 1977), she describes the secure mother/infant pair as flexibly related to each other rather than vigilantly and rigidly bound together, avoidantly disconnected, or attached in a disorganized way. The secure mother/infant pair can come together and go apart comfortably. Mother/infant pairs that are too concerned with interactive regulation turn out to be neither secure in themselves nor in their relatedness. These findings are now well documented by child development research (e.g., see Beebe and Lachmann 1994, Beebe and Lachmann 1998, Beebe, Jaffe, and Lachmann 1992, Beebe, Lachmann, and Jaffe 1997, Beebe et al. in press, Hesse and Main 2000, Main 2000). Beebe's video presentation dramatically showed failure of interactive affective regulation between the mother/ infant couple.

Especially impressive were Beebe's examples of clinical interventions to assist mothers in attuning the levels of their responsiveness to their infants. These mothers needed help not to intrusively overwhelm or (depressively) understimulate their infants. They needed to be taught to aim to match their infants' rhythms, movements, moods, and sounds, allowing the infants to come closer as well as to move away. To do so, these mothers needed to responsibly acknowledge and interrupt their misidentification of the present mother/infant couple with their own relationship with their mothers. The mothers who turned to Beebe for help with their infants were deeply troubled about what was wrong and very receptive to Beebe's help. Viewing themselves with their infants on videotape in Beebe's accepting presence enabled these mothers to connect the problems in their present mothering with problems in the mothering they had received. Previous psychotherapy, the urgent need to repair the disrupted mother/infant unit, and Beebe's very accepting attitude all facilitated rapid modification of the mother/infant relatedness. Although, as Robert Michels noted from the audience, Beebe has not yet documented how long such improvement lasts, in Beebe's hands this technique of mother/infant therapy seems very helpful. Applications of aspects of these models to adult treatment, with full recognition of the differences between mother with infant and therapist with adult patient, are also valuable and will be my focus here.

There are applications to be drawn to adult treatment from what has been learned from adult attachment interviews, which are used to assess styles of attachment (Main 2000). Those whose attachment style is classified as secure-autonomous are able to think about themselves and to collaborate with an interviewer. This contrasts with those who instead are "fixed upon 'getting through' the interview rather than collaborating in the task of recalling and reflecting upon childhood feelings and experiences" (Main 2000, p. 1086). Such dismissing interviewees are considered as dismissing (avoidant) of attachment. A preoccupied interviewee "violates . . . the maxims of collaboration: namely, *quantity, relevance,* and *manner* . . . Once launched upon attempts to describe her experiences, she seems to focus upon them so persistently, albeit confusedly, that she cannot simultaneously maintain collaborative discourse" (Main 2000, p. 1087). Main's emphasis on the form rather than the content of such interviews is relevant to adult treatment. I would not seek to merely classify a patient's attachment status but to work toward understanding problems in preserving a collaborative focus in treatment. Especially prominent here are needs to flee rather than seek help from the other and difficulty with tolerating and integrating contradictory feelings towards the other without becoming overwhelmed and confused. More difficult patients will tend not to preserve a collaborative focus in treatment. Drawing on models of problematic attachment can help us to grasp why it is so difficult to understand our more difficult patients, who simultaneously do and do not want our help.

I imagine that if Beatrice Beebe were to videotape adult treatments to assist therapists to view themselves with their patients, most therapists would be able to newly see aspects of what was transpiring between themselves and their patients. Here too, therapists in Beebe's accepting presence, availing themselves of their own personal treatment experiences and of their need to repair disruptions with their patients, would be able to recognize how their own needs were now interfering with their patients' needs. Of course, this is the model of self-examination, consultation with a colleague, or presentation to a peer group. The rapid efficacy of mother/infant therapy reminds us of the value of seeking help from others about difficult treatments because our own needs can so easily interfere with our attention to our patients' needs. Much of what allows us access to the interference of our own needs as we treat others comes from our own personal treatments that have opened up our tolerance of the childlike, irrational, demanding aspects of ourselves in relation to others. I cannot imagine how I could work with my more difficult patients had I not had my own personal analyses; I could never have tolerated, in them and in myself, what they continue to find so unbearable. Without access to the repudiated aspects of ourselves not only can we not assist our patients to reclaim repudiated aspects of themselves but we cannot monitor ourselves in relation to our patients. So, I find it helpful to imagine Beatrice Beebe filming my difficult treatments and then enabling me to see what had led to the disruption between my patient and me.

Beebe's presentation was the third paper on child research that I have discussed at the Association for Psychoanalytic Medicine (besides work by Paulina Kernberg and Susan Coates). However, I confess that I have not, but should have had, child analytic training. I was especially delighted at the end of a two-day workshop on applications of child analytic technique to adult analysis at the American Psychoanalytic Association some years ago that the others, all Philadelphia-trained child analysts, thought that I too was a child analyst. They thought so despite my repeated questioning why the analyst should not just *talk* about what an adult patient, whose mother had died when she was 15 months old, needed and wanted from the analyst, rather than actually provide it, as if she really were a developmentally arrested child. They treated my questions with respect and concern, without disdain, as we considered the pros and cons of an approach they all shared that was foreign to me. So perhaps the hallmark of child analytic training is heightened empathy and acceptance of others. If so, then we all need *some* immersion in child analytic training or at least more exposure to work such as Beebe's. I'm currently relishing the opportunity to listen to detailed four-time-per-week analytic process material of a very young child in my peer supervision study group. I especially value the opportunity to enhance my empathic skills by trying to feel and imagine my way into this young child's affective experience.

When I first read a draft of Beebe's work, I found myself thinking about rhythmic patterns between Professor N., a narcissistic patient, and me. Indeed, I later found such concern with matching adult patients' rhythms the most novel application to adult treatment by Beebe and her collaborators. When Professor N. would retreat behind his narcissistic protections, tuning out and dismissing what had previously touched him a little, I'd often feel disappointed and annoyed, as if we were writing on water. I'd been acutely aware of Professor N.'s sensitivity to feeling controlled and intruded upon, resentfully refusing to provide what he thought I wanted from him. Of course, I talked with him about the awfulness of his expectation that the only way I'd have any interest in him would be if he fulfilled my needs of him. Reading Beebe's draft got me thinking that his narcissistic retreat led to my interpretive pursuit of him, not quite a dodge-and-chase sequence, but one he had to experience as my intrusion into his space.   .

Indeed, I expect that good clinical writing will have such an effect on me, as I make it my own and apply it to what I'm currently finding difficult in my work with more challenging patients. My favorite clinical papers are those, which when I reread them, no matter how many times, help me to see something new with a patient I am finding difficult. For example, in teaching psychopathology to candidates, I enjoy their reading Betty Joseph's (1983) paper, "On understanding and not understanding." With each rereading, I imagine Betty Joseph newly saying to me, "Can't you *now* see what your patient can't bear to have you and he understand?"

I wondered whether Professor N. and I might do better if I didn't intrude on him so often to interpret that he'd again withdrawn narcissistically. No matter how I'd word my interpretation, he'd hear me as the critical parent, dissatisfied with his functioning on my couch. Often, of course, he was right about me. Other times, I certainly could remain empathic with his fearful hesitation to make use of me. Now I imagined Beatrice Beebe was with us, observing, filming our interaction. I slowed down, listening to Beatrice Beebe's mellifluous tones in my head, trying to wait for my patient to approach me again before I intervened. When he did speak, I tried to respond appreciatively to his again making himself available rather than comment on his retreat. I tried harder than I had done previously not to impinge on him, to follow his lead rather than my own. For a week, I liked how we were with each other, as I waited for Professor N. to approach me, trying hard not to expect anything of him. This certainly was not the first time we'd enjoyed being with each other. But our new-found pleasurable way of being with each other ran dry. Perhaps Beatrice Beebe hadn't gone on speaking loudly enough inside my head.

Professor N. didn't really seem to care about what we'd done differently, even that we'd both enjoyed our experience together. Once more, he had gone back inside himself. We could talk about his fear of allowing himself to care about what had been good between us, which he'd extinguished. Once more it felt like there was nothing he wanted from me, nothing good he had ever gotten from me. I had to feel for myself, and to bear for Professor N., the terror of being vulnerable in needing me that fueled his aloofness, detachment, control, rejection, arrogance, and negativism. I had to respect his need for detachment, distance, control, and self-sufficiency. Sometimes, we could explore how easily he felt impinged upon by me. I imagined more than I had previously how he'd had to cope with his intrusively demanding mother throughout his entire childhood, not just during his infancy. I think that whatever helps a therapist preserve or restore his empathic appreciation of his patient's terror in the therapeutic situation is valuable. Beatrice Beebe helped me to do so with Professor N., as I imagined his need to protect himself from maternal impingement now *by me*.

So, I also believe that when I internalize certain accepting women, like Beatrice Beebe or Betty Joseph, I feel better contained so that I can then become more patient, tolerant, and focused on my patients' difficulties. But that's not all! Beebe's model of infant-mother interaction helps me to feel my way into what certain more difficult patients do and don't need from me. I think Beebe has brought from her research to adult treatment heightened sensitivity to certain important themes that play out *throughout* the life cycle. I'd object to too literal attempts to translate infant–mother interaction into the therapeutic situation. But I certainly would encourage all of us to be acutely aware of how easily we may impinge upon our patients with our needs, wishes, expectations, and priorities.

I'm less convinced than Beebe or than Aron and Bushra (1998) that the therapeutic couple mutually regulate each other's affect states, as do infant and mother. However, I'm vitally interested in how each therapeutic partner affects the other's ease and comfort and how each can interfere with the other's ability to fully experience dangerous affects. I'm concerned with how therapists' discomfort with passion exacerbates patients' affect intolerance. I've come to believe that in the face of the affect intolerance of our most difficult patients, the therapist must feel and contain the affect(s) that the patient dreads, over a prolonged time, before the therapist will be able to find creative ways to return these feelings in metabolized form to such patients (see Chapter 7). I now believe the therapist needs to feel for, and with, those of his patients who are terrified to feel more directly for themselves. Thereby, the therapist can remain empathic with the patient's affective terrors and rigorous needs for protection, so as to make the therapeutic situation viable for both partners. I would want to address whatever has led the patient, from any developmental level, to fear experiencing these affects.

I've been treating a number of patients, like Professor N., who experienced themselves as having been intruded upon by a parent, usually the mother, during childhood. I have learned to become exquisitely attuned to these patients' extreme sensitivity to intruding my own feelings, expectations, and needs on them. Sixteen years earlier, in discussing work by Paulina Kernberg at the Association for Psychoanalytic Medicine, I learned that the therapist of a child who has been intruded upon needs to be exceptionally careful not to introduce anything other than what the child brings to the treatment. I still had to relearn this affectively in the room with my own adult patients. I take for granted that such patients and I will become caught up in repeating invasion and undermining of the other, as we alternate roles. Much of the analysis of my patient's mistrust, in contrast to other patients' ability to explore their mistrust primarily as their own internal problem, occurs as he repeatedly confronts his sensitivity to my intrusion, dismissal, and obliteration of his perceptions, feelings, and needs. To the degree that I'm able to encourage him to examine what I've done with him, without becoming defensive, critical, or rejecting, he sees me as sharply different from his intrusive parent. But so long as he needs to hate and attack me as the bad, deficient, intrusive parent, neither of us *should* seek to escape this repetition, much as both of us may very much wish to do so.

Freud would have liked the frequency of the word *overstimulation* in Beebe's work as used to describe the infant's affective response to himself and to his mother. That is, a word count of Beebe's writings would probably reveal that *overstimulation* is one of the most frequently recurring terms. But I wonder which affects or proto-affects are overly stimulating or disturbing so that they need to be calmed and contained. Rather than focus on levels of arousal and stimulation, I wonder about the young child's need to manage or regulate specific difficult affects within herself (precursors of anger and disappointment at mother's impingement, unavailability, unresponsiveness, lack of empathic attunement), and between her and the other (mother's anxiety, depression, anger). To my mind, restricting our focus to levels of arousal and stimulation seems overly physiological, insufficiently psychological, as compared with consideration of specific affects or proto-affects. But we need more data on how early we can begin to differentiate the precursors of discrete affects in very young children.

I imagine the young child's affective reaction to perceptions of mother's, or father's, rage. I think of guilty accounts by several of my patients of shaking their newborn child before my patients were able to feel their enraged wish to kill their baby. Once my patients could feel their rage, then they could stop themselves, tell themselves they needed to contain their rage until the following day when they could talk to me. What did these young children feel when their parents wanted to shake them to death? At what age do young children feel terror as they experience their parents as hating and wanting to destroy them, when the parents see these children as bad, destructive, or persecutory? What are the precursors of terror, the affective building blocks from which the young child learns to dread his parents' affects and behavior with him?

At the other pole, Adrienne Harris (1997) would have Beebe put "jouissance" into her view of the child's experience of the mother. How can we say no to delight? I'm delighted that pleasure has been restored to attachment theory by Stern (1990), Schore (1994), and Eagle (1995), that we're not content that very young infants' levels of arousal merely be optimum. Better that we put pleasure, joy, exuberance, love back into what we expect between mothers and their infants. Shouldn't the potential for passion already begin in infancy? I'm delighted with what I've learned from Beatrice Beebe, Susan Coates, and from other infant researchers and attachment theorists, such as Stern, Fonagy and his collaborators, Schore, Eagle, and many others. In the future, I'd want to learn more from them about the finer shadings of proto-affects in the very young child. In Chapter 7, I draw on applications of this work to adult treatment by Killingmo, Tähkä, Settlage, Akhtar, and D. Silverman.

11

The Pleasures and Pitfalls of Interpretation

T he death of Erik Erikson in 1993 invited clinicians to begin to assess the impact of his contributions to our field, which many believe has been insufficiently acknowledged. Traditional psychoanalysts have reflected a similar ambivalence toward Erikson as he seemed to have shown toward us. I had an even more personal reason for this study: the death the same year of Paul Bradlow, my teacher, supervisor, and friend, who introduced me to Erikson's dream specimen paper, to the communicative functions of dreams, and to the research study of the manifest content of dreams (Bradlow 1971, 1973, 1974, Bradlow and Coen 1975, Coen and Bradlow 1985). My early reading of Erikson, especially his dream specimen paper and his review of the Freud–Fliess letters the following year (1955), helped me to open my own passions for imaginative resonance and play with the interpersonal dimensions of intensive treatment, of dreams, and of literary texts. This chapter is confined to these two papers of Erikson's.

I especially valued his creative exuberance in arguing against premature closure, in opening up multiple meanings for dreams and for texts that reach beyond the obvious, the narrow, the expected. What is truly deep may only *seem* superficial; what is right in front of us should be questioned rather than rejected. Erikson precedes Lacan (1956), Derrida (1975), and many others (e.g., see *The Purloined Poe*,

1988, ed. Muller and Richardson) who will draw upon Poe's 1844 story, "The Purloined Letter," to show that the seemingly obvious may not be so at all. This chapter will emphasize that original clinical thinkers, such as Freud and Erikson, turn our theory upon itself in order to get us to acknowledge that we cannot know what we think we know. Self-reflexive questioning is now pursued in most academic disciplines (see, e.g., Eagleton 1986, 1990, Scott 1988). By engaging his texts, his patients, and his readers in creative, subjective play and interplay, Erikson helps us to read and work with more spontaneity and pleasure.

We hope that innovative therapists may have sufficient access to their own deeper feelings and needs so that such self-questioning can lead to new discovery. At the least, the interpreter's ability to share with others his questioning of himself and his theories allows others personal access to him and to his theories (see Chapter 9). I believe that such personal connection with the interpreter and his work helps to render his ideas vivid, meaningful, and accessible. If an author refuses us some access to the workings of his mind, we may have little desire to welcome him and his ideas into our hearts and minds.

For example, at a recent clinical workshop, a number of us were intrigued by our guest's masterful approach to clinical material. We kept pressing her to share with us how she knew what she asserted until, at long last, she admitted, to our relief and delight, that what she drew upon most were her own feelings, hunches, and personal clinical experience. Now indeed we could share with her the clinical relevance of her own personal (affective) experience and of the therapeutic reasoning that covered and derived from what she felt. By allowing us access to a bit of her inner world, she enabled us to follow her personal and therapeutic path toward clinical understanding. In sharp contrast to this group experience was another with a distinguished scholar who would not share with us anything personal about his readings of the text under discussion or about how he constructed his critical theories. Without some bits of "clinical context," something psychological in the interpreter as well as in his reading of the text, we were barred from a meaningful connection with the interpreter and with his theories.

Our field, like every other discipline, needs those who will question what we seek to clutch in our anxiety and uncertainty. In contrast to the rigidity and restraint of much of American psychoanalysis in the 1950s, say as described at the Eissler parameter panel at the American Psychoanalytic Association meetings (Panel 1994), rereading Erikson's dream specimen paper now is refreshing. Erikson brings the surface of dreams, writing, play, and imagination passionately to life. What is fresh and exciting for me in Erikson's paper is his imaginative play with his materials: Freud's letters, dreams, and texts and Erikson's own patient's dream and his investigation of how we represent conflict in dreams. He describes Freud's conflicts about creative discovery as he enacts his own scene of creatively revising Freud's discovery of systematic dream interpretation. Erikson writes at his best both as a clinical investigator and literary critic as he seeks to explore the meanings of dream texts.

Erikson allows himself and encourages us as readers to participate with him in a creative interpretive reading of Freud's early acts of psychoanalytic creation. Emphasizing translation, transference, interpersonal communication and involvement, Erikson gets himself, his readers, and Freud interconnected in enthusiastic reading of Freud's early writing. Of course, Erikson's emotionally involved readings of Freud have to be subjective, involving Erikson in highly personal interpretation of Freud. But I think for 1954 that is wonderfully exciting. Perhaps Erikson, like the rest of us, is using Freud's conflicts with creativity to engage his own struggles; hence, Erikson's almost joyous celebration of creativity.

A year later in his review of the Freud–Fliess letters, Erikson (1955) emphasizes transference between writer and reader more explicitly. He focuses skillfully on the psychology of interaction between letter writers as he assesses their fervent interchanges as a "rituel à deux." Correspondence, according to Erikson (1955, p. 2), "develops and cultivates particular levels of mood, selected confessions, and habitual admissions, it is apt to indulge in plaintive comparison with the unseen recipient's person or fate, and in expressions of hopes for a reunion; often it invites some kind of mutual *correspondence-transference*" (emphasis added).

Erikson encourages passionate exchange between the child and adult within one's own mind, between patient and therapist, and between writer and reader. In other words, he is linking intrapsychic and interpersonal in ways that feel surprising for 1954–1955. In his writing, Erikson seems to be describing and enacting another antinomy about openness versus restraint. Erikson does well to confront us, clinicians of the 1950's and of the new millenium, with the anxiety-relieving value of dogmatic certainty. Of course, he himself will have to struggle in his paper, as we all must do, with this tension between openness and closure.

Mautner (1991, p. 278) criticized Erikson's essay as "*distracted by a desire to explore his own theory of dreams . . . rather than concentrating on the Irma dream itself* [emphasis added]. I disagree. Even Mautner's interesting interpretation of Freud's Irma dream as related to childhood sexual aggression against Freud's sister, Anna, shows this same inescapable subjective interest within the author's focus. Mautner's argument (objectively) hinges on the connection of the Irma dream with the "Dream of the Botanical Monograph" in the original 1900 German edition of the *Dreambook*. I think it is better that we acknowledge our own subjective wishes to transform, translate, rob, and capture as we reinterpret our heroes' work.

The literary critic Murray Schwartz (1975) specifically chose Erikson's dream specimen paper as a psychoanalytic link with literary critical writing. Interpretation is formed by the author's (Schwartz, 1975, p. 763) "actively mixing himself with his subject" not by "the elimination of 'irrelevant' subjective responses and ideas." For Schwartz, Erikson encourages a "process of interplay" within a subjective, emotional literary relationship involving reader and writer. I thoroughly agree with Schwartz's view. This is the important link Erikson offers between reading and interpreting literary and dream texts through intimate interpersonal resonance between author (of literary or dream text) and interpreter. Here, Erikson is way ahead of his time as a reader-response critic and as a clinician working at the edge of a model of mutual interpenetration between the therapeutic couple that leads to the conjoint creation of meanings. Opening up resonance and exploration of communication and transference between dreamer or author and therapist or reader brings therapy and reading vividly to life. Although Erikson does not explicitly use the language of countertransference, then beginning in the 1950s to be explored constructively (see Chapter 7), he helps to move us into this same arena by his focus on understanding interpersonal experience in analyzing and in reading.

When I listen to a patient's dream or read a novel or even when I read Freud, I aim to reverberate with my own personal fantasies, images, longings, and feelings. I then struggle to sort out which of these responses have to do primarily with my patient (or text) and which are idiosyncratic to me. Then I try to determine how to use my fantasy responses to advance my patient's treatment. When I do not get carried away into my own reveries and strong feelings, I wonder what is going on between patient (or text) and me that is interfering. As I work with patients, I especially enjoy resampling bits of my own passions. It is a pleasure to be able to help a patient with something I have been able to master.

Erikson's paper shows a striking contrast between playful, excited, expansive, triumphant writing and a much more restrained, slower, tight, quasi-scientific presentation that includes lists, tables, charts, subsections, and outlines. For example, Erikson introduces the Irma dream by telling us that it "may, in fact, carry the historical burden of being *dreamed in order to be analyzed, and analyzed in order to fulfill a very special fate*" (p. 8, my italics). A few lines later, writing about Breuer and Freud, Erikson writes: "The junior worker felt increasingly committed to these ideas; he had begun to feel, with a pride often overshadowed by despair, that he was destined to make a revolutionary discovery *by (I shall let this stand) undreamed-of-means*" (my italics).

Author and reader share an excitement through creative writing about Freud and revising Freud that is soon tempered by much more sober prose. Salman Akhtar, as an editorial reader of the paper that became this chapter, suggested that I consider further the manifest configuration of Erikson's paper as Erikson does with Freud's dream: its length, vast scope, striking language, "terse statements ready to become psychoanalytic aphorisms." An example of the latter is "to reinterpret a dream means to reinterpret the dreamer" (p. 7). And indeed Erikson is reinterpreting Freud, Freud's dream, and Freud's approach to dream interpretation and to psychoanalysis. I think that all of this may point in the same direction: the writer's grand, competitive, offering of himself, his words and his ideas to replace Freud's, while, simultaneously, restraining himself with much more tempered prose.

Erikson suggests that Freud wished to have a dream that he would be able to analyze in detail, that the Irma dream is in fact the fulfillment of such a wish. Erikson argues against "premature closure" in dream understanding in favor of *communication*, receptivity, and responsiveness between the therapeutic couple. He focuses the communicative function of dreams nicely as he points out that the memory of having told a dream "becomes inextricably interwoven with the memory itself" (p. 18). The dream's "style of representation," he argues, is "no mere shell to the kernel, the latent dream" (p. 21). Erikson would unsettle us from the smugness that we do indeed know what is covering what. He connects translation with transfer, noting the difficulties of moving meanings between childhood and adulthood and between patient and therapist. Mahony (1980) will later expand the interconnections of translation, metaphor, and transference as he describes dynamic movement from the unconscious of one person to its preconscious grasp by another person. Such dynamic interaction occurs within the literary encounter among the author's unconscious, the text, and the reader's resonating preconscious apprehension of the text, much as Erikson is doing with Freud (see also Coen 1994a).

While claiming that he is not immediately "'going deeper' than Freud did" (p. 16), Erikson shows how to probe the surface, the manifest content of the dream, in a novel, rich way, as he gives "new depth to the surface" (p. 16). Erikson's analysis of *his* patient's dream is masterful, especially in its focus on language, vision and exhibitionism, sensation, time, motion, light, dark, absence and presence, aloneness or connection with others, and affect. That is, he divides the manifest configuration of the dream into seven areas: verbal, sensory, spatial, temporal, somatic, interpersonal, and affective. He wants us to consider what is present and what is absent within each category, to link the manifest with the latent dream material, and then attempt to understand the latent dream material in relation to the dreamer's life cycle and ego identity. In the section on dream transference, Erikson makes clear that the dreamer, as he dreams, has an audience in mind, Fliess for Freud, the therapist for the patient. This dream audience is the lens through which to understand the dreamer's transferences. At the same time, the dreamer may regard his dream as a "secret love life" (p. 46), a longed-for mother, separate and apart from the therapist—as—audience.

With "the shortest illustration" of a dream from his practice (p. 18), Erikson temporarily upstages Freud's Irma dream. A young woman patient dreamed of the word "S{E}INE," light against a dark background. Erikson plays with "Seine (the river), "sehn" (to see, German), "seine (his, German), "E" first letter in Erik Erikson, "sine" (without, Latin), and finally, "sin." He combines these elements into the rebus, "To see (E) without his . . . . in Paris" (p. 19). We are led to the image of Christ without his loincloth as now transferred onto the therapist, Erikson, as therapeutic savior. And indeed the reader is filled with phallic awe, envy, and admiration at Erikson's lexical and imaginative prowess in deconstructing the manifest content of this dream. Is the author exhibiting himself as a psychoanalytic Christ—savior to the reader as admiring woman? Erikson emphasizes sacrilegious looking, as he demonstrates the meaningfulness of what is absent ("spatial extension, motion, shading, color, sound," [p. 19] and people). What is absent "may shine" (p. 21) nevertheless. What *shines* to this reader is Erikson himself as he plays exuberantly with Freud's dream model. At least, there is striking tension in Erikson's paper between expansive creative revision of Freud and a much more subdued, restrained, plodding, sober presentation. We can speculate that this tension represents Erikson's own conflict about wanting to supplant Freud or that this contrasting writing style is intended to help gain acceptance from Freud's followers as Erikson outshines Freud and then quickly allows himself to fade behind Freud's shadow.

Pulver (1987) has recently reassessed the position of the manifest dream in clinical work. Following Erikson, Pulver focuses closely on what is present and what is absent in the manifest dream, even concluding with an appendix of an Erikson-like table. Pulver argues that we cannot identify a *single* manifest dream apart from how the dream is narrated to another person. He notes that patients may gain conviction about early traumatic experiences when these childhood memories can be recovered from undisguised manifest dream images. Bradlow and I (Bradlow and Coen 1975, Coen and Bradlow 1985) studied manifest dreams containing mirrors as well as the analyst undisguised in the initial dream in psychoanalysis. When looking seems especially dangerous, patients may need to feel the reassuring presence of the therapist more concretely. This may help to differentiate dangerous transference from reality (by trying to see who the therapist really is) and to manage frightening affects and wishes. The manifest dream image of the therapist undisguised or of a mirror, as well as fantasy preoccupation with the therapeutic transference and the therapist, may help to differentiate and modulate dangerous transference and dangerous affects. Unlike Erikson, Bradlow hoped to be able to use very unusual manifest dream elements (murder, incest) reported early in analysis to predict (un)analyzability.

There are many examples in colleagues' writing about the Irma dream of presenting *evidence* that they have drawn from their own connections with Freud's various written statements about himself in different texts or parts of texts. I shall offer two such examples. Without providing evidence, Hartman (1983) regards Freud and Fliess's treatment of Emma Eckstein as a repetition of Freud's and his nephew John's mistreatment of John's younger sister, Pauline. Or Blum (1981, p. 545) presents a lovely interpretation of the chemical formula printed in heavy type in the Irma dream as "the formula for the interpretation of dreams." How do we know this? Blum bypasses such questions of evidence. Although Blum's reading is similar to Erikson's and I like it very much, I want us to acknowledge our own *subjective play* with this material. For example, Mahony (1977) wonders why Freud did not write out the formula that Freud saw in the dream; Mahony suggests that this omission may point to Freud's need for censorship.

I believe we are contending here with the inevitability of subjective interpretation that must, at some point, intersect with what we want to do to the material at hand. We risk closing off meanings if we believe that we are somehow privileged to be able to claim certainty. In writing about Freud, our progenitor, we need to be sufficiently aware of our competitive aims so that we can imagine but not actually pin him down with overly certain interpretive spears. More than most authors who followed him in writing about the Irma dream, Erikson seems implicitly to acknowledge his own competitive agenda with Freud, including his wish to redefine dreaming and dream interpretation as, at least partly, transference-driven ego activity that can be adaptive and transformative. So, from our subjective, playful, creative resonance with patients and texts, we must then argue the relevance of our "evidence" for the tasks of understanding and interpreting. And in both psychoanalytic literary criticism and in the therapeutic situation, the best interpretation is conservative, spare, and elegant when it stays close to the evidence and succeeds in persuading us that the interpreter's understanding is relevant. We are put off by wild interpretation of texts and of patients.

Erikson emphasizes the loving intimacy Freud feels toward his dream and its analysis; this extends all the way to impregnation and conception as Freud creates the psychoanalytic technique of self-analysis. Freud, Erikson suggests, has given birth to psychoanalysis through an incestuous dream woman. Using his own work on gender differences in play styles, Erikson describes the dream's emphasis on phallic investigation. Erikson plays the tension between Freud's becoming his own patient in the Irma dream as a defensive surrender to stronger men against Freud's creative (and triumphant) new step in becoming his own patient so as to explore the human psyche.

When Erikson interprets his own patient's graduation dream from treatment as a tonsure, he is emphasizing the positive aspects of success over negative, destructive concerns. I am skeptical of his contention about this dream. It reads like a reassuring argument that creative success should indeed be accepted by others rather than attacked by them (tonsure versus censure). Erikson contends that his patient preferred interpretation of the therapist's attack rather than of his "infantile wishes to belong to and to believe in organizations providing for collective reassurance against individual anxiety" (p. 40).

In contrast, Erikson interprets Freud's defensive retreats from phallic masculine competition toward dependence on others. Why not similar interpretation here too of the patient's movement from aggressive challenge toward "belonging"? Erikson certainly does discuss conflict in creativity, conflict between multiple identifications and wishes, and especially the phallic-oedipal meanings of unveiling the unknown, that mysterious and forbidden mother. He adds an adaptive perspective to the instinctual and defensive aspects of dreaming and creating. Erikson posits that "at the height of consummation," the creative individual achieves a kind of transcendence in which he is able to integrate paternal, maternal, and infantile identifications, paternal potency, maternal fertility, and "his own reborn ideal identity" (p. 49). Unlike the ordinary person, Erikson believes, the creative individual needs repeatedly to face his late adolescent conflicts through his creative work. I sense a tension here between conflict in creativity and an idealized illusion that creativity should somehow transcend such conflict, at least for a while.

Erikson does not provide reasonable evidence for his arguments for the role of religion in the Irma dream. Indeed he uses his own patient's tonsure dream, information about Freud's religious Czech caretaker from the Freud–Fliess letters, and Freud's B'nai B'rith speech (1926) as if these lent credibility to Erikson's wish to privilege (religious) identity in understanding the Irma dream.

Erikson follows Freud's style of offsetting doubt by assuring the reader of his *certainty* (cf. Mahony 1982, 1986) when he uses Freud's childhood memory of his father's reprimand that he would never amount to anything as related to concerns about feelings of inadequacy in the Irma dream. He continues the same forced indoctrination on the following page as he writes, "It thus becomes *clearer* than ever why Dr. Otto had to take over the severe designation of a dirty little squirt" (p. 42) (my italics). Now Erikson is free to describe a cultural pattern in which fathers' humiliation of their sons leads to Freud's (everyman's) inner tyrant. He continues the same disregard for arguing from evidence as he refers to Freud's conflicted relationship with his one-year-older nephew.

In contrast, Erikson's section on transference in the Irma dream is convincing and imaginative. He extends the idea of Freud's dream discoveries as the forbidden knowledge of women. Earlier, Erikson (p. 37) had focused on Freud's "terrifying discovery" in his investigations, seeing what is not to be seen. Freud, Erikson suggests, has given birth to psychoanalysis through an incestuous dream woman. By translating "Nabel" as the navel of the dream, Erikson connects the examination of women more immediately with confrontation with "the unknown." Erikson refers repeatedly to "unveiling" the mystery of the dream, playing on Freud's metaphor. In describing Fliess as the recipient of both a creative and therapeutic transference, Erikson considers that Freud *invented* the image of Fliess that he needed. He argues that Freud could allow himself to draw on his feminine side in creating as a kind of impregnation, conception, and birth. Erikson can discuss his own ideas of developmental sequence and ego identity as he builds to the climax of his paper, affirming Freud's (and his own) need to investigate alone, to face his own inner terrors, and to commit himself to his work. Erikson optimistically emphasizes the constructive aspects of dreaming, investigation, and creativity.

Later Hartman (1983) will provide an interesting piece from the Freud–Abraham correspondence in which Freud writes that what he kept hidden in the Irma dream was his "sexual megalomania," his wish to have his daughters' three godmothers for himself. Hartman sets the Irma dream temporally in relation to Freud's father becoming ill. His attempt to change the identity of Irma from Emma Eckstein to Anna Hammerschlag Lichtheim misses Mahony's (1977, pp. 122-

123) earlier play with turning Emma into Irma as "Freud's own phonemic 'operation' on the name" in parallel with Fliess's nasal surgery on Emma. Mahony emphasizes the sound "Ir" in Irma as linked with "irr" as in "in error, wrong, delirious, insane." Hartman's revision of Irma's identity does not, however, change much in Erikson's interpretation.

As Freud tells us about wanting his women to yield to him, he does indeed seem to stop short. Freud writes (1900, p. 111): "For Irma seemed to me foolish because she had not accepted my solution. Her friend would have been wiser, that is to say, she would have yielded sooner. She would then have *opened her mouth properly*, and have told me more than Irma." Freud then adds this footnote: "I had a feeling that the interpretation of this part of the dream was not carried far enough to make it possible to follow the whole of its concealed meaning. If I had pursued my comparison between the three women, it would have taken me far afield. There is at least one spot in every dream at which it is unplummable—a navel, as it were, that is its point of contact with the unknown." Two pages later (p. 113) when Freud associates to "in spite of her dress," he writes about examining women patients, clothed or unclothed, and again pulls himself and the reader up short: "Further than this I could not see. Frankly, I had no desire to penetrate more deeply at this point."

Freud (1900, p. 525; I use the translation by Weber 1982, p. 75) will tell us more about the navel of the dream: "Even in the best interpreted dreams, there is often a place [*eine Stelle*] that must be left in the dark, because in the process of interpreting one notices a tangle of dream-thoughts arising [*anhebt*] which resists unravelling but has also made no further contributions [*keine weiteren Beiträge*] to the dream-content. This, then, is the navel of the dream, the place where it straddles the unknown [*dem Unerkannten aufsitzt*]. The dream-thoughts, to which interpretation leads one, are necessarily interminable [*ohne Abschluss*] and branch out on all sides into the netlike entanglement [*in die netzartige Verstrickung*] of our world of thought. Out of one of the denser places in this meshwork, the dream-wish rises [erhebt sich] like a mushroom out of its mycelium."

Weber reads "netlike entanglement" to imply something like "the snares of a trap," a place where we cannot preserve our bearings but must become unsettled.

Weber (1982), not a clinician but a literary critic, illuminates the path Freud follows in the *Dreambook* to reach this spot of the dream's navel. Freud introduces the section on "The Psychology of the Dream Processes" with a very brief chapter that features the "model dream," which requires no interpretation. Freud introduces the dream as transparent, playing with images of light and dark (1900, p. 509; translation by Weber 1982, p. 69): "A father has been watching beside his child's sick-bed day and night on end. After the child has died, he goes into an adjoining room to rest, leaves the door open, however, so that from his bed chamber [*Schlafraum*; literally, sleeping space] he can look into the room where the corpse of the child lies in state, surrounded by tall candles. An old man has been hired to keep watch and sits next to the corpse, murmuring prayers. After a few hours' sleep, the father dreams that the child is standing at his bedside, grasps him by the arm and whispers reproachfully to him, 'Father, don't you see that I'm burning?' He wakes up, notices a bright light coming from the next room [*Leichenzimmer*], hurries there, finds the old watchman dozed off, the coverings [*die Hüllen*] and one arm of the cherished body burned by a lighted candle that had fallen on them."

When Freud notes that the old man assigned to watch the corpse of the dream-father's son might be "incompetent to carry out his task," the reader begins to become unsettled. Then Freud begins to complicate the task as he introduces other meanings to this model dream (1900, p. 510; translation by Weber 1982, p. 70) which he had contended posed "no problem of interpretation, [whose] meaning is obvious and unveiled [*dessen Sinn unverhüllt gegeben ist*]." Freud proceeds to darken what had seemed so clear and light, playing with such images, until he arrives at the above passage about the unfathomable navel of the dream. Freud has indeed unsettled traditional dream interpreters who presume to understand dreams as clear and simple. He has gotten us lost in "the snares of a trap." The dream's veils [or coverings] cannot be so simply removed. That the navel of the dream straddles the unknown, Weber translates from the German into being duped or deluded, by the unknown. Weber argues against Strachey's translation and Lacan's view that the navel of the dream is something definite, even like Lacan's abyss. That is, Weber argues that there is no center to the dream; the dream work does not have a starting point. Interpretation involves deception by the unknown.

Here is a literary critic using psychoanalytic theory to decenter itself. I am less concerned with Weber's adherence to French Freud (Lacan, Derrida) than with the usefulness of questioning whether we can indeed pin down unconscious conflict. Put another way, interpretation seeks to render the uncertain certain; hence as we interpret, we should be wary of what we seek to foreclose and avoid, mindful of what must lie beyond and outside of our interpretation. Although American psychoanalysts would claim more privilege for compromise formation and for the adaptive and integrative roles of the ego, most of us would insist that conflict is interminable, endless, the very stuff of life. Better that we not close off too much in our interpretations of patients or texts of the vitality of human struggles. This is another, more pragmatic argument in favor of self-reflexive questioning of our interpretive positions. Such self-reflexive investigation of our interpretive positions should include consideration of the emotional paths we have followed and the personal psychic gains which accrue.

Goldberg (1990) proposes that therapists' rigid adherence to fixed systems of thought, especially with static, mechanical models, forecloses the best kind of open psychoanalytic exploration with our patients and within ourselves. Such exploration, he advises, should feature curiosity, open inquiry, and ongoing creative efforts toward new integration. Unfortunately, as I (1993) have argued previously, Goldberg's project is marred by his exempting his own position from such (self) inquiry. Scholars in most disciplines now argue that issues of belief, bias, influence, and power may determine our basic assumptions (for an excellent discussion, see Scott 1988). Self-inquiry may help to keep us less deluded. We would hope that psychoanalysts and psychotherapists would be especially capable of such honest self-examination. However, psychoanalysts and psychotherapists, like everyone else, can be motivated by power, politics, or any other need and seek to advance *only* their own position.

When Erikson (p. 21) claims that the dream's "style of representation" is "no mere shell to the kernel, the latent dream," he makes our study of the veils of the dream legitimate. Erikson heightens the interpersonal drama between dreamer and dream-interpreter as they become caught in the passions of a netlike entanglement of veiling and unveiling, seeking connection, penetration, conception, and meaning as they approach each other. Erikson's emphasis on transference in dreams and their interpretation focuses interpersonal communication, desire, need, and interpenetration within which each subject cannot remain fully apart.

Erikson has gotten us solidly into our own contemporary debates about how much each member of the therapeutic couple affects the other. One pole of this gradient of influence is that the therapist is relatively uninfluenced by the patient and the patient is or should be relatively uninfluenced by the therapist, except by the therapist's "objective" interpretations which are made from a position of affective neutrality. In this view the therapist's attempts to influence the patient will interfere with full analysis of conflict, substituting a defensive illusion for the achievement of full autonomy. The therapist's caring, wanting to help, and so on will interfere with full analysis of the patient's conflicts.

The other pole of this gradient is that both patient and therapist exert great emotional influence on the other and that we do well to appreciate, understand, and interpret how each influences the other. This second pole would question whether therapists can interpret in dispassionate ways without attempting to influence their patients. Put in other terms, there is a gradient from insisting on the autonomy and separateness of patient and therapist, each of whom is capable of staying outside of the other's conflicts and influence, to a view of interpenetration of conflict and influence that cannot be avoided except through denial and foreclosure. In my reading, Erikson was making early attempts to engage us in such debates about mutual influence and joint creation. Nor could he get fully beyond his own constraints and the constraints of American psychoanalytic ego psychology of the 1950s.

Perhaps Erikson's, and Freud's, enthusiastic advocacy of self-inquiry can modify such sharp dichotomy between these two differing positions about the interpenetration of influence in the therapeutic situation. That is, in this ideal psychoanalytic self-inquiry, advocates of each position would keep wondering about their investment in their position and about what may lie behind and outside of it. Two, among many, obvious possibilities that these therapists could reclaim would be that those who argue against mutual influence may obscure their own wishes to influence their patients in ways they themselves would find objectionable; and that those who argue in favor of mutual influence may obscure their own wishes to be separate from and uninfluenced by their patients. Erikson and Freud certainly would have encouraged contemporary therapists to persevere with such ongoing constructive self-examination, of our psyches and of our theories. As Goldberg (1990) argued, honest self-exploration of our emotional and theoretical positions tends to reduce rigidity, conformity, and idealization, enhancing freer, less restrained, more exuberant personal and therapeutic attitudes.

Today Erikson's optimism about psychoanalysis as a general psychology and his tilting of psychoanalysis toward positive adaptive tasks seems insufficiently balanced by the interminability of conflict. Freud's vision in the *Dreambook* preserves unconscious conflict at the core or navel. Although unconscious conflict cannot be fully known or tamed, we seek to follow it into the unknown, where we must become lost and unsettled. As Junker (1992) has argued recently, Strachey rendered Freud's "Analysis Terminable and Interminable" (1937) in an overly pessimistic way. That conflict may be interminable need not mean that we must feel hopeless and defeated by it. On the contrary, there is something affirmative of the ongoing vitality of life processes in our feeling able to continue struggling with our conflicts rather than surrendering to despair or disgust. Erikson might have regarded such struggle as marks of integrity or generativity. Despite Erikson's discussion of conflicts in creativity, I read this essay as, in part, idealizing creativity, that tempting seductress, as somehow allowing us to transcend the id and the interminability of conflict. Better that we keep together the ego's potential for creativity with the burdens and joys of our relentless passions and desires.

Although I may quibble whether Erikson would like to move (his own) creativity beyond conflict, I appreciate his encouraging the rest of us to engage in optimistic, joyful, intersubjective play with texts and patients. I have argued that Erikson's approach preceded reader-response (literary) criticism, most of clinical writing on the constructive uses of countertransference, and our own contemporary fascination with how patient and therapist and reader and text each influences the other and how they, patient and therapist and reader and text, construct meanings within the therapeutic and literary situations. By helping us to enjoy *playing* with our materials—texts and patients—Erikson not only was way ahead of his time but he showed us that both treatment and literary criticism could be less constrained and more pleasurable. Erikson's early attempts to deconstruct meanings with patients and texts has contributed to our movement away from interpretive certainty toward the more exciting, interminable search for meanings.

References

Abend, S. (1982). Serious illness in the analyst: countertransference considerations. *J. Amer. Psychoanal. Assn.* 30:365–379.

Akhtar, S. (1994). Needs, disruptions, and the return of ego instincts: some explicit and implicit aspects of self psychology. In *Mahler and Kohut: Perspectives on Development, Psychopathology, and Technique*, ed. S. Kramer & S. Akhtar, pp. 97–116, Northvale, N. J.: Jason Aronson.

———. (1995). *Quest for Answers*. Northvale, N. J.: Jason Aronson.

———. (1996). "Someday" and "if only" fantasies: pathological optimism and inordinate nostalgia as related forms of idealization. *J. Amer. Psychoanal. Assn.* 44: 723–753.

———. (unpublished). Discussion of "How much does the analyst at work need to feel" by S.J. Coen, American Psychoanalytic Association Meetings, Chicago, IL, 2000.

Arlow, J. A. (1971). Character perversion. In *Psychoanalysis: Clinical Theory and Practice*. Madison, CT: Internat. Univ. Press, 1991, pp. 177–194.

———. (1986). The relation of theories of pathogenesis to therapy. In *Psychoanalysis: The Science of Mental Conflict*, ed. A.D. Richards & M. S. Willick, pp. 49–63. Hillsdale, N. J.: The Analytic Press.

———. (1995). Stilted listening: psychoanalysis as discourse. *Psychoanal. Quart.* 64: 215–233.

Aron, L. and Bushra, A. (1998). Mutual regression: altered states in the psychoanalytic situation. *J. Amer. Psychoanal. Assn.* 46: 389–412.

Asch, S. (1976). Varieties of negative therapeutic reaction and problems of technique. *J. Amer. Psychoanal. Assn.* 24:383–407.

Bach, S. (1977). On the narcissistic state of consciousness. *Internat. J. Psycho-Anal.* 58: 209–233.

———. (1985). *Narcissistic States and the Therapeutic Process*. New York: Aronson.

Bader, M. (1994). The tendency to neglect therapeutic aims in psychoanalysis. *Psychoanal. Quart.* 63: 246–270.

————. (1995). Authenticity and the psychology of choice in the analyst. *Psychoanal. Quart.* 64: 282–305.

Balint, M. (1968). *The Basic Fault: Therapeutic Aspects of Regression.* London & Southampton: Tavistock Publications.

Balsam, R. (1997, unpublished). Discussion of "How to help patients (and analysts) bear the unbearable". Association for Psychoanalytic Medicine, New York.

Barratt, B. (1994). Critical notes on the psychoanalyst's theorizing. *J. Amer. Psychoanal. Assoc.* 42: 697–725.

Barthes, R. (1973). *The Pleasure of the Text.* Translated R. Miller. New York: Hill & Wang, 1975.

————. (1979). From work to text. In *Textual Strategies: Perspectives in Post-Structuralist Criticism*, Ed. J. V. Harari, pp. 73–81. Ithaca, NY: Cornell University Press.

Basch, M. (1981). Self-object disorders and psychoanalytic theory: A historical perspective. *J. Amer. Psychoanal. Assn.* 29:337–351.

Beebe, B. (unpublished). Brief Mother-Infant Treatment using Psychoanalytically Informed Video Microanalysis: Integrating Procedural and Declarative Processing. Presented to the Association for Psychoanalytic Medicine, N.Y.C., 2000.

Beebe, B., Jaffe, J., & Lachmann, F. (1992). A dyadic systems view of communication. In *Relational Perspectives in Psychoanalysis*, N. Skolnick & S. Warshaw (Eds.). Hillsdale, N. J.: The Analytic Press.

Beebe, B., Jaffe, J., Lachmann, F., Feldstein, S., Crown, C., & Jasnow, M. (2000). Systems models in development and psychoanalysis: the case of vocal rhythm coordination and attachment. *Infant Mental Health*: 21: 99–122.

Beebe, B. & Lachmann, F. (1994). Representation and internalization in infancy: three principles of salience. *Psychoanalytic Psychology* 11: 127–165.

Beebe, B. & Lachmann, F. M. (1998). Co-constructing inner and relational processes: self- and mutual regulation in infant research and adult treatment. *Psychoanalytic Psychol.* 15: 480–516.

Beebe, B., Lachmann, F., & Jaffe, J. (1997). Mother-infant structures and presymbolic self- and object-representations. *Psychoanalytic Dialogues* 7: 133–182.

Bergmann, M. (Unpublished). Retraumatization anxiety and the negative therapeutic reaction. Presented, American Psychoanalytic Association Meetings, Toronto, Canada, 1998.

Berman, E. (1997). Psychoanalytic supervision as the crossroads of a relational matrix. In *Psychodynamic Supervision: Perspectives of the Supervisor and the Supervisee*, ed. M. H. Rock, Northvale, N.J. & London: Jason Aronson, pp. 161–186.

Bion, W. R. (1959). Attacks on linking. *Internat. J. Psycho-Anal.* 40: 308–315.

————. (1962). *Learning from Experience.* Northvale, N.J. & London: Jason Aronson, Inc. (1994).

———— (1967). *Second Thoughts: Selected Papers on Psychoanalysis*. Northvale, N.J. & London: Jason Aronson Inc. (1993).

———— (1970). *Attention and Interpretation*. New York: Basic Books.

Bleich, D. (1967). The determination of literary value. *Literature and Psychology* 27: 19–30.

————. (1975). The subjective character of critical interpretation. *College English* 36: 739–755.

————. (1976). The subjective paradigm in science, psychology, and criticism. *New Literary History* 7: 313–334.

————. (1977). The logic of interpretation. *Genre* 10: 363–394.

————. (1978). *Subjective Criticism*. Baltimore: The Johns Hopkins University Press.

Blum. H. P. (1981). The forbidden quest and the analytic ideal: the superego and insight. *Psychoanal. Quart.* 50: 535–556.

Boesky, D. (2000). Affect, language and communication. *Internat. J. Psycho-Anal.* 81: 257–262.

Bollas, C. (1984/85). Loving hate. *Annual Psychoanal.*, *12/13*, 221–237.

Bollas, C. & Sundelson, D. (1995). *The New Informants: The Betrayal of Confidentiality in Psychoanalysis and Psychotherapy*. Northvale, N. J.:Jason Aronson.

Bolognini, S. (1997). Empathy and 'empathism.' *Internat. J. Psycho-Anal.* 78:279–293.

————. (unpublished). A look at the analyst's emotions: obstacle and asset. International Psychoanalytical Association Congress, Santiago, Chile, 1999.

Booth, W. (1979). *Critical Understanding: The Powers and Limits of Pluralism*. Chicago: University of Chicago Press.

Bradlow, P. A. (1971). Murder in the initial dream in psychoanalysis. *Bull. Phila. Assoc. Psycho-Anal.* 21: 70–81.

————. (1973). On reporting an initial dream in psychoanalysis of undisguised sexual activity between family members. (Abstract in *Bull. Assoc. Psychoanal. Medicine* 12: 18–22.

————. (1974). The very late first dream reporter in psychoanalysis. (Paper presented to the American Psychoanalytic Association in December, 1974; unpublished).

Bradlow, P. A. & Coen, S. J. (1975). The analyst undisguised in the initial dream in psychoanalysis. *Internat. J. Psycho-Anal.* 56:415–425.

————. (1984). Mirror masturbation. *Psychoanal. Quart.* 53:267285.

Brenner, C. (1982). *The Mind in Conflict*. New York: International Universities Press.

Britton, R. (1994). Publication anxiety: conflict between communication and affiliation. *Internat. Jour. Psychoanal.*, 75:1213–1224.

Bromberg, P. M. (1982). The supervisory process and parallel process. *Contemp. PsychoAnal.* 18: 92–111.

————. (1983). The mirror and the mask: on narcissism and psychoanalytic growth. *Contemp. PsychoAnal.* 19: 359–387.

———. (1984). The third ear. In *Clinical Perspectives on the Supervision of Psychoanalysis and Psychotherapy*, ed. L. Caligor, P. M. Bromberg, & J. D. Meltzer, pp. 29–44. New York & London: Plenum.

———. (2000). Potholes on the royal road: or is it an abyss? *Contemp. PsychoAnal.* 36: 5–28.

Buechler, S. (1999). Searching for a passionate neutrality. *Contemp. PsychoAnal.* 35: 213–227.

Busch, F. (1993). In the neighborhood: aspects of a good interpretation and its relationship to a "developmental lag" in ego psychology. *Journal of the American Psychoanalytic Association* 41: 151–178.

———. (1994). Some ambiguities in the method of free association and their implications for technique. *Journal of the American Psychoanalytic Association* 42: 363–384.

———. (1995). Do actions speak louder than words? A query into an enigma in analytic theory and technique. *Journal of the American Psychoanalytic Association* 43 (1).

Butler J., (1990). *Gender Trouble: Feminism and the Subversion of Identity*. New York & London: Routledge.

——— (1993). *Bodies that Matter: On the Discursive Limits of "Sex."* New York & London: Routledge.

Butler J. & Scott, J. W., Eds., (1992). *Feminists Theorize The Political*. New York & London: Routledge.

Carvajal, G. (1999). An experience of rage. Contribution to the panel: Rage in the analytic setting, International Psychoanalytical Association Congress, Santiago, Chile, 1999.

Casement, P. J. (1982). Some pressures on the analyst for physical contact during the reliving of an early trauma. *Internat. Rev. Psychoanal.*, 9:279–286.

Castle, T. (1993). *The Apparitional Lesbian: Female Homosexuality and Modern Culture.* New York: Columbia Univ. Press.

Chessick, R. D. Poststructural psychoanalysis or wild analysis? *Jour. Amer. Acad. Psychoanal.* 23:47–62.

Coates, S. (1992). The etiology of boyhood gender identity disorder: an integrative model. In *Interface of Psychoanalysis and Psychology*, ed. J. W. Barron, M. N. Eagle, & D. L. Wolitzky, p. 262. Washington, D. C.: American Psychological Association.

———. (1998). Having a mind of one's own and holding the other in mind: commentary on paper by Peter Fonagy and Mary Target. *Psychoanal. Dial.* 8: .

Coen, S. J. (1981). Notes on the concepts of selfobject and preoedipal object. *J. Amer. Psychoanal. Assn.* 29:395–411.

———. (1982a). Louis-Ferdinand Céline's *Castle to Castle*: The author–reader relationship in its narrative style. *Amer. Imago* 39:343–368.

———. (1982b). Essays on the relationship of author and reader: transference implications for psychoanalytic literary criticism: an introduction. *Psychoanal. Contemp. Thought* 5: 3–15.

——. (1984). The author and his audience: Jean Genet's early work. *Psychoanal. Study Society* 10:301–320.

——. (1985). Freud and Fliess: A supportive literary relationship. *Amer. Imago* 42: 385–412.

——. (1987). The analyst's uses and misuses of clinical theory: interpretation. *Yearbook of Psychoanal. & Psychother.*, 2:200–224.

—— (1988a). Superego aspects of entitlement. *J. Amer. Psychoanal. Assn.*, 36:409–427.

—— (1988b). How to read Freud: a critique of recent Freud scholarship. *J. Amer. Psychoanal. Assn.* 36:483–515.

——. (1989). Intolerance of responsibility for internal conflict. *J. Amer. Psychoanal. Assn.* 37:943–964.

——. (1992). *The Misuse of Persons: Analyzing Pathological Dependency.* Hillsdale, N. J. & London: The Analytic Press.

——. (1993). Book review of *The Prisonhouse of Psychoanalysis* by A. Goldberg (1990). Hillsdale, N. J.: The Analytic Press, *Psychoanal. Quart.* 62:656–658.

——. (1994a). *Between Author and Reader: A Psychoanalytic Approach to Writing and Reading.* New York: Columbia Univ. Press.

——. (1994b). Barriers to love between patient and analyst. *J. Amer. Psychoanal. Assn.* 42: 1107–1135, 1994.

——. (1997a). How to help patients (and analysts) bear the unbearable: paradoxes in psychoanalytic technique. *J. Amer. Psychoanal. Assn.* 45: 1183–1207.

——. (1997b). Book Review of *Fantasy and Reality in History* by Peter Loewenberg 1995, NY: Oxford University Press. *Internat. J. Psycho-Anal.* 78: 199–202.

——. (1998a). Perverse defenses in neurotic patients. *J. Amer. Psychoanal. Assn.* 1998, 46: 1169–1194.

——. (1998b). Book Notice of *Writing in Psychoanalysis*, edited by Emma Piccioli, Pier Luigi Rossi, & Antonio Alberto Semi (1996). The Analytic Press for Rivista di Psicoanalisi. *J. Amer. Psychoanal. Assn.* 46: 1323–1324, 1998.

——. (2000a). Clinical discussants as psychoanalytic readers. *J. Amer. Psychoanal. Assn.* 48: 471–495.

——. (2000b). Why we need to write openly about our clinical cases. *J. Amer. Psychoanal. Assn.* 48: 449–470.

——. (2000c). The wish to regress in patient and analyst. *J. Amer. Psychoanal. Assn.* 48: 785–810.

——. (unpublished). How Do We Bear Our Patients' Rage and Our Own? Contribution to the Panel: Rage in the Analytic Setting. International Psychoanalytical Association Congress, Santiago, Chile, 1999.

Coen, S., & Bradlow, P. A. (1985). "The common mirror dream, dreamer, and the dream mirror." *J. Amer. Psychoanal. Assn.* 33:797–820.

Coltart, N. (1986). Slouching toward Bethlehem . . . or thinking the unthinkable in psychoanalysis. In *Slouching Toward Bethlehem* . . . by N. Coltart, 1992, New York & LondonL Guilford Press, pp. 1–14.

———. (1991). The silent patient. In *Slouching Toward Bethlehem.* by N. Coltart, pp. 79–94. New York & London: Guilford Press, 1992.

———. (1992a). On the tightrope: therapeutic and non-therapeutic factors in psychoanalysis. In *Slouching Toward Bethlehem* . . . by N. Coltart, pp. 95–110. New York & London: Guilford Press, 1992.

———. (1992b). What does it mean: 'Love is not enough'? In *Slouching Toward Bethlehem* . . . by N. Coltart, pp. 111–127. New York & London: Guilford Press, 1992.

———. (1996). The baby and the bathwater. In *The Baby and the Bathwater*, pp. 155–166. London: Karnac Books.

Cooper, S. (1996). Facts all come with a point of view: some reflections on fact and formulation from the 75th Anniversary Edition of the *International Journal of Psycho-Analysis. Internat. J. Psycho-Anal.* 77:255–273.

———. (1998). Analyst subjectivity, analyst disclosure, and the aims of analysis. *Psychoanal. Quart.* 67: 379–406.

Davies, J. M. (1994). Love in the afternoon: a relational reconsideration of desire and dread in the countertransference. *Psychoanal. Dialogues* 4:153–170.

———. (1996). Dissociation, repression, and reality testing in the counter-transference: the controversy over memory and false memory in the psychoanalytic treatment of adult survivors of childhood sexual abuse. *Psychoanal. Dialogues* 6:189–218.

———. (1999). Getting cold feet, defining "safe-enough" borders: dissociation, multiplicity, and integration in the analyst's experience. *Psychoanal. Quart.* 68: 184–208.

———. (Unpublished). What in the world is the relationship? Getting down to basics in an age of complexity and diversity. American Psychoanalytic Association Meetings, May, 1999, Washington, D. C.

Davies, J. M., & Frawley, M. G. (1994). *Treating the Adult Survivor of Childhood Sexual Abuse: A Psychoanalytic Perspective.* New York: Basic Books.

Davison, W., Bristol, C., Pray, M. (1986). Turning aggression on the self: study of psychoanalytic process. *Psychoanalytic Quarterly* 55: 273–295.

Davison, W., Pray, M., Bristol, C. (1990). Mutative interpretation and close psychoanalytic monitoring. *Psychoanalytic Quarterly* 59: 599–628.

DeLaurette, T. (1994). *The Practice of Love: Lesbian Sexuality and Perverse Desire.* Bloomington & Indianapolis: Indiana Univ. Press.

Derrida, J. (1975). The purveyor of truth. Trans. Willis Domingo et al. In *Graphesis: Perspective in Literature and Philosophy. Yale French Studies* 52: 31–113.

Deutsch, H. (1926). Occult processes occurring during psychoanalysis. In

Psychoanalysis and the Occult, ed. G. Devereux, pp. 133–146. New York: International Universities Press, 1953.

Dewald, P. (1982). Serious illness in the analyst: transference, countertransference, and reality responses. *J. Amer. Psychoanal. Assn.* 30:347–363.

Dorpat, T. L. (1987). A new look at denial and defense. *Annual Psychoanal.* 15:23–47.

Eagle, M. (1995). The developmental perspectives of attacment and psychoanalytic theory. In *Attachment Theory: Social, Developmental, and Clinical Perspectives*, ed. S. Goldberg, R. Muir, J. Kerr. pp. 123–150. Hillsdale, N.J. & London: The Analytic Press.

Eagleton, T. (1986). *Against the Grain, Essays 1975–1985*. London & New York: Verso.

———. (1990). *The Significance of Theory*. Oxford, U.K. & Cambridge, MA: Blackwell.

Edelson, M. (1986). Causal explanation in science and in psychoanalysis: implications for writing a case study. *Psychoanal. Study Child* 41: 89–127.

Eigen, M. (1997). Being too good. In *Psychodynamic Supervision: Perspectives of the Supervisor and the Supervisee*, ed. M. H. Rock, 1997, pp. 57–72. Northvale, N.J. & London: Jason Aronson.

Epstein, L. (1977). The therapeutic function of hate in the countertransference. *Contemp. PsychoAnal.* 13: 422–461.

———. (1979). The therapeutic use of countertransference data with borderline patients. *Contemp. PsychoAnal.* 15: 248–275.

———. (1981). Countertransference and its influence on judgments of fitness for analysis. *Contemp. PsychoAnal.* 17: 35–68.

———. (1984). An interpersonal-object relations perspective on working with destructive agression. *Contemp. PsychoAnal.* 20: 651–662.

———. (1987). The bad analyst feeling. *Modern Psychoanalysis* 12: 35–45.

———. (1999). The analyst's "bad-analyst feelings": a counterpart to the process of resolving implosive defenses. *Contemp. PsychoAnal.* 35: 311–325.

Erikson, E. H. (1954). The dream specimen of psychoanalysis. *J. Amer. Psychoanal. Assn.* 2:2–56.

———. (1955). Freud's "The Origin of Psychoanalysis". *Int. J. PsychoAnal.* 36: 1–15.

Etchegoyen, H. (1978). Some thoughts on transference perversion. *Internat. J. Psycho-Anal.* 59: 45–54.

Felman, S. (1977). Turning the screw of interpretation. *Yale French Studies* 55/56: 94–207.

———. (1987). *Jacques Lacan and the Adventure of Insight: Psychoanalysis in Contemporary Culture*. Cambridge, MA: Harvard University Press.

Fish, S. (1980). *Is There a Text in This Class? The Authority of Interpretive Communities*. Cambridge, MA: Harvard University Press.

Fonagy, P. (1991). Thinking about thinking: some clinical and theoretical considerations in the treatment of a borderline patient. *Internat. Jour. Psycho-Anal.* 72: 639–656.

Fonagy, P. & Target, M. (1996). Playing with reality. I. *Internat. Jour. Psycho-Anal.* 77: 217–234.

Fonagy, P., Steele, M., Moran, G., Steele, H. & Higgitt, A. (1993). Measuring the ghost in the nursery: an empirical study of the relation between parents' mental representations of childhood experience and their infants' security of attachment. *J. Amer. Psychoanal. Assn.* 41: 929–989.

Fonagy, P., Steele, M., Steele, H., Leigh, T., Kennedy, R., Mattoon, G., & Target, M. (1995). Attachment, the reflective self, and borderline states: the predictive specificity of the adult attachment interview and pathological emotional development. In *Attachment Theory: Social, Developmental and Clinical Perspectives*, ed. Goldberg, S., Muir, R. & Kerr, J., pp. 233–278. J. Hillsdale, N. J.: The Analytic Press.

Freud, A. (1952). A connexion between the stats of negativism and of emotional surrender. (Summary). *Internat. J. Psycho-Anal.* 33: 264.

Freud, S. (1900). The interpretation of dreams. *S. E.* 4 & 5.

———. (1909). Notes upon a case of obsessional neurosis. *Standard Edition* 10:153–250. London: Hogarth Press, 1955.

———. (1911). Formulations on the two principles of mental functioning. *Standard Edition*, 12: 213–226. London: Hogarth Press, 1961.

———. (1912). The dynamics of transference. *Standard Edition* Vol. 12. (1915). London: Hogarth Pess.

———. (1915). Observations on transference love (further recommendations on the technique of psychoanalysis, III). *Standard Edition* Vol. 12. London: Hogarth Press.

——— (1924). The loss of reality in neurosis and psychosis. *Standard Edition*. 19: 183–187. London: Hogarth Press, 1961.

——— (1927). Fetishism. *Standard Edition*. 21:147–157. London: Hogarth Press, 1961.

———. (1937). Constructions in analysis. *S.E.*, 23: 255–269.

——— (1940a). An outline of psycho-analysis. *Standard Edition*, 23:140–207. London: Hogarth Press, 1961.

——— (1940b). Splitting of the ego in the process of defense. *Standard Edition*, 23:271–278. London: Hogarth Press, 1961.

———. (1926). Ansprache an die Mitglieder des Vereins B'nai B'rith. *Gesammelte Werke*, Vol. XVI. London: Imago Publishing Co., 1941. [as cited in Erikson, 1954].

Friedman, L. (1991). A reading of Freud's papers on technique. *Psychoanal. Quart.* 60: 564–595.

———. (1997). Ferrum, ignis and medicina: return to the crucible. *J. Amer. Psychoanal. Assn.* 45: 20–36.

Furlong, A. (1998). Should we or shouldn't we? Some aspects of the confidentiality of clinical reporting and dossier access. *Internat. Jour. Psycho-Anal.* 79: 727–739.

Fuss, D., Ed. 1991. *Inside/Out: Lesbian Theories, Gay Theories.* New York & London: Routledge.

Gabbard, G. O. (1991). Technical approaches to transference hate in the analysis of borderline patients. *Internat. Jour. Psycho-Anal.* 72: 625–638.

———. (1994). On love and lust in erotic transference. *J. Amer. Psychoanal. Assn.* 42:385–403.

Gabbard, G. and Lester, E. (1995). *Boundaries and Boundary Violations in Psychoanalysis.* New York: Basic Books.

Gadamer, H. G. (1975). *Truth and Method.* New York: The Seabury Press.

Galatzer-Levy, R. (1991). Reporter: Presentation of clinical evidence. *Jour. Amer. Psychoanal. Assoc.* 39: 727–740.

Garber, M. (1995). *Vice Versa: Bisexuality and the Eroticism of Everyday Life.* New York, London, Toronto, Sydney, Tokyo, Singapore: Touchstone (Simon & Schuster).

Gediman, H. & Wolkenfeld, F. (1980). The parallelism phenomenon in psychoanalysis and supervision: its reconsideration as a triadic system. *Psychoanal. Quart.* 49: 234–255.

Gedo, J. E. (1979). *Beyond Interpretation: Toward a Revised Theory for Psychoanalysis.* New York: International Universities Press.

——— (1984). *Psychoanalysis and Its Discontents.* New York: Guilford Press.

Gill, M. M. (1963). *Topography and Systems in Psychoanalytic Theory. Psychological Issues, Monograph 18.* New York: International Universities Press.

Giovacchini, P. (1967). Frustration and externalization. *Psychoanal. Q.,* 36:571–583.

Goldberg, A. (1990). *The Prisonhouse of Psychoanalysis.* Hillsdale, N.J.: The Analytic Press.

———. (1997). Writing case histories. *Internat. Jour. Psycho-Anal.* 78: 435–438.

Gorney, J. E. (1980). The field of illusion in literature and the psychoanalytic situation. *Psychoanalysis and Contemp. Thought* 2: 527–550.

Gray, P. (1973). Psychoanalytic technique and the ego's capacity for viewing intrapsychic conflict. *Journal of the American Psychoanalytic Association* 21: 474 494.

———. (1982). "Developmental lag" in the evolution of technique for psychoanalysis of neurotic conflict. *Jour. Amer. Psychoanal. Assoc.* 30: 621–655.

———. (1994). *The Ego and Analysis of Defense.* Northvale, N. J.: Jason Aronson.

Green, A. (1978). The double and the absent. In *Psychoanalysis, Creativity, and Literature: A French-American Inquiry,* ed. A. Roland, pp. 271–292. New York: Columbia University Press.

Greenacre, P. (1953). Certain relationships between fetishism and the faulty development of the body image. In *Emotional Growth*, Vol. I. New York: International Universities Press, 1971, pp.9–30.

———— (1967). The influence of infantile trauma on genetic patterns. In *Emotional Growth, Vol. I.*, 1971, pp. 260–299. New York: International Universities Press.

Grossman, L. (1992). An example of "character perversion" in a woman. *Psychoanal. Quart.* 61:581–589.

———— (1993). The perverse attitude toward reality. *Psychoanal. Quart.* 62:422–436.

———— (1996). "Psychic reality" and reality testing in the analysis of perverse defences. *Internat. J. Psycho-Anal.* 77: 509–517.

Grossman, W. I. (1986). Notes on masochism: A discussion of the history and development of a psychoanalytic concept. *Psychoanal. Q.* 55:379–413.

Grotstein, J. (1996). Unpublished. Two-day clinical workshop, American Psychoanalytic Association Meetings, December, 1996, New York, N.Y.

Holland, N. (1982). Why this is transference, nor am I out of it. *Psychoanal. & Contemp. Thought*, 5: 27–34.

———— (2000). The mind and the book: a long look at psychoanalytic literary criticism. *Jour. Applied Psychoanal. Studies*, 2:13–23.

Hamilton, N. G. (1986). Positive projective identification. *Internat. Jour. Psycho-Anal.* 67: 489–496.

Harris, A. (1997). The enduring encounter: commentary on paper by Beebe, Lachmannn, and Jaffe. *Psychoanalytic Dialogues* 7: 197–206.

Hartman, F. R. (1983). A reappraisal of the Emma episode and the specimen dream. *J. Amer. Psychoanal. Assn.* 31: 555–585.

Heiman, P. (1950). On counter-transference. *Internat. Jour. Psycho-Anal.* 31: 81–84.

Hesse, E. & Main, M. (2000). Disorganized infant, child, and adult attachment: collapse in behavioral and attentional strategies. *J. Amer. Psychoanal. Assn.* 48: 1097–1127.

Holland N. (1968). *The Dynamics of Literary Response*. New York: Norton.

————. (1970). Discussion of "Criticism and the experience of interiority" by G. Poulet. In *The Structuralist Controversy: The Languages of Criticism and the Sciences of Man*, ed. R. Macksey & E. Donato, pp. 86–87. Baltimore & London: The Johns Hopkins University Press.

————. (1973). *Poems in Persons: An Introduction to the Psychoanalysis of Literature*. New York: Norton.

————. (1975a). *5 Readers Reading*. New Haven & London: Yale University Press.

————. (1975b). Unity, identity, text, self. *PMLA* 90: 813–822.

————. (1976). The new paradigm: subjective or transactive? *New Literary History* 7: 335–346.

————. (1978). Literary interpretation and three phases of psychoanalysis. In

Psychoanalysis, Creativity, and Literature: A French-American Inquiry, pp. 233–247. New York: Columbia University Press.

———. (unpublished). The mind and the book: a long look at psychoanalytic literary criticism.

Hurwitz, M. (Unpublished). Comments at 2–Day Clinical Workshop on Process and Technique, American Psychoanalytic Association Meetings, Washington, D. C., May, 1999.

Inderbitzin, L. & Levy, S. (2000). Regression and psychoanalytic technique: the concretization of a concept. *Psychoanal. Quart.* 69: 195–223.

Isakower, O. (1963). Minutes of faculty meeting of the New York psychoanalytic Institute, October 14 and November 20.

Isay, R. (1985). On the analytic therapy of homosexual men. *Psychoanal. Study Child,* 40:235–254.

——— (1986). The development of sexual identity in homosexual men. *Psychoanal. Study Child,* 41:467–489.

——— (1987). Fathers and their homosexually inclined sons in childhood. *Pyschoanal. Study Child,* 42:275–294.

——— (1989). *Being Homosexual: Gay Men and Their Development.* New York: Avon Books.

Iser, W. (1978). *The Act of Reading: A Theory of Aesthetic Response.* Baltimore & London: The Johns Hopkins University Press.

Issacharoff, A. (1984). Countertransference in supervision: therapeutic consequences for the supervisee. In *Clinical Perspectives on the Supervision of Psychoanalysis and Psychotherapy,* ed. L. Caligor, P. M. Bromberg, & J. D. Meltzer, pp. 89–105. New York & London: Plenum.

Joseph, B. (1975). The patient who is difficult to reach. In *Psychic Equilibrium and Psychic Change, Selected papers of Betty Joseph,* Ed. E. B. Spillius & M. Feldman, 1989, London & New York: Tavistock/Routledge, pp. 75–87.

———. (1982). Addiction to near-death. In *Psychic Equilibrium and Psychic Change, Selected papers of Betty Joseph,* ed. E. B. Spillius & M. Feldman, 1989, London & New York: Tavistock/Routledge, pp. 127–138.

———. (1983). On understanding and not understanding: some technical issues. In *Psychic Equilibrium and Psychic Change, Selected papers of Betty Joseph,* ed. E. B. Spillius & M. Feldman, (1989), pp. 139–150. London & New York: Tavistock/Routledge.

———. (1987). Projective identification: some clinical aspects. In *Psychic Equilibrium and Psychic Change, Selected papers of Betty Joseph,* ed. E. B. Spillius & M. Feldman, (1989,) pp. 168–180. London & New York: Tavistock/Routledge.

———. (1993). A factor militating against psychic change: nonresonance. In: *Psychic Structure and Psychic Change: Essays in Honor of Robert S. Wallerstein, M. D.,* Madison, CT: Internat. Univ. Press, pp. 311–325.

Junker, H. (1992). Standard translation and complete analysis. In *Translating Freud*, ed. D. G. Ornston, pp. 48–62. New Haven & London: Yale Univ. Press.

Kantrowitz, J. (1997). A different perspective on the therapeutic process: the impact of the patient on the analyst. *J. Amer. Psychoanal. Assn.* 45:127–153.

Kanzer, M. (1952). The transference neurosis of the Rat Man. *Psychoanal. Quart.* 21:81–189.

Kaplan, L. (1991a). Women masquerading as women. In *Perversions and Near Perversions in Clinical Practice*, ed. G. Fogel & W. Myers. New Haven: Yale Univ. Press.

——— (1991b). *Female Perversions: The Temptations of Emma Bovary*. New York, London, Toronto, Sydney, Auckland: Doubleday.

Katz, G. (1998) Where the action is: the enacted dimension of analytic process. *J. Amer. Psychoanal. Assn.* 46: 1129–1167.

Kermode, F. (1974). Novels: recognition and deception. *Critical Inquiry* 1: 103–121.

Kernberg, O. F. (1992a) *Aggression in Personality Disorders and Perversions*. New Haven & London: Yale Univ. Press.

———. (1992b, unpublished). Love in the analytic setting. Presented at the Panel, "Love in the analytic setting", American Psychoanalytic Association meetings, New York City, December, 1992.

———. (1993). Convergences and divergences in contemporary psychoanalytic technique. *Internat. J. Psycho-Anal.* 74:659–673.

———. (1994). Love in the analytic setting. *J. Amer. Psychoanal. Assn.* 42:1137–1157.

Kernberg, P. (1984). Unpublished. Reflections in the Mirror: Mother-Child Interactions, Self-Awareness, and Self-Recognition. Presented to the Association for Psychoanalytic Medicine, New York City.

Khan, M. M. R. (1962). The role of polymorph-perverse body experiences and object-relations in ego-integration. *Brit. J. Med. Psychol.* 35:245–261.

——— (1964). The role of infantile sexuality and early object relations in female homosexuality. In *Pathology and Treatment of Sexual Deviations*, ed. I. Rosen. London: Oxford University Press, pp. 221–292.

——— (1965a). The function of intimacy and acting out in perversions. In *Sexual Behavior and the Law*, ed. R. Slovenko. Springfield, IL: Thomas, pp. 397–412.

——— (1965b). Foreskin fetishism and its relation to ego-pathology in a male homosexual. *Internat. J. Psycho-Anal.* 46:64–80.

——— (1969). Role of the "collated internal object" in perversion-formations. *Internat. J. Psycho-Anal.* 50:555–565.

Killingmo, B. (1989). Conflict and deficit: Implications for technique. *Internat. Jour. Psycho-Anal.* 70:65–79.

Klein, G. S. (1976a). Freud's two theories of sexuality. In *Psychoanalytic Theory: An*

Exploration of Essentials. New York: International Universities Press, pp. 72–102.

Kiersky, S. & Beebe, B. (1994). The reconstruction of early nonverbal relatedness in the treatment of difficult patients: a special form of empathy. *Psychoanalytic Dialogues* 4: 389–408.

Klein, M. (1946). Notes on some schizoid mechanisms. *Internat. Jour. Psycho-Anal.* 27: 99–110.

Kohut, H. (1971). *The Analysis of the Self.* New York: International Universities Press.

Kris, A. (1977). Either/or dilemmas. *Psychoanal. Study Child*, 32:91–117.

—— (1983). Determinants of free association in narcissistic phenomena. *Psychoanal. Study Child*, 38:439–458.

—— (1985). Resistance in convergent and in divergent conflicts. *Psychoanal. Quart.* 54:537–568.

—— (1990). Helping patients by analyzing self-criticism. *Jour. Amer. Psychoanal. Assn.* 38:605–636.

Kris, E. (1950). On preconscious mental processes. *Psychoanal. Quart.* 19: 540–560.

——. (1952). *Psychoanalytic Explorations in Art.* New York: International Universities Press.

Krystal, H. (1975). Affect tolerance. *Annual Psychoanal.* 3 179–219.

——. (1978a). Trauma and affects. *Psychoanal. Study Child* 33: 81–116.

——. (1978b). Self representation and the capacity for self care. *Annual Psychoanal.* 6: 209–246.

Lacan, J. (1956). Le séminaire sur "La lettre volée." *Le Psychanalyse*, 2: 1–44. (English translation "Seminar on 'The Purloined Letter'" by J. Mehlman, 1972, in *French Freud: Structural Studies in Psychoanalysis, Yale French Studies*, 48: 38–72.

Lachmann, F. M. & Beebe, B. (1996). The contribution of self- and mutual regulation to therapeutic action: a case illustration. Ed. A. Goldberg, *Progress in Self Psychology*, 12: 123–140.

LaFarge, L. (2000). Interpretation and containment. *Internat. Jour. Psycho-Anal.* 81: 67–84.

Langs, R. J. (1980). The misalliance dimension in the case of the Rat Man. In *Freud and His Patients, Volume II, Downstate Psychoanalytic Institute Twenty-Fifth Anniversary Series*, pp. 215–231. New York & London: Jason Aronson.

Laplanche, J. and Pontalis, J.-B. (1973). *The Language of Psychoanalysis.* Trans. D. Nicholson-Smith. New York: W. W. Norton. Inc.

Lasky, R. (1990). Catastrophic illness in the analyst and the analyst's emotional response to it. *Internat. J. Psycho-Anal.* 71:455–473.

Lear, J. (1998). *Open Minded: Working Out the Logic of the Soul.* Cambridge, Ma. & London: Harvard Univ. Press.

Leavy, J. H. (1998). Understanding repetition and the treatment crisis: a view of Paul Russell's theoretical orientation. In *Trauma, Repetition, and Affect Regulation:*

The Work of Paul Russell, ed. J. G. Teicholz & D. Kriegman, pp. 123–145. New York: The Other Press.

Levenson, E. (1982) Follow the fox. *Contemp. PsychoAnal.* 18: 1–15.

Levy, S. T. & Inderbitzin, L. (1989). Negativism and countertransference. *J. Amer. Psychoanal. Assn.* 37:7–30.

Lewin, B. D. (1955). Dream psychology and the analytic situation. *Psychoanal. Quart.* 24:169–199.

Limentani, A. (1981). On some positive aspects of the negative therapeutic reaction. *Internat. J. Psycho-Anal.* 62:379–390.

Lipton, E. (1991). The analyst's use of clinical data and other issues of confidentiality. *Jour. Amer. Psychoanal. Assoc.* 39: 967–985.

Lipton, S. (1977). The advantages of Freud's technique as shown in his analysis of the Rat Man. *Internat. Jour. Psychoanal.* 58: 255–274.

Loewald, H. W. (1960). On the therapeutic action of psychoanalysis. In *Papers on Psychoanalysis.* New Haven & London: Yale University Press, 1980, pp. 221–256.

———. (1970). Psychoanalytic theory and the psychoanalytic process. *Psychoanal. Study Child* 25:45–68.

———. (1975). Psychoanalysis as an art and the fantasy character of the psychoanalytic situation. *J. Amer. Psychoanal. Assn.* 23:277–299.

Loewenberg, P. (1995). *Fantasy and Reality in History.* New York & Oxford: Oxford University Press.

Mahony, P. (1977). Friendship and its discontents. *Contemp. PsychoAnal.* 15: 55–109.

———. (1982). *Freud as a Writer.* Madison, CT: International Universities Press.

———. (1984a). *Cries of the Wolf Man.* Madison, CT: International Universities Press.

———. (1984b). Further reflections on Freud and his writing. *J. Amer. Psychoanal. Assn.* 32: 847–864.

———. (1986). *Freud and the Rat Man.* New Haven & London: Yale University Press.

———. (1987). *Psychoanalysis and Discourse.* London and New York: Tavistock Publications.(1989).

———. (1989a). *On Defining Freud's Discourse.* New Haven & London: Yale University Press.

———. (1989b). Aspects of nonperverse scopophilia within an analysis. *J. Amer. Psychoanal. Assn.* 37:365–399.

———. (1993). Freud's cases: are they valuable today? *Internat. Jour. Psycho-Anal.* 74: 1027–1035.

———. (1996). *Freud's Dora: A Psychoanalytic, Historical, and Textual Study.* New Haven & London: Yale Univ. Press.

Main, M. (2000). The organized categories of infant, child, and adult attachment:

flexible vs. inflexible attention under attachment-related stress. *J. Amer. Psychoanal. Assn.* 48: 1055–1096.

Maroda, K. J. (1991). *The Power of Countertransference.* New York: Wiley.

———. (1999). *Seduction, Surrender, and Transformation: Emotional Engagement in the Analytic Process.* Hillsdale, N. J. & London: The Analytic Press.

Mautner, B. (1991). Freud's Irma dream: a psychoanalytic interpretation. *Internat. J. Psycho-Anal.* 72: 275–286.

Mayer, E. L. (1994). Some implications for psychoanalytic technique drawn from analysis of a dying patient. *Psychoanal. Quart.* 63: 1–19.

Mayer, E. L. (1996). Subjectivity and intersubjectivity of clinical facts. *Internat. J. Psycho-Anal.* 77:709–737.

McLaughlin, J. T. (1981). Transference, psychic reality, and countertransference. *Psychoanal. Quart.* 50:639–664.

Modell, A. H. (1961). Denial and the sense of separateness. *J. Amer. Psychoanal. Assn.*, 9:533–547.

——— (1965). On having the right to a life: an aspect of the superego's development. *Internat. J. Psycho-Anal.* 45:323–331.

——— (1971). The origin of certain forms of pre-oedipal guilt and their implications for a psychoanalytic theory of affects. *Internat. J. Psycho-Anal.* 52:337–346.

——— (1976). The "holding environment" and the therapeutic action of psychoanalysis. *J. Amer. Psychoanal. Assn.* 24:285–307.

——— (1990). *Other Times, Other Realities: Toward a Theory of Psychoanalytic Treatment.* Cambridge: Harvard University Press.

Moore, B. E. & Fine, B. D. (Eds.). (1990). *Psychoanalytic Terms and Concepts.* New Haven & London: The American Psychoanalytic Association and Yale University Press.

Morris, H. (1993). Narrative representation, narrative enactment, and the psychoanalytic construction of history. *Internat. J. Psycho-Anal.* 74: 33–54.

Muller, J. P. and Richardson, W. J. eds. (1988). *The Purloined Poe: Lacan, Derrida, and Psychoanalytic Reading.* Baltimore & London: The Johns Hopkins Univ. Press.

Muslin, H. L. 1979. Transference in the Rat Man case: the transference in transition. *J. Amer. Psychoanal. Assn.* 27: 561–57.

The New Shorter Oxford English Dictionary on Historical Principles. (1993). New York: Oxford University Press.

Novick, J. (1990). (Unpublished). Presentation, Symposium on Perversion, Michigan Psychoanalytic Society, Dearborn, MI, 1990.

Novick, J. and Novick, K. K. (1996). *Fearful Symmetry: The Development and Treatment of Sadomasochism.* Northvale, NJ & London: Jason Aronson.

Novick, K. K. and Novick, J. (1987). The essence of masochism. *Psychoanalytic Study of the Child.* 42:353–384.

Nydes, J. (1950). The magical experience of the masturbation fantasy. *Amer. J. Psychother.* 4:303–310.

Ogden, T. H. (1989a). On the concept of an autistic-contiguous position. *Internat. Jour. Psycho-Anal.* 70: 127–140.

———. (1989b). *The Primitive Edge of Experience.* Northvale, N. J.: Jason Aronson/ London:Karnac.

———. (1994). The analytic third: working with intersubjective clinical facts. *Internat. J. Psycho-Anal.* 75:3–19.

———. (1997a). On the use of language in psychoanalysis. In *Reverie and Interpretation: Sensing Something Human*, pp. 201–231. Northvale, N. J. & London: Jason Aronson.

———. (1997b, originally published 1995). Analyzing forms of aliveness and deadness. In *Reverie and Interpretation: Sensing Something Human*, pp. 21–63. Northvale, N. J. & London: Jason Aronson.

———. (1997c). Reverie and interpretation. In *Reverie and Interpretation: Sensing Something Human*, pp. 155–197. Northvale, N. J. & London: Jason Aronson.

———. (1997d). Reverie and metaphor: some thoughts on how I work as a psychoanalyst. *Internat. J. Psycho-Anal.* 78:719–732.

Olinick S. (1964). The negative therapeutic reaction. *Internat. J. Psycho-Anal.* 45:540–548.

———. (1969). On empathy, and regression in the service of the other. *Brit. Jour. Med. Psychol.* 42: 41–49.

———. (1970). Reporter: Negative therapeutic reaction. *J. Amer. Psychoanal. Assn.* 18: 655–672.

———. (1975). On empathic perception and the problems of reporting psychoanalytic processes. *Internat.J. Psycho-Anal.* 56: 147–154.

Olinick, S. L., Poland, W. S., Grigg, K. A., & Granatir, W. L. (1973). The psychoanalytic work ego: process and interpretation. *Internat.J. Psycho-Anal.* 54: 143–151.

Opatow, B., (1996). Panel report: Meaning in the clinical moment. *J. Amer. Psychoanal. Assn.* 44:639–648.

Panel (1994). K. R. Eissler's (1953) "The effect of the structure of the ego on psychoanalytic technique", reported by K. Kelly, *J. Amer. Psychoanal. Assn.* 42: 875–882.

Panel (1994a). Hate in the analytic setting. G. O. Gabbard, Chair, J. A. Winer, reporter. *J. Amer. Psychoanal. Assn.* 42:219–231.

Panel (1994b). Classics Revisited: K. R. Eissler's "The effect of the structure of the ego on psychoanalytic technique." L. Friedman, Chair, K. Kelly, reporter. *J. Amer. Psychoanal. Assn.* 42:875–882.

Panel (1994c). Impasses in psychoanalysis. R. Wallerstein, Chair, S. J. Coen, reporter. *J. Amer. Psychoanal. Assn.* 42:1225–1235.

Panel (1994d). What are the boundaries of psychoanalytic work? S. J. Coen, Chair, D. E. Harris, reporter. *J. Amer. Psychoanal. Assn.* 42:1209–1224.

Panel, 1996. Unpublished. The Patient's Processing of the Analyst's Interpretations. American Psychoanalytic Association Meetings, May, 1996, Los Angeles, Ca.

Panel, 1999. What in the world is the relationship? American Psychoanalytic Association Meetings, Washington, D. C.

Pao, P.–N. (1965). The role of hatred in the ego. *Psychoanal. Quart.* 34:257–264.

Peltz, M. (1992). The wish to be soothed as a resistance. *Psychoanal. Quart.* 61: 370–399.

Piccioli, E., Rossi, P. L., & Semi, A. A. (eds.). (1996). *Writing in Psychoanalysis*, Psychoanalytic Issues Monograph Series I. Hillsdale, N. J. & London: The Analytic Press for Rivista di Psicoanalisi.

Poulet, G. (1970). Criticism and the experience of interiority. In Ed. R. Macksey & E. Donato. *The Structuralist Controversy: The Languages of Criticism and the Sciences of Man*, pp. 56–72. Baltimore & London: The Johns Hopkins University Press.

Pulver, S. E. (1987). The manifest dream in psychoanalysis: a clarification. *J. Amer. Psychoanal. Assn.* 35: 99–118.

Racker, H. (1957). The meanings and uses of countertransference. *Internat. Jour. Psycho-Anal.* 34: 313–324.

———. (1958). Psychoanalytic technique and the analyst's unconscious masochism. *Psychoanal. Quart.* 27:555–562.

———. (1968). *Transference and Countertransference.* New York: Internat. Univ. Press.

Rapaport, D. (1953). Some metapsychological considerations concerning activity and passivity. In *The Collected Papers of David Rapaport*, ed. M. M. Gill. New York: Basic Books, 1967, pp. 530–568.

——— (1960). *The Structure of Psychoanalytic Theory: A Systematizing Attempt.* Psychological Issues, Vol. 2, No. 2, Monograph No. 6. New York: Internat. Univ. Press.

Reed, G. S. (1982). Toward a methodology for applying psychoanalysis to literature. *Psychoanal. Quart.* 51: 19–42.

———. (1985). Psychoanalysis, psychoanalysis appropriated, psychoanalysis applied. *Psychoanal. Quart.* 54: 234–269.

———. (1993, unpublished). The transference perversion. Presented to the Association for Psychoanalytic Medicine, N.Y.C.

——— (1997). The analyst's interpretation as fetish. *Jour. Amer. Psychoanal. Assn.* 45: 1153–1181.

Renik, O. (1991). One kind of negative therapeutic reaction. *J. Amer. Psychoanal. Assn.* 39:87–105.

———. (1992). Use of the analyst as a fetish. *Psychoanal. Quart.* 61: 542–563.

———. (1993). Countertransference enactment and the psychoanalytic process. In: M. J. Horowitz, O. F. Kernberg, and E. M. Weinshel (Eds.), *Psychic Structure* and *Psychic Change, Essays in Honor of Robert S. Wallerstein*, Madison, CT: Internat. Univ. Press, pp. 135–158.

———. (1994). Presentation of clinical facts. *Internat. Jour. Psycho-Anal.* 75: 1245–1250.

———. 1995). The role of an analyst's expectations in clinical technique: reflections on the concept of resistance. *J. Amer. Psychoanal. Assn.* 43: 83–94.

———. (1998). Getting real in analysis. *Psychoanal. Quart.* 67: 566–593.

———. (unpublished). Panel: Affective Self-disclosure by the analyst. International Psychoanalytical Association Congress, Santiago, Chile, 1999.

Richards, A. K. (1996). Ladies of fashion: pleasure, perversion or paraphilia. *Internat. J. Psycho-Anal.* 77:337–351.

Rizzuto, A. M. (2000). Reporter: Panel: Rage in the analytic setting. International Psychoanalytical Association Congress, Santiago, Chile, 1999. *Internat. Jour. Psycho-Anal.* 81: 575–578.

Rosenblatt,L. (1938). *Literature as Exploration*, rev. ed. New York: Noble & Noble, 1968.

Roth, L. (1994). Being true to a false object: a view of identification. *Psychoanal. Inquiry.* 14:393–405.

Rothstein, A. (1998). *Psychoanalytic Technique and the Creation of Analytic Patients. Second Edition.* Madison, CT: Internat. Univ. Press.

Russell, P. (1998). *Trauma, Repetition, and Affect Regulation: The Work of Paul Russell,* ed. J. G. Teicholz & D. Kriegman. New York: The Other Press.

Sander, L. (1977). The regulation of exchange in the infant-caretaker system and some aspects of the context-content relationship. In *Interaction, Conversation, and the Development of Language,* M. Lewis & L. Rosenblum (eds.). N. Y.: Wiley, pp. 133–156.

Sandler, J. (1976). Countertransference and role-responsiveness. *Internat. Rev. Psycho-Anal.* 3: 43–47.

Sandler, J. & Sandler, A.-M. (1998). *Internal Objects Revisited.* Madison, CT: Internat. Univ. Press.

Sandler, J. with Freud, A. (1985). *The Analysis of Defense: The Ego and the Mechanisms of Defense Revisited.* New York: International Universities Press.

Schafer, R. (1977). The interpretation of transference and the conditions for loving. *J. Amer. Psychoanal. Assn. 25,* 335–362.

———. (1983). *The Analytic Attitude.* New York: Basic Books.

———. (1985). Wild analysis. *J. Amer. Psychoanal. Assn.* 33: 275–300.

———. (1992). Unpublished. Contribution to the Panel: Classics Revisited: Eissler's The effect of the structure of the ego on psychoanalytic technique. American Psychoanalytic Association Meetings, December, 1992, New York City.

———. (1993). Five readings of Freud's "Observations on transference love", pp. 75–95. In E. S. Person, A. Hagelin, & P. Fonagy (eds.), *On Freud's "Observations on transference love".* New Haven & London: Yale Univ. Press.

———. (1996, Unpublished). Defenses against goodness. Presented to the Association for Psychoanalytic Medicine, N.Y.C., October, 1996.

———. (1997). Vicissitudes of remembering in the countertransference. *Internat. J. Psycho-Anal.* 78, 1151–1163.

Schore, A. N. (1994). *Affect Regulation and the Origin of the Self.* Hillsdale, N. J. & Hove, U. K.: Lawrence Erlbaum.

Schwaber, E. (1981). Empathy: a mode of analytic listening. *Psychoanal. Inq.* 1:351–392.

———. (1983). Psychoanalytic listening and psychic reality. *Internat. Rev. Psycho-Anal.* 10: 379–392.

———. (1995). A particular perspective on impasses in the clinical situation: further reflections on psychoanalytic listening. *Internat. Jour. Psycho-Anal.* 76: 711–722.

———. (1998). From whose point of view? The neglected question in analytic listening. *Psychoanal. Quart.* 67: 645–661.

Schwartz, M. M. (1975). Where is literature? *College English* 36: 756–765.

———. (1978). Critic: define thyself. In *Psychoanalysis and the Question of the Text,* ed. G. Hartman, pp. 1–17. Baltimore & London: The Johns Hopkins Univ. Press.

———. (1980). Shakespeare through contemporary psychoanalysis. In *Representing Shakespeare: New Psychoanalytic Essays,* ed. M. M. Schwartz & C. Kahn, pp. 21–32. Baltimore & London: The Johns Hopkins University Press.

———. (1982). The literary use of transference. *Psychoanal. & Contemp. Thought* 5: 35–44.

Schwartz, M. M., & Willbern, D. (1982). Literature and psychology. In *Inter-relations of Literature,* ed. J-.P. Berricelli & J. Gibaldi, pp. 205–224. New York: Modern Language Association.

Scott, J. W. (1988). *Gender and the Politics of History.* New York, Oxford: Columbia University Press.

———. (1991). The evidence of experience. *Critical Inquiry* 17: 773–797.

———. (1992). Multiculturalism and the politics of identity. *October,* No. 61, Summer 1992: 12–19.

Searles, H. (21969). Oedipal love in the countertransference. *Internat. J. Psycho-Anal.* 40, 180–190.

Settlage, C. F. (1994). On the contribution of separation-individuation theory to psychoanalysis: developmental process, pathogenesis, therapeutic process and technique. In *Mahler and Kohut: Perspectives on Development, Psychopathology, and Technique,* ed. S. Kramer & S. Akhtar, Northvale, N. J. & London: Jason Aronson, pp.17–52.

Shapiro, D. (1981). *Autonomy and Rigid Character.* New York: Basic Books.

Shengold, L. L. (1991). Coda: the problem of evil. In *"Father, Don't You See I'm Burning?"* New Haven & London: Yale Univ. Press, pp. 164–170.

———. (1999). Murder, violence, and soul murder: "Did it really happen?" and a note on therapy. In *Soul Murder Revisited: Thoughts About Therapy, Hate, Love, and Memory*, pp. 257–286. New Haven & London: Yale Univ. Press.

Sherwood, M. (1969). *The Logic of Explanation in Psychoanalysis*. New York & London: Academic Press.

Silver, A.-L. (1982). Resuming the work with a life-threatening illness. *Contemp. PsychoAnal.* 18:314–326.

Silverman, D. (1998). The tie that binds: affect regulation, attachment, and psychoanalysis. *Psychoanal. Psychol.* 15: 187–212.

Skura, M. A. (1981). *The Literary Use of the Psychoanalytic Process*. New Haven: Yale University Press.

Spence, D. (1981). Psychoanalytic competence. *Internat. Jour. Psycho-Anal.* 62: 113–124.

———. (1986). When interpretation masquerades as explanation. *Jour. Amer. Psychoanal. Assoc.* 34: 3–22.

———. (1990). The rhetorical voice of psychoanalysis. *Jour. Amer. Psychoanal. Assoc.* 38: 579–603.

Stein, M. (1981). The unobjectionable part of the transference. *J. Amer. Psychoanal. Assn.* 29:869–892.

———. (1988a). Writing about psychoanalysis: I. Analysts who write and those who do not. *Jour. Amer. Psychoanal. Assoc.* 36: 105–124.

———. (1988b). Writing about psychoanalysis: II. Analysts who write, patients who read. *Jour. Amer. Psychoanal. Assoc.* 36: 393–408.

Steiner, J. (1993). *Psychic Retreats*. London & New York: Routledge.

Sterba, R. (1957). Oral invasion and self-defense. *Internat. J. Psycho-Anal.* 38:204–208.

Stern, D. N. (1990). Joy and satisfaction in infancy. In *Pleasure Beyond the Pleasure Principle*, ed. R. A. Glick & S. Bone, pp. 13–25. New Haven: Yale Univ. Press.

Stimpson, C. R. (1985). The somagrams of Gertrude Stein. In *The Lesbian and Gay Studies Reader*, ed. H. Abelove, M. A. Barale, & D. M. Halperin, pp. 642–65. New York & London: Routledge, 19932.

Stoller, R. J. (1975). *Perversion: The Erotic Form of Hatred*. New York: Pantheon.

——— (1979). *Sexual Excitement: Dynamics of Erotic Life*. New York: Pantheon.

———. (1988). Patients' responses to their own case reports. *Jour. Amer. Psychoanal. Assoc.* 36: 371–392.

Symposium (a), 1996. Unpublished. Experiencing the Other: Emotional Contact in the Therapeutic Situation. Association for Psychoanalytic Medicine, March, 1996, New York, N. Y.

Symposium (b), 1996. The limits of analysis, impasse and unanalyzability: perspectives on analytic failures, New York Psychoanalytic Society Extension Division. Parts of this are in press, *J. Clin. Psychoanal.*

Tähkä, V. (1993). *Mind and Its Treatment: A Psychoanalytic Approach.* Madison, CT: Internat. Univ. Press.

Thompson, P. G. (1980). On the receptive function of the analyst. *Internat. Rev. Psycho-Anal.* 7:183–205.

Tuckett, D. (1991). Editorial: Fifteen clinical accounts of psychoanalysis, a further invitation. *Internat. Jour. Psycho-Anal.* 72: 377–381.

———. (1993). Some thoughts on the presentation and discussion of the clinical material of psychoanalysis. *Internat. Jour. Psycho-Anal.* 74: 1175–1189.

———. (1994). The conceptualization and communication of clinical facts in psychoanalysis. *Internat. Jour. Psycho-Anal.* 75: 865–870.

Tustin, F. (1980). Austistic objects. *Internat. Rev. Psycho-Anal.* 7: 27–40.

———. (1984). Autistic shapes. *Internat. Rev. Psycho-Anal.* 11: 279–290.

Valenstein, A. F. (1971). The defense mechanisms and activities of the ego: some aspects of a classificatory approach. In *The Unconscious Today*, ed. M. Kanzer. New York: International Universities Press, pp. 127–136.

Wallerstein, R. S. (1993). On transference love: revisiting Freud. In E. S. Person, A. Hagelin, and P. Fonagy (Eds.), *On Freud's "Observations on transference love"*, New Haven & London: Yale Univ. Press, pp. 57–74.

Wasserman, M. (1999). The impact of psychoanalytic theory and a two-person psychology on the empathising analyst. *Internat. Jour. Psycho-Anal.* 80: 449–464.

Weber, S. (1982). *The Legend of Freud.* Minneapolis: University of Minnesota Press. (Originally, *Freud Legende: Drei Studien Zum Psychoanalytischen Denken.* Olten, Switzerland: Walter Verlag AG. Rev. & trans. by the author).

Weinshel, E. (1966). Reporter: Severe regressive states during analysis. *J. Amer. Psychoanal. Assn.* 14:538–568.

Weissman, P. (1962). The psychology of the critic and psychological criticism. *J. Amer. Psychoanal. Assn.* 10: 745–761.

Winer, J. (1994) Reporter, Panel: Hatred in the analytic setting, American Psychoanalytic Association Meetings, 1991. *Jour. Amer. Psychoanal. Assn.* 42: 219–231.

Winnicott, D. W. (1956). The antisocial tendency. In *Through Paediatrics to Psychoanalysis.* New York: Basic Books, 1975, pp. 306–315.

———. (1967). The location of cultural experience. In *Playing and Reality*, pp. 95–103. New York: Basic Books, 1971.

———. (1968). The use of an object and relating through identifications. In *Playing and Reality*, pp. 86–94. London: Tavistock, 1971.

———. (1971). Playing: creative activity and the search for the self. In *Playing and Reality*, pp. 53–64. New York: Basic Books, 1971.

Wyman, H. M. & Rittenberg, S. (1992). Reflections on the written presentation of psychoanalytic clinical data: necessary source and perennial problem. *Jour. Clin. PsychoAnal.* 1: 323–331.

Zetzel, E. (1949). Anxiety and the capacity to bear it. *Internat. J. Psycho-Anal.* 30:1–12. (Note author's name was "Rosenberg" in 1949).

———. (1966). 1965: Additional notes upon a case of obsessional neurosis: Freud 1909. *Internat. J. Psycho-Anal.* 1966, 47, 123–129.

Index

ABOUT THE AUTHOR

Stanley J. Coen, M.D. is a Training and Supervising Analyst at the Columbia University Center for Psychoanalytic Training and research, Clinical Professor of Psychiatry at the Columbia University College of Physicians & Surgeons, and a member of the editorial boards of the *Journal of the American Psychoanalytic Association*, *Journal of Clinical Psychoanalysis*, and the *Journal of Applied Psychoanalytic Studies*. He is the author of *The Misuse of Persons: Analyzing Pathological Dependency* (1992), and *Between Author and Reader: A Psychoanalytic Approach to Writing and Reading* (1994). He was awarded the Alexander Beller Memorial Prize for Psychoanalytic Writing and the George E. Daniels Merit Award for Excellence in Psychoanalysis, and has been the Victor Calef Memorial Lecturer. He has chaired the Interdisciplinary Colloquium on Psychoanalysis and Literary Criticism at the American Psychoanalytic Association since 1984. He has published and lectured extensively on problems in clinical psychoanalysis and psychoanalytic literary criticism.